'The authors give a comprehensive view of a timely topic-the role of gender in family entrepreneurship. I applaud the authors for addressing this important issue that is taking on more relevance daily around the world.'

Dianne H.B. Welsh, *Hayes Distinguished Professor of Entrepreneurship, University of North Carolina Greensboro, USA*

'In this edited book, a team of international scholars, including Ratten, Ramadani, Dana, Hisrich and Ferreira, is addressing a set of important issues at the crossroads of gender and family entrepreneurship. This useful book combines both perspectives with the aim to bring value to entrepreneurship scholarship, policy and practice.'

Alain Fayolle, *Entrepreneurship Distinguished Professor, Director of Research Centre, Emlyon Business School, France*

'Family business is one of the most important and significant areas of business management as it relates to social issues. This book about gender and family entrepreneurship brings together international scholars that focus mostly on the changing societal trends towards females in family business. It has a range of topics from the role of self-employment for female lawyers in the United States, to the dowager principle of females in family business in the United Kingdom, to rehabilitation through entrepreneurship in Spain. The book takes a different perspective by highlighting the role gender plays in family entrepreneurship.'

Pramodita Sharma, *Professor & Daniel Clark Sanders Chair, Grossman School of Business, UVM, and Visiting Professor, Kellogg School of Management, USA*

'A remarkable team has put together a collection of studies hitting on important and controversial topics in family entrepreneurship. Drawing from top scholars around the globe, they attack subjects that have been ignored or downplayed in business education. The findings reported here enable academics to offer more value to students, consultants to better assist their family business clients, and practitioners to improve their abilities to manage the family and business relationships.'

Frank Hoy, *Professor, Director of the Collaborative for Entrepreneurship & Innovation, Worcester Polytechnic Institute, USA*

'Family business, or family entrepreneurship, is the right approach to understand most of the entrepreneurial activity in today's world and in the future. It is also a homogeneous view because it is transversal and present in all industrial sectors. We are dealing with a book that brings the particular study from the perspective of gender and from the most current approach, which no longer focuses on purely biological differences. At a global level, old social roles are also being overcome, perhaps not with sufficient speed, and the new research focuses on more promising aspects such as attitudes, values and cultural dimensions. The good news is that there is no longer essential a feminist approach to analyse and describe the situation of "Gender and Family Entrepreneurship".'

Salvador Roig, *Dpto. Dirección de Empresas, Universitat de València, Spain*

Gender and Family Entrepreneurship

This book focuses on gender and family entrepreneurship, as they are interrelated concepts particularly important in today's global society. The book highlights the significance of the role of gender in the development and growth of family businesses. It helps readers understand the role of family dynamics in business, particularly in terms of succession planning, strategic development and internationalization.

Often, both gender and family entrepreneurship are studied independently, but this book aims to marry both perspectives with a novel approach. This creates a synergy between gender and family entrepreneurship that increases the potential value to entrepreneurship scholarship, policy and business practice. This edited book is a useful and insightful addition to the entrepreneurship field.

Vanessa Ratten is Associate Professor of Entrepreneurship and Innovation at the Department of Management and Marketing, La Trobe University, Australia.

Veland Ramadani is Associate Professor at South East European University, Macedonia.

Leo-Paul Dana is Professor at Montpellier Business School, France.

Robert D. Hisrich is the Bridgestone Chair of International Marketing and Associate Dean of Graduate and International Programs at the College of Business Administration at Kent State University, USA.

Joao Ferreira is Associate Professor at the University of Beira Interior, Portugal.

Routledge Frontiers of Business Management

For a full list of titles in this series, please visit www.routledge.com/series/rfbm

5 **Japanese Management**
International Perspectives
Hitoshi Iwashita

6 **Strategic Human Resource Management in China**
A Multiple Perspective
Min Min, Mary Bambacas and Ying Zhu

7 **Fostering Local Entrepreneurship in a Multinational Enterprise**
Joe J. Amberg and Sara L. McGaughey

8 **Digital Business and Sustainable Development**
Asian Perspectives
Yongrok Choi

9 **Management Control Systems in Japan**
Takashi Shimizu

10 **Internal Marketing**
Another Approach to Marketing for Growth
Tatsuya Kimura

11 **Entrepreneurship, Innovation and Smart Cities**
Vanessa Ratten

12 **Japanese Management in Evolution**
New Directions, Breaks and Emerging Practices
Edited by Tsutomu Nakano

13 **Gender and Family Entrepreneurship**
Edited by Vanessa Ratten, Veland Ramadani, Leo-Paul Dana, Robert D. Hisrich and Joao Ferreira

Gender and Family Entrepreneurship

Edited by Vanessa Ratten,
Veland Ramadani, Leo-Paul Dana,
Robert D. Hisrich and Joao Ferreira

LONDON AND NEW YORK

First published 2018
by Routledge

2 Park Square, Milton Park, Abingdon, Oxfordshire OX14 4RN
52 Vanderbilt Avenue, New York, NY 10017

Routledge is an imprint of the Taylor & Francis Group, an informa business

First issued in paperback 2019

British Library Cataloguing-in-Publication Data
A catalogue record for this book is available from the British Library

Library of Congress Cataloging-in-Publication Data
Names: Ratten, Vanessa, editor. | Ramadani, Veland, editor.
Title: Gender and family entrepreneurship / edited by Vanessa Ratten, Veland Ramadani, Leo-Paul Dana, Robert D. Hisrich and Joao Ferreira.
Description: First Edition. | New York : Routledge, 2017. | Series: Routledge frontiers of business management ; 13 | Includes bibliographical references and index.
Identifiers: LCCN 2017013786 | ISBN 9781138228870 (hardback) | ISBN 9781315391427 (ebook)
Subjects: LCSH: Family-owned business enterprises. | Women-owned business enterprises. | Sex role. | Family-owned business enterprises—Succession.
Classification: LCC HD62.25 .G456 2017 | DDC 658.4/21—dc23
LC record available at https://lccn.loc.gov/2017013786

ISBN: 978-1-138-22887-0 (hbk)
ISBN: 978-0-367-37473-0 (pbk)

Typeset in Galliard
by Apex CoVantage, LLC

Contents

Figures

Tables

Contributors

Hyrije Abazi-Alili is Assistant Professor at South-East European University, Republic of Macedonia.

Emna Baccari-Jamoussi graduated with a doctoral degree in management from the University of Nice, France. Her field of research is entrepreneurship and strategy.

María Barreiro-Gen is Assistant Professor at the University of A Coruña.

Paolo Pietro Biancone is full Professor of Financial Management and Islamic Finance at the University of Torino.

Börje Boers is a Senior Lecturer at the school of business, University of Skovde, Sweden.

Nuria Calvo is Associate Professor at the University of A Coruña.

So Young Choi is a graduate student at Ewha School of Business, Ewha Womans University.

Leo-Paul Dana is Professor at Montpellier Business School, France.

Joao Ferreira is Associate Professor at the University of Beira Interior, Portugal.

Vishal K. Gupta is Associate Professor at the University of Mississippi.

Robert D. Hisrich is the Bridgestone Chair of International Marketing and Associate Dean of Graduate and International Programs at the College of Business Administration at Kent State University.

Angelka Ilioska is Brand Manager at ALMA M.

Golshan Javadian is Assistant Professor of Management at Morgan State University.

Sang-Joon Kim is Assistant Professor at Ewha School of Business, Ewha Womans University.

Aleš Kubíček is Assistant Professor with the Department of Strategy, Faculty of Business Administration, University of Economics, Prague, Czech Republic.

Carmem Leal is Assistant Professor of Knowledge Management at University of Trás-os-Montes and Alto Douro.

Severine Leloarne-Lemaire is Associate Professor of Entrepreneurship at Grenoble EM.

Marlene Loureiro is Assistant Professor in the Department of Arts and Communication of the University of Trás-os-Montes and Alto Douro and Member of the LabCom.IFP Research Center.

Adnane Maâlaoui graduated with a doctoral degree in management from the University of Toulon, France.

Ondřej Machek is Assistant Professor at Faculty of Business Administration, University of Economics, Prague, Czech Republic.

Galvão Meirinhos is Assistant Professor at the University of Trás-os-Montes and Alto Douro (UTAD) and researcher at LABCOM.IFP – Communication, Philosophy and Humanities Research Unit of University of Beira Interior.

Etayankara Muralidharan is Assistant Professor at MacEwan University's School of Business, Canada.

Isabel Novo-Corti is Lecturer in the Faculty of Economics and Business and Director of the Department of Economic Analysis and Business Administration at the University of A Coruña.

Saurav Pathak is Assistant Professor in Entrepreneurship at Kansas State University.

Veland Ramadani is Associate Professor at South-East European University, Republic of Macedonia.

María Ramil-Díaz is Lecturer in the Faculty of Economics and Business and the Faculty of Sociology at the University of A Coruña.

Vanessa Ratten is Associate Professor of Entrepreneurship and Innovation at La Trobe University, Melbourne, Australia.

Gadaf Rexhepi is Associate Professor at South-East European University of Tetovo.

Vahid Jafari Sadeghi is a PhD candidate involved in the business and management program at the University of Turin, Italy.

Anil Boz Semerci is Researcher and Lecturer at Hacettepe University, Department of Business Administration.

Robert P. Singh is Professor of Management in the Graves School of Business and Management at Morgan State University.

Robert Smith is Professor of Enterprise and Innovation at the University of the West of Scotland, Dumries.

Foreword

In recent years, women's involvement in family entrepreneurship activities has attracted increasing attention amongst both academics and practitioners. Scholars have discussed the topic since the 1980s (e.g., Lyman, Salganicoff, & Hollander, 1985), but a clear understanding of the role of gender in family entrepreneurship activities is far from being clear and attention to women's involvement in family entrepreneurship has grown considerably.

This timely book challenges the prevalent assumption that most entrepreneurship studies are about male business people and makes an important step forward in advancing our understanding of the role of gender in family entrepreneurship. Overall, the book provides a clear and well-reasoned overview of how men, women, asexual and transgender individuals affect decision-making processes and behaviours in the context of family businesses.

More specifically, the volume offers a systematization of existing knowledge that is useful to understand the effect of gender relations and their structures on entrepreneurship. The different chapters shed light on a number of important topics, including the intention and/or ability to create and manage businesses based on gender and the role gender plays on key behaviours such as professional development or family business succession.

The five co-editors and the authors of the various chapters discuss in a clear and comprehensive way the importance of taking a gender and family view in business, and the volume offers important contributions to the existing body of knowledge on gender based studies.

I strongly recommend this reading to anyone interested in appreciating the role of gender but also family in society and to those scholars who are eager to know how adopting a gender based lens can influence the creation of new ventures and the management of existing family businesses. The five co-editors have succeeded in the important task of disseminating the latest research insights to the benefit of a large community of stakeholders that extends well beyond the academic network.

Alfredo De Massis
Professor of Entrepreneurship & Family Business
Free University of Bozen-Bolzano and
Lancaster University Management School
Director of the Unibz Knowledge Platform on
Family Business Management and Co-Director
of the LUMS Centre for Family Business

Acknowledgements

Due to our passion for family business, gender studies and entrepreneurship we had noticed that there were few books focusing specifically on gender, family and entrepreneurship. This meant that in researching the literature and practical significance of these topics we came up with the idea to edit a book on Gender and Family Entrepreneurship. We thank our Editor, Yongling Lam, for her championing of the idea and for constructive feedback about suggestions. We also thank Samantha Phua for her assistance in helping us with this book. In terms of our family, each of us would like to thank the following:

I thank my mum for telling me when I was young that instead of being a teacher, I should be a Professor, and that is a dream, which did come true. So thank you mum (Kaye Ratten) for everything you did for me and continue to do but in a spiritual way. I also thank my dad (David Ratten) for his advice and always being there, listening to my academic discussions about this book. Lastly, I thank my brothers (Stuart Ratten and Hamish Ratten) for their sense of fun and style and of course, humour.

Vanessa Ratten

To my sons Rron and Rrezon
Veland Ramadani

I dedicate this volume to Naomi Josephine and to Jake (Jakob) Theodore
Leo-Paul Dana

I thank my family
Robert D. Hisrich

I thank my family
Joao Ferreira

1 Gender and family entrepreneurship

An overview

Vanessa Ratten, Veland Ramadani, Leo-Paul Dana, Robert D. Hisrich and Joao Ferreira

Introduction

Entrepreneurship traditionally is viewed as being focused on business creation and the role of gender has been diminished, although this is important to understanding the way family businesses in particular are managed. This is the result of the assumption that most entrepreneurship studies are about male business people but this has changed in recent times with the increase in the role of females in the workplace. In addition, there has been an increased interest in gender based studies about entrepreneurship due to the realization that it impacts decision-making processes and gender rather than being purely biological can also be in the attitudes and behaviors of a person. For this reason, it is important to understand how gender entrepreneurship is impacted by contextual influences on business behavior in family businesses, which comprise a large proportion of overall businesses.

This chapter will provide an overview of gender and family entrepreneurship to enhance our understanding of different entrepreneurial behaviors between men, women, asexual and transgender individuals and how they are integrated specifically into business. Due to the trend toward gender neutrality in society, there is a changing perception about the role of gender in entrepreneurship. This chapter suggests that gender is not so important in today's society but rather the person's capability to be an entrepreneur. This means extending previous research by incorporating a gender-neutral stance on entrepreneurial behaviors but acknowledging that in certain environmental contexts there are gender differences. As there is a complex understanding about gender in society it is important to acknowledge that younger generations are being taught both masculine and feminine behaviors as part of their education. It is proposed that in more developed countries the conceptualization of gender is no longer based on biological conditions but rather on the way a person behaves in society.

This chapter is organized as follows. The next section discusses the importance of gender to entrepreneurship by explaining its embeddedness in society. The changing role of gender in society is then discussed with a view to suggesting current conceptualizations of gender entrepreneurship. Finally the conclusion summarizes the main findings and suggests ways to move forward.

Gender entrepreneurship

Feminist studies are useful to understand entrepreneurship due to their emphasis on gender relations and their structures (Berg, 1997). Researchers have different conceptualizations of gender and its impact on society depending on their beliefs. Berg (1997: 259) states there is "diversity in both femininity and masculinity, i.e. differences among women and differences among men, as well as gender differences". There is also growing recognition of asexual individuals who classify themselves as neither male nor female. Therefore, the way we study entrepreneurship needs to consider gender because of its significance in behavioral aspects of business management (Ferreira, Ratten, and Dana, 2017).

Entrepreneurship is an embedded phenomenon that needs to be understood in the appropriate environmental context (Diaz-Garcia and Jimenez-Moreno, 2010). Some environments are more conducive to certain types of entrepreneurship (Gerguri, Rashiti, Ramadani, Abazi-Alili, Dana, and Ratten, 2017). This is due to culture and society playing an important role in entrepreneurial behavior (Ratten and Ferreira, 2017). There is a perception in society that masculine traits and behaviors are considered better for business than females ones (Marlow and Patton, 2005). This has resulted in a socially constructed gender belief system influencing entrepreneurial intentions and the development of business ventures.

There are stereotypes about the role of women in business that bias entrepreneurial activity (Nilsson, 1997). This has meant that women are generally perceived as being less entrepreneurial than men (Langowitz and Minniti, 2007). For these reasons gender has influenced the ability of females to be entrepreneurs and their inclusion as business owners in the workforce. A study by Menzies and Tatroff (2006) found that male students are more likely to choose an entrepreneurial course as part of their business degree. Thus, the education and training of entrepreneurs has tended to bias males, although this is changing.

Females tend to identify opportunities differently because of their gender and environmental characteristics (DeTienne and Chandler, 2007). In business, masculine styles of management are still considered to be better despite changing society attitudes (Diaz-Garcia and Jiménez-Moreno, 2010). This has meant that the gender of a manager influences their ability to be promoted and considered as an authority figure in business (Ratten, 2007). Society tends to view managers as having behavior that is more conducive to entrepreneurship (Langowitz and Minniti, 2007).

Women are conditioned by societal norms in terms of expected behavior, which influences their entrepreneurial intention (Welter, Smallbone, Isakova, and Aculai, 2007). Concurrent with the growth in entrepreneurship research has been studies about females and their role in the entrepreneurial process (Sullivan and Meek, 2012). These studies have focused on how entrepreneurship is associated with creativity and innovation, which has contributed to a more diverse workforce (Ratten, 2017). Part of this change in workforce participation has been the increase in women entrepreneurs (Brush, De Bruin, and Welter, 2009).

Processes in the internal and external environment provide a useful way to understand the gender issues in entrepreneurship. The process model of entrepreneurship views entrepreneurs as applying their ideas, knowledge, skills and talents to business endeavours (Baron and Henry, 2011). There are four main stages to the process model of entrepreneurship: 1) motivation, 2) opportunity recognition, 3) acquiring resources and 4) entrepreneurial success/ performance (Sullivan and Meek, 2012). Firstly, motivations for female entrepreneurs might be necessity-based as they need an income or opportunity and this influences their ability to see a gap in the market. The motivational factors reflect the reasons why females decide to be self-employed rather than employed by others. Secondly, opportunity recognition refers to how females realize and evaluate opportunities in the market. Some female entrepreneurs pursue business ideas because of personal experience. This means that gender can play a role in the type of businesses established by female entrepreneurs.

Thirdly, acquiring resources for female entrepreneurs might depend on their financial capacity or social networks. These resources are both financial and non-financial and are important to establish business ventures but also to maintain existing ones. Fourthly, entrepreneurial success can be brand reputation or profitability, which influences the perception of a female entrepreneur in the business world. The performance of a business venture may depend on market position. Females often pursue entrepreneurship due to frustration over career opportunities (Buttner and Moore, 1997). This has meant that females are increasingly seeing entrepreneurship as a way to advance their careers and to be independent. In addition, females wanting to create a better work environment based on their personal preferences are motivated to become entrepreneurs (Sullivan and Meek, 2012). The flexibility associated with entrepreneurship is another driving force affecting females to be involved with entrepreneurial ventures.

Despite the hard work and long hours many entrepreneurs face, female entrepreneurs consider the autonomy of choosing their own work hours as an advantage. Carter, Gartner, Shaver, and Gatewood (2003) found that women value independence as more important than financial success. The rationale for this is due to females often having more responsibility for family related matters, which makes having flexibility and independence with work matters being important for them (DeMartino and Barbato, 2003). Females are also considered to associate more value from working from home due to their role in family life. These gender differences between males and females with family responsibilities are changing as more men choose to stay at home to raise children.

Matthews and Moser (1996) found that both males and females are more motivated to become an entrepreneur if their parents were entrepreneurs. Parents play a role in influencing individuals, regardless of gender, to become entrepreneurs. Some parents, regardless of culture or religion, motivate their children to become entrepreneurs. However, there are cultural factors that affect the role of women in society and their ability to be entrepreneurs (Sullivan and Meek, 2012). Some research has suggested that in free market economies females are better able to pursue entrepreneurship (Zapalska, 1997). Therefore, the economic stage of development for a country may affect the gender differences for entrepreneurship. This is evident in work by Sullivan and Meek (2012) highlighting how a country's social norms supporting entrepreneurship will result in more female entrepreneurs. Moreover, Caputo and Dolinksy (1998) found that self-employed husbands positively impact the likelihood of females deciding to also be self-employed.

Females are socialized differently to males, which affects their entrepreneurial behavior. Orhan and Scott (2001), in a study on French female entrepreneurs, found that these situations affect decisions to become entrepreneurs: dynastic compliance, natural succession and pure entrepreneur. A need for achievement influences both males and females to become entrepreneurs. This has led to there being both push and pull factors affecting the decision of females to start a business (Orhan and Scott, 2001). Push factors include need for flexibility, financial reasons and dissatisfaction with current job whilst pull factors involve independence and social status. Females often perceive entrepreneurship as enabling them to maintain child-rearing responsibilities whilst having a professional position.

There are gender neutral characteristics associated with entrepreneurship such as having a vision, need for achievement and being competitive. In business soft leadership traits associated with females are consensus and discussion in decision-making (Orhan and Scott, 2001). Feminine management traits are becoming increasingly valued in business because of an acknowledgement they are useful in organizations. Females become entrepreneurs often because they are bored and require an outlet for their business ideas.

Female owned businesses usually start with less financial resources than male owned businesses (Coleman, 2000). In addition, there has been a feminization of the labour force that has positively affected female entrepreneurship (Humbert and Drew, 2010). Humbert and Drew (2010: 192) states "the importance of diversity (in race/ethnicity, sexual orientation, age, etc.) intersecting with gender would facilitate an investigation into the multiplicative effects of being female (or male) when entering a male (female) world".

Family entrepreneurship

The definition of a family business is still elusive due to the differing ways to conceptualize both a family and business entity (De Massis, Sharma, Chua, and Chrisman, 2012). Most definitions focus on the level of involvement by family members in a business. This involvement can be in terms of control both from a financial and non-financial perspective. Financial control includes degree of ownership in the form of shareholding or equity. Non-financial control means voting rights or managerial positions in the business.

Firms that want to increase their competitiveness need to combine both strategy and entrepreneurship. This enables firms to create business opportunities that will lead to increased wealth. As industries go through different lifecycles, firms that take a strategic posture to business activity can be more flexible. This is helpful for family businesses that see business segments evolve based on consumer demand (De Massis, Frattini, Pizzurno, and Cassia, 2015).

Dyer and Handler (1994) proposed that there were four career nexuses that were important to family entrepreneurship. First, the experiences from the entrepreneur's family shape business decisions. This includes whether an entrepreneur was part of a family who had international experiences or grew up in a family of entrepreneurs. Second, an entrepreneur's family can be involved in the establishment of the business from providing sources of funding to working in the business. This means that family member ideas and attitudes can shape start-up decisions and internationalization strategies. Third, family members are employed in the firm due to it being entrepreneurial and in the start-up phase. This means that the employment can be volunteer-based until the enterprise has started to make money and become profitable. Fourth, family members can be involved in the succession, thereby transforming the business into new fields.

An entrepreneur's family plays a role in the development of their behaviours and personality (Dyer and Handler, 1994). For entrepreneurial activity to occur there needs to be a conducive environment and this often occurs from a family. Often entrepreneurs come from families that have been involved in business and are self-employed. This has led to there being a variety of ways individuals can become entrepreneurs by having the right environment to build a learning capability.

Families, particularly parents, can influence the confidence, skills and values that children have, which affects their entrepreneurial capabilities (Dyer and Handler, 1994). Bird (1989) developed the psychodynamic view of entrepreneurship to understand behavior. In this model the cultural, economic, historical and social context together with childhood dynamics result in behavior that influences an individual's choice to become an entrepreneur. As part of Bird's (1989) model parents play a crucial role in the identification of entrepreneurial behaviors. This is due to parents playing an important nurturing and supportive role in their children's development (Ronstadt, 1984). Individuals who have a high need for achievement are influenced into an entrepreneurial role due to their need for independence. In Bird's (1989) model it is also acknowledged the role adulthood plays in terms of entrepreneurial behavior. This includes the rebelliousness and suspicion that might be part of young adulthood. In addition, the conscious decisions an individual makes are influenced by their level of planning and work environment.

Research about family businesses has increased due to the awareness about their role in promoting economic development. Bird, Welsch, Astrachan, and Pistrui (2002) view family controlled enterprises as part of society from the new world discovery period, Middle Ages, Roman Empire, Industrial Revolution and knowledge economy. The historical significance of family businesses can be seen in the initiatives based on family loyalty. However as Al-Dajani, Bika, Collins, and Swail (2014:219) states "less than a quarter of family businesses survive to the second generation and only about a seventh survive to the third generation".

In most studies about family business the concept of a family is undifferentiated and considered the same regardless of context (Al-Dajani et al., 2014). The word 'family' has different meanings depending on the societal environment. This is seen in studies of family business preferring to focus on succession and other areas about family business rather than dissecting what a family means to people (Miller, Steier, and Le Breton-Miller, 2003). Moreover, instead of recognizing the changing role of family in society, issues around succession planning and financial matters have taken precedence. Karra, Tracey, and Phillips (2006) indicate that a family is automatic as a result of blood or marriage. However, with the growing public acceptance of alternative conceptualizations of a family the definition needs to be adapted. Therefore, this book defines a family as a mutual respect, bond and love existing within a group of people.

Gender and family entrepreneurship

Familiness is a term used to describe the linkages between people in a family that provide mutual benefit (Habbershon and Williams, 1999). The role of family businesses is important due to the increased recognition of the way males and females differ in business. This has been the result of changes in the roles females and males play in business. The composition of families has led to new business opportunities. In family businesses, women are often seen as being marginalized at the expense of males. This stereotype of females in supporting rather than domineering positions in business has changed in recent decades. Part of this change has been the result of demographic changes, such as increased participation of females in the workforce.

The traditional view of females in a family was as a housewife who did the cooking and cleaning rather than having their own professional career. Despite the decreased gender gap some studies still stereotype entrepreneurs as males (Al-Dajani et al., 2014). Family entrepreneurship enables the exploration of innovative business activity in a family setting. This is useful for informing the practice of family business but also for potential avenues to increase entrepreneurship. Policy makers can implement changes to encourage family entrepreneurship in terms of decisions and strategies based on gender equality. Family business research needs to realize that there is an inherent entrepreneurial capability of families when they work together for innovative outcomes.

A reconsideration of family businesses as being gender based and entrepreneurial is needed due to the misleading understanding by many that they are resistant to change. There is still much debate about whether family businesses outperform non-family businesses depending on the context and arguments proposed. Parental altruism means that a family business will prosper. The level of family capital influences whether the business performs well. Regardless of this there is an agreement that family businesses are different in attitude compared to non-family businesses, and gender plays a role in their development.

Family businesses have two main types of social capital: family and organizational. Family social capital involves the relationship individuals have as part of their family connections that are built across time. Organizational social capital involves the networks firms have that form business relationships. Family businesses have a stable management that encourages other businesses to partner with them. These business networks are developed in family businesses as forms of long-term relationships. Some networks might focus more on other family members at the expense of other businesses that are considered outsiders and not trustworthy. This has restricted the development of some networks by family businesses as they are considered as competitors.

Family networks and resulting social networks are a powerful form of social capital as it endures for many years. As a result of family social capital it has meant that some family businesses restrict business's relationships to kin members. This has led to family businesses having a competitive advantage due to their unique social capital and organizational culture. In addition, family human capital can help with access to other resources and networks.

Networks are built around relationships that are managed with key stakeholders in a family business. The reputation of a family business comes from their social capital, which influences management practices and inter-organizational harmony. The long-term success of family businesses revolves around the organizational culture and resulting use of human capital. This helps family businesses create a sense of familiness that leads to a market-orientated culture.

Overview of chapters

The chapters in this book range in topics from a focus just on gender or family entrepreneurship to an integration of how both are interlinked and important determinants of business success. The first chapter (this chapter) has provided an overview of gender and family entrepreneurship, which is a dynamic way to understand behavior and cultural traits. The second chapter titled 'Culturally endorsed leadership styles and entrepreneurial behaviors of women' by Saurav Pathak and Etayankara Muralidharan focuses on how culture affects leadership styles and influences the intention to create businesses based on gender. The third chapter titled 'Moving beyond the barriers: Examining the impact of self-efficacy and stereotype reactance on women's entrepreneurial intentions' by Golshan Javadian, Robert P. Singh and Vishal K. Gupta also examines the role of gender by focusing on behavioural traits such as perceived ability to manage a business based on gender stereotypes. The fourth chapter titled 'Representations of gender: The *media* as the mirror of gender roles' by Marlene Loureiro, Galvão Meirinhos, Carmem Leal and Vanessa Ratten discusses the role the media plays in establishing gender roles in the workforce. The fifth chapter titled 'Gendered perspectives in succession process of family businesses: A conceptual review' by Anil Boz Semerci focuses on gender more broadly by reviewing the literature about family business succession. The sixth chapter titled 'Family embeddedess and gendered professional entrepreneurship: Evidence from the self-employment of female lawyers in the U.S.' by Sang-Joon Kim and So Young Choi examines the role gender plays in professional development.

The seventh chapter titled 'Could women ex-offenders reinvent their future? An entrepreneurial approach' by Isabel Novo-Corti, María Ramil-Díaz, Nuria Calvo and Maria Barreiro-Gen examines the positive role entrepreneurship can play in society. The eighth chapter titled 'Exploring the drivers of gender entrepreneurship: Focus on the motivational perspectives in USA, Italy and France' by Vahid Jafari Sadeghi and Paolo Pietro Biancone discusses the international differences towards gender and entrepreneurship. The ninth chapter titled 'The impact of family structure, marital status and the parental mode on the business creation process among young Tunisian entrepreneurs' by Emna Baccari-Jamoussi, Adnane Maâlaoui and Severine Leloarne-Lemaire demonstrates the role of parenting and marriage on business creation. The tenth chapter titled 'Heteronormativity and the family firm: Will we ever see a queer family business?' by Börje Boers discusses the changing societal norms about the meaning of family. The eleventh chapter titled 'Family business management challenges: Understanding generational differences' by Veland Ramadani, Angelka Ilioska, Gadaf Rexhepi and Hyrije Abazi-Alili examines success issues in family business. The twelfth chapter titled 'Father-daughter succession in family businesses: Current state of knowledge and future research challenges' by Aleš Kubíček and Ondřej Machek provides a holistic understanding about the role of father daughter relationships in family entrepreneurship. The thirteenth chapter titled 'The "Dowager" and her role in the governance, and leadership of the entrepreneurial family business' by Robert Smith focuses on the different perceptions of individuals based on gender in family entrepreneurship.

Conclusion

This introductory chapter of this book has discussed the importance of taking a gender and family view in business. There are changes happening internationally in terms of how we conceptualize and understand the role of gender but also family in society. These changes are influencing business venture creation and the management of existing family businesses. In this chapter, we have discussed the need for gender dimensions to be addressed within studies of family entrepreneurship that can help practice but also inform policy.

References

Al-Dajani, H., Bika, Z., Collins, L., and Swail, J. (2014). Gender and family business: New theoretical directions. *International Journal of Gender and Entrepreneurship*, 6(3), 218–230.

Baron, R.A., and Henry, R.A. (2011). Entrepreneurship: The genesis of organizations. In S. Zedeck (Ed.), *APA Handbook of Industrial and Organizational Psychology, 1*, American Psychological Association (pp. 241–273). Washington, DC.

Berg, N.G. (1997). Gender, place and entrepreneurship. *Entrepreneurship & Regional Development*, 9, 259–268.

Bird, B.J. (1989). *Entrepreneurial Behavior.* Glenview, IL: Foresman.

Bird, B., Welsch, H., Astrachan, J.H., and Pistrui, D. (2002). Family business research: The evolution of an academic field. *Family Business Review*, XV(4), 337–350.

Brush, C., De Bruin, A., and Welter, F. (2009). A gender aware framework for women's entrepreneurship. *International Journal of Gender and Entrepreneurship*, 1(1), 8–24.

Buttner, E.H., and Moore, D.P. (1997). Women's organizational exodus to entrepreneurship: Self-reported motivations and correlates with success. *Journal of Small Business Management*, 35(1), 34–46.

Caputo, K., and Dolinksy, A. (1998). Women's choice to pursue self-employment: The role of financial and human capital of household members. *Journal of Small Business Management*, 36(3), 8–17.

Carter, N.M., Gartner, W.B., Shaver, K.G., and Gatewood, E.J. (2003). The career reasons of nascent entrepreneurs. *Journal of Business Venturing*, 18(1), 13–39.

Coleman, S. (2000). Access to capital and terms of credit: A comparison of men and women owned small businesses. *Journal of Small Business Management*, 38(3), 37–52.

De Martino, R., and Barbato, R. (2003). Differences between women and men MBA entrepreneurs: Exploring family flexibility and wealth creation as career motivators. *Journal of Business Venturing*, 18(6), 815–832.

De Massis, A., Frattini, F., Pizzurno, E., and Cassia, L. (2015). Product innovation in family versus nonfamily firms: An exploratory analysis. *Journal of Small Business Management*, 53(1), 1–36.

De Massis, A., Sharma, P., Chua, J.H., and Chrisman, J.J. (2012). *Family Business Studies: An Annotated Bibliography*. Cheltenham, UK: Edward Elgar.

DeTienne, D.R., and Chandler, G.N. (2007). The role of gender in opportunity identification. *Entrepreneurship Theory and Practice*, 30(1), 365–386.

Diaz-Garcia, M.C., and Jimenez-Moreno, J. (2010). Entrepreneurial intention: The role of gender. *International Entrepreneurship and Management Journal*, 6, 261–283.

Dyer, W.G., and Handler, W. (Fall 1994). Entrepreneurship and family business: Exploring the connections. *Entrepreneurship Theory & Practice*, 19(1) 71–83.

Ferreira, J., Ratten, V., and Dana, L.-P. (2017). Knowledge spillover based strategic entrepreneurship. *International Entrepreneurship and Management Journal*, 13(1): 161-167.

Gerguri, R. S., Ramadani, V., Abazi-Alili, H., Dana, L.-P., and Ratten, V. (2017). ICT, innovation and firm performance: The transition economies context. *Thunderbird International Business Review*, 59(1), 93–102.

Habbershon, T.G., and Williams, M.L. (1999). A resource-based framework for assessing the strategic advantages of family firms. *Family Business Review*, 12(1), 1–25.

Humbert, A.L., and Drew, E. (2010). Gender, entrepreneurship and motivational factors in an Irish context. *International Journal of Gender and Entrepreneurship*, 2(2), 173–196.

Karra, N., Tracey, P., and Phillips, N. (2006). Altruism and agency in the family firm: Exploring the role of family, kinship and ethnicity. *Entrepreneurship Theory and Practice*, 30(6), 861–877.

Langowitz, N., and Minniti, M. (2007). The entrepreneurial propensity of women. *Entrepreneurship Theory and Practice*, 31(3), 341–365.

Marlow, S., and Patton, D. (November 2005). All credit to men? Entrepreneurship, finance and gender. *Entrepreneurship Theory & Practice*, 29(6): 717–735.

Matthews, C.H., and Moser, S.B. (1996). A longitudinal investigation of the impact of family background and gender on interest in small firm ownership. *Journal of Small Business Management*, 34(2), 29–43.

Menzies, T.V., and Tatroff, H. (2006). The propensity of male versus female students to take courses and degree concentrations in entrepreneurship. *Journal of Small Business and Entrepreneurship*, 19(2), 203–218.

Miller, D., Steier, L., and Le Breton-Miller, I. (2003). Lost in time: Intergenerational succession, change and failure in family business. *Journal of Business Venturing*, 18(4), 513–531.

Nilsson, P. (1997). Business counseling services directed towards female entrepreneurs: Some legitimacy dilemmas. *Entrepreneurship and Regional Development*, 9(3), 239–258.

Orhan, M., and Scott, D. (2001). Why women enter into entrepreneurship: An explanatory model. *Women in Management Review*, 16(5), 232–243.

Ratten, V. (2007). Organisational learning: How can it foster alliance relationships? *Development and Learning in Organisations: An International Journal*, 22(1), 20–21.

Ratten, V. (2017). Social media innovations and creativity. In A. Brem and E. Viardot (Eds.), *Revolution of Innovation Management* (pp. 199–220). Palgrave, UK.

Ratten, V., and Ferreira, J. (2017). Future research directions for innovation and entrepreneurial networks. *International Journal of Business and Globalisation*, 18(1), 1–8.

Ronstadt, R. (1984). *Entrepreneurship: Text, Cases and Notes*. Dover, MA: Lord.

Sullivan, D.M., and Meek, W.R. (2012). Gender and entrepreneurship: A review and process model. *Journal of Managerial Psychology*, 27(5), 428–458.

Welter, F., Smallbone, D., Isakova, N., and Aculai, E. (2007). The role of gender for entrepreneurship in a transition context. In L. Iandoli, M. Raffa and H. Landstrom (Eds.), *Frontiers in European Research*. Cheltenham, UK: Edward Elgar.

Zapalska, A. (1997). A profile of women entrepreneurs and enterprises in Poland. *Journal of Small Business Management*, 35(4), 76–82.

2 Culturally endorsed leadership styles and entrepreneurial behaviors of women

Saurav Pathak and Etayankara Muralidharan

Introduction

Extant research has yet to find leadership patterns that are particularly relevant to entrepreneurship (Vecchio, 2003). While the entrepreneurial process has previously been seen in the same vein as that of leadership (Cogliser and Brigham, 2004), the links between leadership styles and women entrepreneurship has not been understood. Leadership and entrepreneurship studies have been conducted against a masculine backdrop (Bryans and Mavin, 2003). Although recent studies have begun to explore the relationship between the two fields (Cogliser and Brigham, 2004; Vecchio, 2003), there are limited studies considering the relationship from a gender perspective (Patterson, Mavin, and Turner, 2012). Considering that entrepreneurs are embedded in contexts (Welter, 2011), our study specifically seeks to address the above gap by examining how culturally endorsed leadership styles influence women's entrepreneurial behaviors.

Differences between leadership effectiveness and performance outcomes have been explained by the moderating influences of institutional or cultural variables (Atwater, Wang, Smither, and Fleenor, 2009; Spreitzer, Perttula, and Xin, 2005). Implicit leadership theories (ILTs) have been posited as normative institutions that legitimize behaviors, attributes, and motivations of leaders, and these theories influence individuals' choices in terms of who they will accept and categorize as leaders (Lord, Foti, and de Vader, 1984; Lord and Maher, 1991). Culturally endorsed leadership traits (CLTs) build on implicit leadership theory (Lord and Maher, 1991) and are, consequently, manifestations of normative institutions in a country. Our findings contribute to the above discussions by establishing CLTs as normative institutions, which subsequently influences leadership styles that induce women entrepreneurial behaviors in societies. Exploring the relationship between entrepreneurship and leadership from a gender perspective may facilitate an exchange of insights across disciplines which could support future research (Patterson et al., 2012).

Literature review

Entrepreneurship and women entrepreneurship

Entrepreneurship is an individual's occupational choice to work for his/her own purpose and risk (Hébert and Link, 1982). This career choice to engage in entrepreneurship is a process that unfolds over a time period and it is not a single event (Baron, 2007; McMullen and Dimov, 2013). Extant scholarship on cultural values and entrepreneurship or entrepreneurial behavior has not been consistent. The reasons of this inconsistency may be due to the use of different indicators of entrepreneurship by researchers (Bergmann and Stephan, 2013; Van Der Zwan, Verheul, Thurik, and Grilo, 2011). From the above we infer that entrepreneurs may exhibit different behaviors as they move through the entrepreneurial process. Such influence may be that of societal institutions of culture (Autio, Pathak, and Wennberg, 2013; Bergmann and Stephan, 2013; Van Der Zwan et al., 2011). In our study we associate such entrepreneurial behaviors and the different phases of the entrepreneurial process with the classification of entrepreneurs by the Global Entrepreneurship Monitor (GEM) survey.

The first phase of entrepreneurial process is the intention (which may be goal directed) of individuals to start a new enterprise or venture (Frese, 2009; Gielnik et al., 2014). In the second phase, the entrepreneur proceeds to implement his/her plans in what is termed as nascent entrepreneurship. The third phase, which is immediately after implementation, would be considered as sustained operations of the new enterprise, and this phase reflects that the individual has successfully launched his/her new venture. This phase is termed as the 'new entrepreneur' phase. After the third phase, individuals may or may not continue with their enterprise or operations depending upon the feasibility of their plans, availability of other attractive goals, or because of other external exigencies that may face the venture. This phase is termed as the 'established' phase of the new venture or enterprise.

Extent research examining the rates of the above entrepreneurial phases or behaviors suggest that there is a large variance in entrepreneurship across countries in general (Hayton, George, and Zahra, 2002). This has been particularly observed in women's entrepreneurship (Kelly, Brush, Greene, and Litovsky, 2010). Extant research has particularly adopted individual focused approaches to explain the above behaviors and have, in general, neglected societal factors that account for the variance in the rates of women's entrepreneurial activity across countries (Pathak, Goltz, and Buche, 2013). Such individual behaviors of entrepreneurs may be influenced by the specific cultural context of the society within which it takes place (Welter, 2011; Zahra and Wright, 2011). CLTs are one aspect of the societal cultural context, which is relevant for an individuals' entry and in his or her engagement in entrepreneurship. We first discuss and provide background on CLTs as societal or national institutions more generally before empirically examining their links with women entrepreneurial behavior.

National level institutions

We draw upon institutional theory to develop new insights for entrepreneurship by understanding factors that help to build and manage various relationships within society that facilitate entry and engagement in entrepreneurship (Zahra and Wright, 2011). Institutions refer to aspects of social structure that facilitate or constrain behavior in society (North, 1991; North, 2005; Scott, 2005). These institutions act as implicit guidelines for an individual's actions in society (Powell and DiMaggio, 1991).

Formal institutions relate to explicit incentives and constraints arising from government regulation, for example (Scott, 1995,2005). Informal institutions are implicit, socially constructed, and culturally transmitted (Stephan, Uhlaner, and Stride, 2014). Informal institutions are comprised of normative and cognitive institutions (Scott, 1995). Normative institutions generally model themselves on dominant norms (or practices) in a given societal culture (Javidan, House, Dorfman, Hanges, and Sully De Luque, 2006; Scott, 2005; Stephan and Uhlaner, 2010), elaborating the social obligations and expectations of actions based on existing norms or practices (Bruton, Ahlstrom, and Li, 2010; Stephan and Uhlaner, 2010). Cognitive institutions influence the "schemas, frames, and inferential sets, which people use when selecting and interpreting information," and they reflect the knowledge shared by individuals in a given society (Kostova, 1997: 180). Cognitive institutions are the culturally shared understandings and they are associated with cultural values (Bruton et al., 2010; Stephan and Uhlaner, 2010). In the subsequent section we discuss CLTs as normative institutions.

Culturally endorsed leadership

Leadership is defined as "the nature of the influencing process – and its resultant outcomes – that occurs between a leader and followers and how this influencing processes is explained by the leader's dispositional characteristics and behaviors, follower perceptions and attributions of the leader, and the *context* in which the influencing process occurs [italics added]" (Antonakis, Gianciolo, and Sternberg, 2004:5). Effectiveness of leadership styles may therefore be contingent upon the context within which leadership behaviors are performed (Antonakis and Autio, 2006).

Before discussing the relevance of CLTs on entrepreneurship, we first discuss the general idea of implicit leadership traits (ILTs), of which CLTs are a type. We draw on *implicit leadership theory*, to study the influence of culturally endorsed implicit leadership traits (CLTs) – culturally shared stereotypes of effective and outstanding leaders – on the likelihood of women's' engagement in entrepreneurship. This approach coincides with the *full-range leadership theory* (Bass, 1985, 1998) that contributes by moving beyond just the leader's traits and characteristics to leadership styles, such as transactional, transformational, instrumental, charismatic, visionary, etc., and how these styles affect the influencing process – engaging in entrepreneurial behaviors by women in our case.

ILTs are considered as normative institutions that legitimize behaviors, attributes, and motivations of leaders. These traits influence individuals' preferences in terms of who they will accept and categorize as leaders (Lord et al., 1984; Lord and Maher, 1991). It is established in literature that followers' perceptions of a leader are embedded in societies' cultural values. These values are outcomes of repeated behaviors that shape the cultural expectations and views of ideal leadership, and leaders tend to behave in line with these expectations (House, Dorfman, Javidan, Hanges, and Sully De Luque, 2014). Individuals are more likely to emerge as leaders and be successful in their leadership role if they demonstrate traits that are consistent with the implicit leadership theories held by followers (Epitropaki, Sy, Martin, Tram-Quon, and Topakas, 2013).

Since ILTs are culturally shared and show variations across societies, we can expect different types of leaders to emerge in different cultures, depending on how strongly certain ILTs are culturally endorsed. In summary, CLTs build on implicit leadership theory (Lord and Maher, 1991). They are therefore normative institutions since they refer to individual's stereotypical ideas about the attributes and behaviors of effective leaders (House, Hanges, Javidan, Dorfman, and Gupta, 2004; Javidan et al., 2006). We now discuss culturally endorsed charismatic and participatory leadership styles and empirically examine their effects on women entrepreneurial behaviors.

Leadership styles

We use the notion of *culture-entrepreneurship fit* (Tung, Walls, and Frese, 2007) to propose that individuals are more likely to become entrepreneurs in countries where culturally endorsed leadership theories fit with and are supportive of entrepreneurial attributes and behaviors. We argue that, in particular, charismatic and participative CLTs capture key aspects of entrepreneurial agency and thus can be seen as important cultural predictors of individuals' engagement in entrepreneurship. Global Leadership and Organizational Behavior Effectiveness (GLOBE) performed a cross-cultural research study that extended the understanding of implicit leadership theory and highlighted the concept that individuals' implicit belief systems about ideal leaders are culturally endorsed (House et al., 2004; Javidan et al., 2006). The study showed that although these belief systems varied *between* cultures, there is consensus *within* a culture on the attributes of outstanding leaders (Dorfman, Javidan, Hanges, Dastmalchian, and House, 2012; House et al., 2004). While the GLOBE study examined six different dimensions to describe the content of CLTs (i.e., charismatic, participative, self-protective, humane oriented, team oriented, and autonomous), for the purposes of our study we focused on charismatic and participative CLTs, which hold particular relevance for entrepreneurship.

Charismatic leaders broaden and elevate the interests of their employees and generate awareness and acceptance of their organization's purposes and mission (Schermerhorn, Hunt, and Osborn, 2005). Such leaders, in order to accomplish this objective, use the key entrepreneurial leadership strategies of attention through vision, meaning through communication, trust through positioning, and confidence through respect (Nurmi and Darling, 1997; Ruvio, Rosenblatt, and Hertz-Lazarowitz, 2010). As charismatic leaders, such entrepreneurs have a vision of how things could be, and they clearly communicate this vision to their employees and, through the entrepreneur's own enthusiasm, motivate them to support it. CLTs of charismatic leadership characterize effective leaders as visionary, performance- and future-oriented, and as being able to motivate their employees based on core values, integrity, and vision (House et al., 2004). Therefore, cultures that endorse charismatic leadership provide the required environment within which entrepreneurs are likely to thrive, since their entrepreneurial actions are more likely to be accepted by others in their culture.

Entrepreneurs, who take initiative and shape the future of their organizations to achieve their missions often work cooperatively with other like-minded individuals (Frese and Gielnik, 2014). While they believe in the centrality of their role, they also take care to include their employees in the decision-making and in the operations of the organizations they form (Shaw and Carter, 2007). CLTs of participative leadership capture the followers' expectations that leadership should be non-autocratic (House et al., 2004). Participative leaders therefore strive to motivate and facilitate the involvement of their employees in making decisions since doing so promotes approval and commitment (Yan and Sorenson, 2003). The highest form of participative leadership is in the delegation of decision-making, which includes power-sharing, empowerment, and reciprocal influence processes (Vroom and Yetton, 1973). Cultures that endorse participatory leadership provide the required environment within which entrepreneurs are likely to thrive since their entrepreneurial actions are likely to be accepted by others. Therefore, individuals within societies that endorse participatory leadership are more likely to be motivated to start an entrepreneurial venture.

In summary, we draw upon the insights from *Implicit Leadership Theory* to understand the influence of culturally endorsed implicit leadership traits (CLTs) – culturally shared stereotypes of effective and outstanding leaders – on entrepreneurial behaviors in the entrepreneurship process and empirically examine the effects on women entrepreneurs. These CLTs are considered to be more proximal drivers of cross-societal differences in entrepreneurship as compared with distal cultural values (Stephan and Pathak, 2016). Our approach is in line with the *full-range leadership theory* (Bass, 1985, 1998) that contributes by moving beyond just the leader's traits and characteristics to leadership styles, such as transactional, transformational, instrumental, charismatic, visionary, etc., and the effect of these styles on entrepreneurial behaviors – starting with intentions to engage in entrepreneurship to the establishment of successful ventures. Putting it formally, our study empirically examines the question "*What are the influences of charismatic and participatory CLTs on women entrepreneurial behaviors?*"

In our proposed model, culturally endorsed leadership traits (CLTs) are an important normative institution. We propose and test a multilevel model in which the two institutions of culturally endorsed leadership traits charismatic and participatory leadership styles affect women entrepreneurial behaviors, starting with

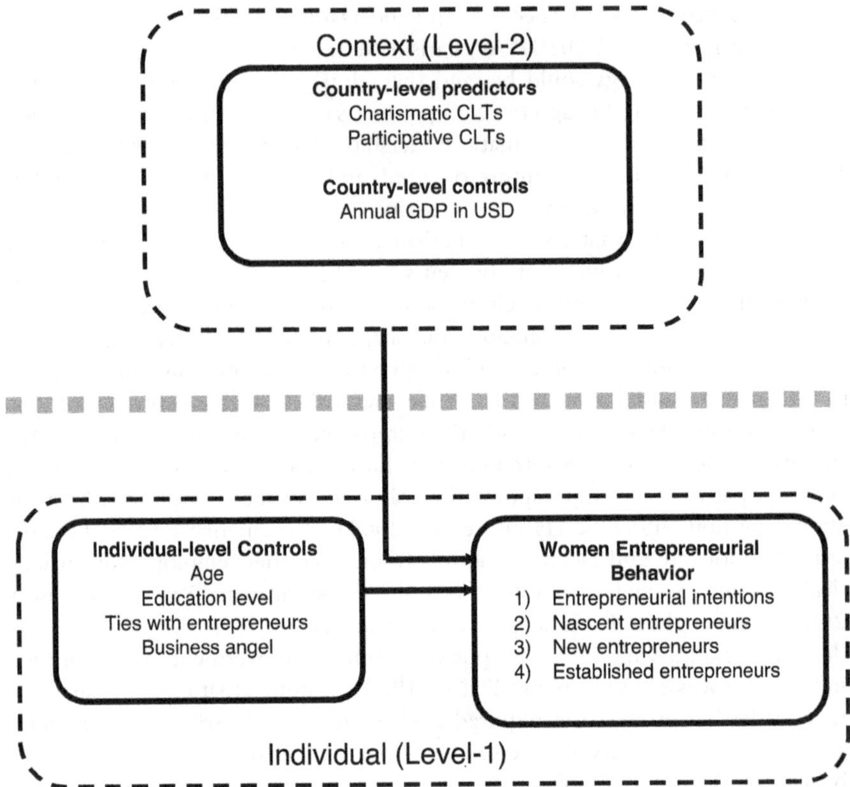

Figure 2.1 Theoretical and empirical model

intentions to engage in entrepreneurship to the establishment of successful ventures. We now discuss the methodology followed to empirically examine the above question and present our findings. *Our empirical model is shown in Figure 2.1.*

Research methodology

In order to empirically examine our research question, "*What are the influences of charismatic and participatory CLTs on women entrepreneurial behaviors?*", we analyzed panel survey data on over 289,888 individual-level responses by women from 41 countries for 2001–2008 obtained from the publicly available Global Entrepreneurship Monitor (GEM) survey (Reynoldset al., 2005) conducted by the Global Entrepreneurship Research Association (GERA). The 41 countries covered in our data set are listed in Table 2.1. GERA, which has been collecting internationally harmonized individual-level data annually since 1998, surveys representative samples of the adult population within each country (18–64 years of age). Through this cross-country survey design, GEM offers one of the most comprehensive and harmonized data sets on internationally comparative data on individual-level entrepreneurial ambitions and behaviors.

GEM survey identifies four types of individuals: (1) individuals with entrepreneurial intentions; (2) *nascent entrepreneurs* (individuals who are active in the process of starting a new firm during the preceding 12 months and with expectations of full or part ownership, but have not yet launched one); (3) *new entrepreneurs* (owner-managers of new firms who have survived for 41 months and have paid wages to any employees for more than three months); and (4) *established entrepreneurs* (owner-managers of firms 42 months old or older). These above indictors of entrepreneurship served as four dependent variables in our study that represented two phases of the entrepreneurial process – *pre-entry* and *post entry.* Finally, we selected a sub-sample that corresponded to all females across each of these four indicators of entrepreneurship.

This data set was subsequently complemented with data on the two country-level predictors – *charismatic* and *participative leadership styles* -–computed as two composite factors using the six leadership dimensions available from the GLOBE study. GLOBE's Leaders Attributes and Behavior Questionnaire is the basis on which CLTs are generated. In the study, GLOBE surveyed 17,000 CEOs/managers across 62 societies. The study started with an *alpha* version of this questionnaire, which listed 56 leader attributes and behavior items. These attributes and items included a wide variety of the traits, skills, behaviors, and abilities that are often associated with leadership emergence and effectiveness. In a subsequent *beta* version, the study enlisted another 56 attributes, thereby totaling 112 leader behaviors.

These leadership attributes were rated from 1 to 7 (a low of 1 indicating "this behavior or characteristic greatly inhibits a person from being an outstanding leader" to a high of 7 indicating "this behavior or characteristic contributes greatly to a person being an outstanding leader"). Using conceptual arguments and various statistical procedures, GLOBE subsequently grouped these 112 disparate leader behaviors into 21 *primary dimensions* of leadership. The study further performed a second-order factor analysis wherein these 21 dimensions were loaded onto six *global dimensions of leadership*: value-based/charismatic, team-oriented, participative, humane-oriented, autonomous, and self-protective. For the purpose of our study, and in line with our empirical framework, we used two out of these six leadership traits – *charismatic and participatory.*

Charismatic is a leadership trait that reflects the leader's ability to inspire, to motivate, and to expect high performance outcomes from others, based on firmly held core values. It includes six out of the 21 primary dimensions of leadership: visionary, inspirational, self-sacrifice, integrity, decisive, and performance-oriented. The charismatic CLT trait showed high internal consistency (Cronbach's Alpha .98, ICC (2) interrater reliability = .95) as well as meaningful within-country agreement. The between-country variation ICC (1) scores for the six subscales ranged from .14 to .19, suggesting that significant variance existed in sub-scales between countries (Hanges and Dickson, 2004). Details on the underlying data source, the operationalization method, and the interpretation of the leadership dimensions can be found in House et al.(2004) and Dorfman et al.(2012).

Participatory is a global leadership trait that reflects the degree to which managers involve other employees or subordinates in the firm's decision-making processes. This trait is statistically linked to two leadership dimensions (both reverse-coded): non-participative and autocratic. In our study, the participative CLT dimension showed high internal consistency (Cronbach's Alpha = .85, ICC (2) interrater reliability = .95) as well as meaningful within-country agreement. The intra-class correlation (ICC) (i.e. between-country variation) ICC (1) scores for the two subscales were .19 for non-participative and .20 for autocratic, suggesting that significant variance existed in sub-scales between countries (Hanges and Dickson, 2004).

Thus, individual-responses were clustered across the 41 countries, yielding a multi-level hierarchical data set. Subsequently, we employed multi-level random effect logistic regression methodology (using *gllamm* command in Stata 13.0 SE version) to estimate the influences of charismatic and participative leadership styles on the individual-level likelihood of women engaging in each of the four stages of entrepreneurship. We ran four separate regressions for the four dependent variables that we just presented.

We employed one control at the country-level – annual GDP in USD (obtained from World Bank). We did not include more country-level controls because of multi-collinearity issues. At the individual-level, we controlled for individual's age (Arenius and Minniti, 2005; Reynoldset al., 2005) and education level (Arenius and Minniti, 2005), ties with other entrepreneurs (1 = knows other entrepreneurs, 0 = otherwise), and business angel status (1 = is a business angel, 0 = otherwise).

Findings

Our data is grouped country wise resulting in a hierarchical and clustered dataset. This type of grouping allows accounting for the variance in the dependent variable that may arise due to country-level specific factors. The significant cross-country variance observed in our four dependent variables across the 41 countries necessitated using multi-level analyses wherein the variance could be explained using the two country-level predictors – charismatic and participatory CLTs. Random-effect logistic regression models report estimates for the fixed part (estimates of coefficients) and random part (variance estimates), as well as providing model fit statistics. The estimates are reported as odds ratios (exponential of the beta coefficients obtained from logistic regressions).

We report our results from four random effect logistic regressions (i.e. examining the effects of charismatic and participative CLTs on the individual-level likelihood of women's engagement in entrepreneurial behaviors) as odds ratios (OR) in Table 2.1. Ratios greater than 1 represent a positive association (percent increase) while ratios less than 1 represent a negative association (percent decrease). Of the four dependent variables 'entrepreneurial intentions' and 'nascent entrepreneurs' represent the *pre-entry* stage and 'new entrepreneurs' and 'established entrepreneurs' represent the *post-entry* stage.

Table 2.1 Effects of CLTs on women entrepreneurial behaviors

	Model 1 Entrepreneurial Intentions	*Model 2 Nascent Entrepreneurs*	*Model 3 New Entrepreneurs*	*Model 4 Established Entrepreneurs*
Fixed part estimates				
Individual-level				
Age	0.97***(0.00)	0.98***(0.00)	0.98***(0.00)	1.02***(0.00)
Education level	1.17***(0.01)	1.17***(0.02)	1.05***(0.02)	1.01***(0.01)
Ties with entrepreneurs	2.44***(0.03)	2.73***(0.06)	2.37***(0.06)	1.96***(0.03)
Business angel	1.97***(0.08)	1.91***(0.09)	1.93***(0.09)	1.66***(0.06)
Country-level				
Annual GDP in USD	1.26***(0.00)	1.32***(0.05)	1.35***(0.05)	1.54***(0.04)
Charismatic CLTs	**1.09***(0.06)**	**1.25***(0.11)**	**1.49*** (0.16)**	**1.43***(0.15)**
Participatory CLTs	**1.09***(0.03)**	**0.82**(0.08)**	**0.77*(0.09)**	**0.77*(0.09)**
Model statistics				
Number of observations	289888	289888	289888	289888
Number of groups (countries)	41	41	41	41

Standard errors in parentheses: p<0.001***; p<.05**; p<0.10*; 2-tailed significance.

Note: 1) Columns present odds ratios (OR) instead of regression estimates. OR values greater than 1 signal positive association. OR values smaller than 1 signal negative association.

2) Country level control of GDP (in USD) was used. Individual level controls of age, gender, and education level of entrepreneurs were used.

3) Model 1, 2, 3, and 4 are results of the separate logistic regressions pertaining to the four dependent variables classified as entrepreneurial intentions, nascent entrepreneurs, new entrepreneurs, and established entrepreneurs respectively.

4) List of countries (N = 41): Argentina, Australia, Austria, Bolivia, Brazil, Canada, China, Colombia, Denmark, Ecuador, Egypt, Finland, France, Germany, Greece, Hong Kong, Hungary, India, Indonesia, Ireland, Israel, Italy, Japan, Malaysia, Mexico, Netherlands, New Zealand, Philippines, Poland, Portugal, Russia, Slovenia, South Africa, South Korea, Spain, Sweden, Switzerland, Thailand, Turkey, UK, USA.

We observed that a one standard deviation increase in charismatic CLT increased the likelihood of women's (1) entrepreneurial intentions by 9 per cent (OR = 1.09; $p < 0.001$), (2) nascent entrepreneurship by 25 per cent (OR = 1.25; $p < 0.01$), (3) new entrepreneurship by 49 per cent (OR = 1.49; $p < 0.001$), and (4) established entrepreneurship by 43 per cent (OR = 1.43; $p < 0.01$). We also observed that a one standard deviation increase in participatory CLT increased the likelihood of women's (1) entrepreneurial intentions by

9 per cent (OR = 1.09; $p < 0.001$) but decreased the likelihood of (2) nascent entrepreneurship by 18 per cent (OR = 0.82; $p < 0.04$), (3) new entrepreneurship by 23 per cent (OR = 0.77; $p < 0.001$), and (4) established entrepreneurship by 23 per cent (OR = 0.77; $p < 0.02$). These findings suggest that while charismatic leadership styles and participatory leadership styles favor entrepreneurial intentions in women in the pre-entry stage, it is the charismatic leadership styles that endure entrepreneurial behaviors through the pre-entry and post-entry stages

Discussions and implications

Entrepreneurship and leadership have been considered as separate fields of study (Vecchio, 2003; Cogliser and Brigham, 2004). Although there have been discussions for the convergence of research in entrepreneurship and leadership to enable an interchange of ideas between the two fields (Czarniawska-Joerges and Wolff, 1991; Cogliser and Brigham, 2004; Vecchio, 2003), there has been little progress made in that direction (Daily, McDougall, Covin and Dalton, 2002). Also, research examining the link from a gender perspective is limited (Patterson et al., 2012).

We attempt to link leadership and entrepreneurship research by introducing a cultural leadership paradigm that improves our understanding of the emergence of entrepreneurial leaders across different cultures. Specifically, we present supporting evidence for the cultural leadership paradigm by using multilevel modeling techniques and by analyzing data that includes population-representative surveys on entrepreneurship, obtained from the GEM survey with regard to women entrepreneurs.

Drawing upon the ***implicit leadership theory***, our study attempts to understand the influence of Culturally-endorsed implicit Leadership Theories (CLTs) – culturally shared stereotypes of effective and outstanding leaders – entrepreneurial behaviors of women in 41 countries. We treat CLTs – ***charismatic*** and ***participatory*** leadership styles – as similar to cultural orientations and theorize to first establish them as a country's ***normative institutional*** context. Cultural orientations manifested by charismatic and participatory leadership styles provide appropriate contexts for entrepreneurs.

Our findings have implications[1] on the effect of leadership on pre-entry and post-entry entrepreneurship, in order to see how women entrepreneurial efforts lead to the successful establishment of enterprises. In other words, how the journey from entrepreneurial intentions to successful establishment of enterprises by women is made possible by leadership styles. While both charismatic and participatory leadership styles may induce entrepreneurial intentions in women, it is the cultural level charismatic leadership styles that endure in women to engage and progress in establishing entrepreneurial ventures. Cultural level participatory, on the contrary, suppresses such behaviors.

We contribute by ascertaining that CLTs are more proximal and domain-specific drivers of cross-national differences in women entrepreneurship compared to general cultural values and add to leadership research investigating drivers of entrepreneurship across cultures. Our contextual perspective highlights the role of the national context in the motivation of women to lead enterprises, in contrast to individual differences that are believed to drive such motivations (Day, 2012). Our study, therefore, contributes to calls for increased consideration of context in examining entrepreneurial behaviors (Zahra and Wright, 2011) and more specifically contributes to the comparative literature on women entrepreneurship.

Limitations and future research

Contextual factors may influence which leadership styles are effective in inducing desired behaviors in followers (Crossan, Vera, and Nanjad, 2008). However, such likelihood is a function of individuals' feasibility assessments and influences arising from other contextual influences in (Levie and Autio, 2011). Therefore, the effects of charismatic and participatory CLTs in inducing entrepreneurial behaviors in women may also be influenced by other national institutions, a factor that leads us to propose a moderating role of other formal and informal institutions on the influence of these CLTs on women entrepreneurship as directions for future research. The more these formal and informal institutions support individual agency, the stronger will be the effects of charismatic and participatory leadership styles on the likelihood of women becoming entrepreneurs.

Note

1 Results are available upon request for all implications referred to, including moderation with cultural variables and results on strategic entrepreneurial leadership aspirations.

References

Antonakis, J., and Autio, E. (2006). Entrepreneurship and leadership. *The Psychology of Entrepreneurship*, 1(1): 189–208.

Antonakis, J., Gianciolo, A.T., Sternberg, R.J. (2004). Leadership: Past, present, and future. In J. Antonakis, A.T. Gianciolo and R.J. Sternberg (Eds.), *The Nature of Leadership* (pp. 3–15). Thousand Oaks, CA: Sage.

Arenius, P., and Minniti, M. (2005). Perceptual variables and nascent entrepreneurship. *Small Business Economics*, 24(3), 233–247.

Atwater, L., Wang, M., Smither, J.W., and Fleenor, J. W. (2009). Are cultural characteristics associated with the relationship between self and others' ratings of leadership? *Journal of Applied Psychology*, 94, 876–886.

Autio, E., Pathak, S., and Wennberg, K. (2013). Consequences of cultural practices for entrepreneurial behaviors. *Journal of International Business Studies*, 44(4), 334–362.

Baron, R. A. (2007). Entrepreneurship: A process perspective. In J. R. Baum, M. Frese and R. A. Baron (Eds.), *The Psychology of Entrepreneurship* (pp. 19–40). Lawrence Erlbaum Associates.

Bass, B. M. (1985). *Leadership and Performance Beyond Expectations.* New York: Collier Macmillan.

Bass, B. M. (1998). *Transformational Leadership: Industry, Military, and Educational Impact.* Mahwah, NJ: Lawrence Erlbaum.

Bergmann, H., and Stephan, U. (2013). Moving on from nascent entrepreneurship: Measuring cross national differences in the transition to new business ownership. *Small Business Economics*, 41(4), 945–959.

Bruton, G. D., Ahlstrom, D., and Li, H.L. (2010). Institutional theory and entrepreneurship: Where are we now and where do we need to move in the future? *Entrepreneurship: Theory and Practice*, 34(3), 421–440.

Bryans, P., and Mavin, S. (2003). Women learning to become managers: Learning to fit in or to play a different game? *Management Learning*, 34(1), 111–134.

Cogliser, C. C., and Brigham, K. H. (2004). The intersection of leadership and entrepreneurship: Mutual lessons to be learned. *The Leadership Quarterly*, 15(6), 771–799.

Crossan, M., Vera, D., and Nanjad, L. (2008). Transcendent leadership: Strategic leadership in dynamic environments. *The Leadership Quarterly*, 19, 569–581.

Czarniawska-Joerges, B., and Wolff, R. (1991). Leaders, managers, entrepreneurs on and off the organizational stage. *Organization Studies*, 12(4), 529–546.

Daily, C. M., McDougall, P. P., Covin, J. G., and Dalton, D. R. (2002). Governance and strategic leadership in entrepreneurial firms. *Journal of Management*, 28(3), 387–412.

Day, D.V. (2012). The nature of leadership development. In D. V. Day and J. Antonakis (Eds.), *The Nature of Leadership* (2nd ed., pp. 108–140). Los Angeles, CA: Sage.

Dorfman, P., Javidan, M., Hanges, P., Dastmalchian, A., and House, R. (2012). GLOBE: A twenty year journey into the intriguing world of culture and leadership. *Journal of World Business*, 47(4), 504–518.

Ensley, M. D., Hmieleski, K. M., and Pearce, C. L. (2006). The importance of vertical and shared leadership within new venture top management teams: Implications for the performance of startups. *The Leadership Quarterly*, 17(3), 217–231.

Epitropaki, O., Sy, T., Martin, R., Tram-Quon, S., and Topakas, A. (2013). Implicit leadership and followership theories 'in the wild': Taking stock of information-processing approaches to leadership and followership in organizational settings. *The Leadership Quarterly*, 24(6), 858–881.

Frese, M. (2009). Towards a psychology of entrepreneurship: An action theory perspective. *Foundations and Trends in Entrepreneurship*, 5(6), 437–496.

Frese, M., and Gielnik, M.M. (2014). The psychology of entrepreneurship. *Annual Review of Organizational Psychology and Organizational Behavior*, 1, 413–438.

Gielnik, M. M., Barabas, S., Frese, M., Namatovu-Dawa, R., Scholz, F. A., and Metzger, J. R. (2014). A temporal analysis of how entrepreneurial goal intentions, positive fantasies, and action planning affect starting a new venture and when the effects wear off. *Journal of Business Venturing*, 29(6), 755–772.

Hanges, P. J., and Dickson, M.W. (2004). The development and validation of the GLOBE culture and leadership scales. In House, R., Hanges, P., Javidan, M., Dorfman, P. and Gupta, V. (Eds) *Culture, Leadership, and Organizations: The GLOBE Study of 62 Societies* (pp. 122–151). New York: Sage.

Hayton, J. C., George, G., and Zahra, S. A. (2002). National culture and entrepreneurship: A review of behavioral research. *Entrepreneurship Theory and Practice*, 26(4), 33–52.

Hébert, R. F., and Link, A. N. (1982). *The Entrepreneurs: Mainstream Views and Radical Critiques.* New York: Praeger.

House, R.J., Dorfman, P., Javidan, M., Hanges, P.J., and Sully De Luque, M. (2014). *Strategic Leadership Across Cultures: GLOBE Study of CEO Leadership Behavior and Effectiveness in 24 Countries.* Thousand Oaks, CA: Sage.

House, R. J., Hanges, P.J., Javidan, M., Dorfman, P.W., and Gupta, V. (2004). *Culture, Leadership and Organizations: The GLOBE Study of 62 Societies.* Thousand Oaks, CA: Sage.

Javidan, M., House, R.J., Dorfman, P., Hanges, P.J., and Sully De Luque, M. (2006). Conceptualizing and measuring cultures and their consequences: A comparative review of GLOBE's and Hofstede's approaches. *Journal of International Business Studies*, 37(6), 897–914.

Kelly, D.J., Brush, C.G., Greene, P.G., and Litovsky, Y. (2010). *GEM 2010 Report on Women and Entrepreneurship: Global Entrepreneurship Monitor Program.* Babson Park, MA: Babson College.

Kostova, T. (1997). *Country Institutional Profile: Concept and Measurement.* Best paper Proceedings of the Academy of Management (pp. 180–184).

Levie, J., and Autio, E. (2011). Regulatory burden, rule of law, and entry of strategic entrepreneurs: An international panel study. *Journal of Management Studies*, 48, 1392–1419.

Lord, R. G., Foti, R. J., and De Vader, C. L. (1984). A test of leadership categorization theory: Internal structure, information processing, and leadership perceptions. *Organizational Behavior and Human Performance*, 34, 343–378.

Lord, R. G., and Maher, K. J. (1991). *Leadership and Information Processing: Linking Perceptions and Performance.* Cambridge, MA: Unwin Hyman.

McMullen, J. S., and Dimov, D. (2013). Time and the entrepreneurial journey: The problems and promise of studying entrepreneurship as a process. *Journal of Management Studies*, 50(8), 1481–1512.

North, D. C. (1991). Institutions. *Journal of Economic Perspectives*, 5(2), 97–112.

North, D. C. (2005). *Understanding the Process of Economic Change.* Princeton, NJ: Princeton University Press.

Nurmi, R., and Darling, J. (1997). *International Management Leadership: The Primary Competitive Advantage.* New York: International Business Press.

Pathak, S., Goltz, S., and Buche, M. W. (2013). Influences of gendered institutions on women's entry into entrepreneurship. *International Journal of Entrepreneurial Behaviour & Research*, 19(5), 478–502.

Patterson, N., Mavin, S., and Turner, J. (2012). Envisioning female entrepreneur: Leaders anew from a gender perspective. *Gender in Management: An International Journal*, 27(6), 395–416.

Powell, W. W., and DiMaggio, P.J. (1991). *The New Institutionalism in Organizational Analysis.* Chicago: University of Chicago Press.

Reynolds, P.D., Bosma, N., Autio, E., Hunt, S., De Bono, N., Servais, I., . . . Chin, N. (2005). Global entrepreneurship monitor: Data collection design and implementation 1998–2003. *Small Business Economics*, 24(3), 205–231.

Ruvio, A., Rosenblatt, Z., and Hertz-Lazarowitz, R. (2010). Entrepreneurial leadership vision in nonprofit vs. for-profit organizations. *The Leadership Quarterly*, 21(1), 144–158.

Schermerhorn, J., Hunt, J., and Osborn, R. (2005). *Organizational Behavior* (9th ed.). Hoboken, NJ: Wiley.

Scott, W. R. (1995). *Institutions and Organizations.* Thousand Oaks, CA: Sage.

Scott, W. R. (2005). Institutional theory: Contributing to a theoretical research program. In K. G. Smith and M. A. Hitt (Eds.), *Great Minds in Management: The Process of Theory Development.* Oxford: Oxford University Press.

Shaw, E., and Carter, S. (2007). Social entrepreneurship: Theoretical antecedents and empirical analysis of entrepreneurial processes and outcomes. *Journal of Small Business and Enterprise Development*, 14(3), 418–434.

Spreitzer, G.M., Perttula, K.H., and Xin, K. (2005). Traditionality matters: An examination of the effectiveness of transformational leadership in the United States and Taiwan. *Journal of Organizational Behavior*, 26(3), 205–227.

Stephan, U., and Pathak, S. (2016). Beyond cultural values? Cultural leadership ideals and entrepreneurship. *Journal of Business Venturing*, 31(5), 505–523.

Stephan, U., and Uhlaner, L.M. (2010). Performance-based vs. socially supportive culture: A cross-national study of descriptive norms and entrepreneurship. *Journal of International Business Studies*, 41(8), 1347–1364.

Stephan, U., Uhlaner, L. M., and Stride, C. (2014). Institutions and social entrepreneurship: The role of institutional voids, institutional support, and institutional configurations. *Journal of International Business Studies*, 46(3), 308–331.

Tung, R.L., Walls, J., and Frese, M. (2007). Cross-cultural entrepreneurship: The case of China. In J.R. Baum, M. Frese and R. Baron (Eds.), *The Psychology of Entrepreneurship* (pp. 265–286). Mahwah, NJ: Lawrence Erlbaum Associates.

Van Der Zwan, P., Verheul, I., Thurik, R., and Grilo, I. (2011). Entrepreneurial progress: Climbing the entrepreneurial ladder in Europe and the United States. *Regional Studies*, 47(5), 803–825.

Vecchio, R. P. (2003). Entrepreneurship and leadership: Common trends and common threads. *Human Resource Management Review*, 13(2), 303–327.

Vroom, V. H., and Yetton, P.W. (1973). *Leadership and Decision Making.* Pittsburgh: University of Pittsburgh Press.

Welter, F. (2011). Contextualizing entrepreneurship: Conceptual challenges and ways forward. *Entrepreneurship Theory and Practice*, 35(1), 165–184.

Yan, J., and Sorenson, R.L. (Fall 2003). Collective entrepreneurship in family firms: The influence of leader attitudes and behaviors. *New England Journal of Entrepreneurship*, 6(2), 37–51.

Zahra, S. A., and Wright, M. (2011). Entrepreneurship's next act. *Academy of Management Perspectives*, 25(4), 67–83.

3 Moving beyond the barriers

Examining the impact of self-efficacy and stereotype reactance on women's entrepreneurial intentions

Golshan Javadian, Robert P. Singh and Vishal K. Gupta

Entrepreneurial intention, which has a significant impact on individuals' decisions to start and grow ventures, is central to entrepreneurship research because it contributes to understanding of the complex process of entrepreneurship. Intentions are defined as the state of mind that focuses an individual's attention and behavior on a specific object or behavioral strategy (Bird, 1988). Intentions result from beliefs and attitudes and lead to behavioral outcomes (Ajzen, 2001; Bird, 1988; Fishbein and Ajzen, 1975).

Research has shown that women generally have lower levels of entrepreneurial intentions than men (Jenning and Brush, 2013). Such differences have been attributed to specific problems faced by women entrepreneurs. In fact, to date, much of women entrepreneurship has been focused on problems and challenges faced by women entrepreneurs, the causes and roots of such problems and on offering explanations for these problems (Jennings and Brush, 2013; James, 2012). Among the identified challenges are the gender stereotypes.

Gender stereotypes are the shared beliefs about the attitudes and characteristics associated with each sex (Powell and Graves, 2003). Such characteristics describe how men and women are, as well as how they should be (Schein, 1994; Heilman, Wallen, Fuchs, and Tamkins, 2004). Negative gender stereotypes, which are predominant in many societies (Heilman and Okimoto, 2007), influence cognitions, attitudes and behaviors (Devine, 1989; Wegener, Lark, and Petty, 2006). Once negative stereotypes have been established, they can influence individuals without any need of a reminder (Devine, 1989). Negative gender stereotypes, specifically, have a crucial impact on women's behavior in many achievement-related domains, including entrepreneurship (Gupta, Turban, and Bhawe, 2008; Nosek, Banaji, and Greenwald, 2002).

In entrepreneurial contexts, negative gender stereotypes have been shown to have a detrimental impact on women's entrepreneurial intentions (Gupta et al., 2008). Such stereotypes impact women's perceptions of their own entrepreneurial capabilities. Women who perceive themselves as similar to males have higher entrepreneurial intentions than those who see themselves as similar to females (Gupta, Turban, Wasti, and Sikdar, 2009). Similarly, negative gender stereotypes affect women's evaluations of business opportunities and their assessment of business ideas (Gupta, Turban, and Pareek, 2013; Gupta, Goktan, and Gunay, 2014; Gupta and Turban, 2012). Women have lower levels of opportunity evaluation and evaluate masculine business ideas more favorably in the presence of masculine stereotypical information (Gupta et al., 2013; Gupta and Turban, 2012).

Much of the literature suggests that entrepreneurship is a masculine activity that usually occurs in a gender stereotypic context (Ahl, 2006; Baron, 1999; Baron, Markman, and Hirsa, 2001; De Bruin, Brush, and Welter, 2006; Fagenson and Marcus, 1991); yet, women continue to start and run businesses in increasing numbers. According to 2014 State of Women owned Business Report by American Express Open, the number of women owned businesses has grown 68 percent over the past 17 years with 11 percent increase in employment and 72 percent increase in revenues. Based on the current research on women entrepreneurship, we do not know how women confront the gender stereotypical context and how they build and run ventures in increasing numbers, despite the challenges caused by such context.

This research aims to explain how women entrepreneurs overcome the negative gender stereotypes through the implications of stereotype reactance/protection theory (Kray et al., 2001; Javadian and Zoogah, 2014) and entrepreneurial self-efficacy. Specifically, we examine how women entrepreneurs confront negative gender stereotypes and form venture creation and venture growth intentions in such masculine context. Taking such an approach, this research addresses James' (2012) call for more focus on women's entrepreneurial successes rather than on their problems. This approach not only seeks to remedy the gap in the literature on this topic, but also strives to move beyond the problems women entrepreneurs face in order to focus on the *solutions* to those problems. Negative gender stereotypes in entrepreneurship are an indisputable problem for women; as a result, it is essential to discover precisely how women form the intentions to start and grow their businesses despite these stereotypes. In addition, a thorough analysis of the process women go through to form the intentions to build and grow businesses in a gender stereotypic context can lead to a better understanding of these processes and can be beneficial in promoting women's entrepreneurship.

Theoretical background and hypothesis development

Associations with different social groups impact individuals' social identities (Ellemers, Spears, and Doosje, 2002). Based on their attachment to different social groups, individuals have different forms of social identities that prescribe their behaviors. Individuals' social identification also depends on their perception of the group and is impacted by the distinctiveness and prestige of the group (Ashforth and Mael, 1989). Social identity leads to differential perceptions of self and others, depending on which identity is most salient (Crisp and Hewstone, 2007; Haslam and Turner, 1992). Although some kinds of group membership are viewed as identity enhancing, others may be viewed as identity jeopardizing based on how that specific group is evaluated within the relevant social context (Ellemers et al., 2002).

Gender is one of the social groups to which individuals belong. It is perhaps the strongest basis for the categorization of people worldwide and surpasses other demographic characteristics, such as race and age, by far (Randel, 2002). Women are affiliated with certain negative gender stereotypes. Negative gender stereotypes are the widely held beliefs about women's inferior abilities, behaviors and attributes (Chalabaev, Stone, Sarrazin, and Croizet, 2008). Negative stereotypes about a group's ability can lead to social inequalities in achievement (Chalabaev et al., 2008). The impact of negative stereotypes on achievement has been examined using stereotype threat theory.

Stereotype threat is defined as being in a position to validate negative stereotypes about one's group. Steele and Aronson (1995) introduced the definition of stereotype threat as "being at risk of confirming a negative stereotype about one's group" (p. 797). Stereotype threat is considered a self-threat, which may interrupt or impede an individual's performance. Steele (1997) argues that stereotype threat is a social-psychological threat that is activated when the subject is put in the stereotype-relevant domain (a threat in the air).

Although studies have shown that people often conform to negative stereotypes, there is evidence to suggest that, in some instances, individuals actually react against the stereotypes and respond positively instead (Hoyt, 2005; Kray et al., 2001). Based on Brehm's (1966) theory of psychological reactance, individuals respond to a perceived threat to their freedom by reasserting their freedom. Therefore, they may respond to the stereotyped expectation of inferiority by engaging in counter-stereotypical behaviors (Hoyt, Johnson, Murphy, and Skinnell, 2010).

Engaging in counter-stereotypical behavior when individuals are confronted with negative stereotypes that disparage the performance of the stereotyped group is termed stereotype reactance (Kray et al., 2001). Stereotype reactance is the positive cognitive response to negative stereotypes, and stereotype protection is the behavioral response resulting from cognitive response (Javadian and Zoogah, 2014). Stereotype protection is defined as "disconfirming a negative stereotype about one's group, which assists the individual in maintaining his/her performance" (Javadian and Zoogah, 2014: 413).

Stereotype reactance has been shown to positively impact the performance of those individuals who have engaged in counter-stereotypical behaviors. Kray et al. (2004) found that when women are bluntly presented with gender and bargaining stereotypes, they outperform men at the bargaining table. Similarly Oyserman, Harrison, and Bybee (2001) found that when African-Americans are aware of racism, connectedness and African-American achievements, they counter the negative stereotypes about math performance and demonstrate an improvement in their math performance instead. In such cases, the stereotyped group apparently copes with the negative stereotypes by eliciting an "I'll show you" reactance response, which motivates these individuals to prove that the stereotypes are wrong (Hoyt et al., 2010).

Previous research has shown that when the target has sufficient self-efficacy to react against the stereotype, he or she responds to stereotypes with reactance as opposed to the more common vulnerability response. The cited studies had shown that when a stereotype group has higher levels of self-efficacy, they are more likely to respond to negative gender stereotypes with reactance rather than vulnerability.

Stereotype reactance and venture creation intentions

When the stereotype reactance theory is applied to the entrepreneurial context, it is expected that the woman who forms the intentions to start a business is in fact acting in counter-stereotypical ways. She is responding to the negative gender stereotypes with reactance by engaging in entrepreneurial activities. In other words, forming the intentions to start a business is contrary to the stereotyped expectations of disqualification. A woman who is interested in starting a business is protecting herself from perceived stereotype threat by engaging in counter-stereotypical behavior. However, the question is what leads women to respond to negative gender stereotypes with reactance and not vulnerability.

Consistent with stereotype reactance research, we argue that entrepreneurial self-efficacy results in stereotype reactance response from women. In other words, when negative gender stereotype are present, entrepreneurial self-efficacy protects women's entrepreneurial intentions from dropping. In general, individuals with higher levels of entrepreneurial self-efficacy have a higher chance of becoming entrepreneurs and running ventures (Markman, Balkin, and Baron, 2002). Those who believe that they have the capability to start and grow a new business are more likely to pursue such a course of action (Arora, Haynie, and Laurence, 2011).

Accordingly, the belief that she has the ability to start a business helps the woman entrepreneur ignore the implication of negative gender stereotypes. In other words, a woman who perceives her entrepreneurial skills to be sufficient to start a business is more likely to have equal levels of venture creation intentions as a man when negative gender stereotypes are activated. On the other hand, a woman who perceives her entrepreneurial skills not to be sufficient to start a business is expected to be more vulnerable to the effects of negative gender stereotypes and thus have lower levels of venture creation as men.

Thus, when entrepreneurial self-efficacy of individuals is high, women tend to have equal levels of venture creation intentions compared to men when negative gender stereotypes are present. However, when entrepreneurial self-efficacy levels are low, consistent with previous studies, women have lower levels of venture creation intentions compared to men when negative gender stereotypes are present. In other words, women with high levels of entrepreneurial self-efficacy experience stereotype protection and those with lower levels of entrepreneurial self-efficacy experience stereotype threat. Thus, the following hypotheses are offered:

> *H1: In low entrepreneurial self-efficacy condition, women have lower levels of venture creation intentions compared to men when negative gender stereotypes are present.*

H2: In high entrepreneurial self-efficacy condition, women have equal levels of venture creation intentions compared to men when negative gender stereotypes are present.

Stereotype reactance and venture growth intentions

Certain negative gender stereotypes exist about women's ability to grow a business. Venture growth is typically used as a criterion for evaluating organizational success (Venkatraman and Ramanujam, 1986). The performance of an entrepreneurial venture is evaluated through the growth of the business (Cooper, 1993). Since women-owned businesses tend to stay small in terms of assets, numbers of employees and profits, women entrepreneurs are seen as inferior entrepreneurs compared to men entrepreneurs (Fischer, Reuber, and Dyke, 1993; Kalleberg and Leicht, 1991). This results in women being stereotyped as not very successful entrepreneurs. Research has shown that this stereotypical view explains why women entrepreneurs face discrimination in terms of acquiring the necessary resources to grow their business (Carter and Rosa, 1998; Coleman and Robb, 2012).

However, women do not always conform to the negative stereotypical expectations of them in regards to growing a business. Based on the stereotype protection theory (Javadian and Zoogah, 2014), stereotype reactance has positive implication for the stereotyped group by improving their behavior. Accordingly, if women entrepreneurs respond to negative gender stereotypes with reactance rather than vulnerability, it is expected that their venture growth intentions improves rather than declines. By reacting to negative gender stereotypes, women entrepreneurs engage in counter-stereotypical behavior, which will protect their growth intentions from the negatives effects of gender stereotypes. Thus, we suggest:

H3: Stereotype reactance positively impacts venture growth intentions.

The impact of stereotype reactance on venture growth intentions is dependent on women's entrepreneurial self-efficacy. Entrepreneurial self-efficacy is crucial to growth intentions for two reasons. First, entrepreneurial self-efficacy is known to impact entrepreneurial behavior and actions (Boyd and Vozikis, 1994). As Bandura (1991) explains, if a certain behavior is perceived to be beyond the ability of a person, he or she will not act. Given the link between entrepreneurial intentions and actions, Boyd and Vozikis (1994) argue that entrepreneurial self-efficacy influences entrepreneurial behavior through its impact on entrepreneurial intentions. Second, entrepreneurial self-efficacy is important to performance of new ventures. Research has shown that entrepreneurial self-efficacy increases risk taking (Krueger and Dickson, 1994), which is important to venture performance and growth (Bromiley, 1991). Entrepreneurial self-efficacy also influences venture performance positively through its effect on entrepreneurial orientation (Poon, Ainuddin, and Junit, 2006). Accordingly, entrepreneurial self-efficacy influences the actual growth of the venture by influencing entrepreneur's intention to grow the venture.

We argue that women who have high levels of entrepreneurial self-efficacy are more likely to have improved venture growth intentions as a result of stereotype reactance. In other words, entrepreneurial self-efficacy is argued to moderate the relationship between stereotype reactance and growth intentions. Women with high levels of entrepreneurial self-efficacy are more likely to have increased ventured growth intentions as a result of stereotype reactance. These women have the ability to not only react to stereotypes, but they also perceive their ability to grow their business to be sufficient. Accordingly, as stereotype reactance increases, we expect women with high levels of self-efficacy to have higher levels of growth intentions compared to those who have low levels of self-efficacy since they believe they do have the ability to grow their venture. In fact, those who believe they do not have the sufficient skills and abilities to grow their venture are less likely to form growth intentions despite their ability to react to stereotypes. Thus we offer the following hypothesis:

> *H4: Entrepreneurial self-efficacy moderates the relationship between stereotype reactance and growth intentions such that women with high levels of entrepreneurial self-efficacy have higher levels of growth intentions as their stereotype reactance increases compared to those who have low levels of self-efficacy.*

Methodology

Two separate studies were conducted to examine the hypotheses of this research. The purpose of the first study was to understand the effects of negative stereotype activation on venture creation intentions when entrepreneurial self-efficacy levels are high versus low. The second study aimed to examine the effects of reactance to negative stereotypes on venture growth intentions and the moderating role of entrepreneurial self-efficacy. In other words, the first study examines the process of stereotype protection in regards to venture creation intentions and the second study examines the process of stereotype protection in regards to venture growth intentions.

The first study used a sample of students drawn from two business schools. Three scenarios were developed and the study had a quasi-experimental design. The three scenarios each correspond to one of the gender stereotypes conditions: positive, negative and neutral. The scenarios related to gender stereotypes that are specific to venture creation. Both male and female students were asked to read a scenario and answer questions related to entrepreneurial self-efficacy and venture creation intentions. The second study used a sample of women entrepreneurs. The entrepreneurs were asked about their reactance to negative stereotypes and their venture growth intentions. Below are the details of each study and their results.

Study 1

Participants

Data was collected from undergraduate business and engineering students at two Northeastern universities. A total of 345 students were approached in class in one school and through email in the other. There were 310 students who completed the survey (response rate: 89 percent) who responded to the two follow up questions correctly. Since the focus of study one was on potential entrepreneurs, surveys from respondents who already owned businesses were eliminated. This left 267 respondents out of which 149 were female and 118 were male. The sample was predominantly Black or African American (67.2 percent) with average full-time work experience of 3 years. The majority of the students were in their senior year (60.2 percent), 9.2 percent were engineering students and the rest were from business school.

Procedure

Participants were randomly assigned to three conditions where they were asked to read a short (fictitious) news article about entrepreneurship. The three stereotype activation conditions included: negative gender stereotypes, positive gender stereotypes and nullified stereotype. Using a news article to manipulate stereotypes had been used in previous research (Gupta et al., 2008,2009; Smith and White, 2002) and the news article was adapted from previous research (Gupta et al., 2008).

In the negative condition, entrepreneurs were identified as having masculine characteristics, such as aggressiveness, risk taking and independence. In the positive condition, entrepreneurs were identified as having feminine characteristics, such as passion, affection and social adoptability. In the nullified condition, entrepreneurs were identified as having neutral characteristics, such as creative, steady and generous. After reading the article, to ensure the participants had read the article carefully, they were asked two questions on the content of the article. A total of 119 students responded to negative gender stereotype condition, 86 responded to positive gender stereotype condition and 62 responded to nullified condition.

These numbers are different since the surveys were distributed randomly. Following the two questions, the participants responded to a set of questions related to venture creation intentions and entrepreneurial self-efficacy.

Measures

Venture creation intentions: Six items developed by Zhao, Seibert, and Hills (2005) were used to measure venture creation intentions. This measure was used in other studies such as in Gupta et al. (2008) and Gupta et al. (2009). Sample items included "I am ready to do anything to be an entrepreneur," and

"I am determined to create a firm in the future." The respondents rated on a 5-point Likert scale (1 = strongly disagree, 5 = strongly agree) the extent to which they were interested in starting a business. The internal consistency of the scale was .934.

Entrepreneurial self-efficacy: Six items developed by De Noble, Jung, and Ehrlich (1999) was used to measure entrepreneurial self-efficacy. This measure was used in several other studies, such as in Hmieleski and Corbett (2008) and Hmieleski and Baron (2008). Sample items included "I can originate new ideas and products," and "I can recruit and train key employees." The respondents rated on a 5-point Likert scale (1 = strongly disagree, 5=strongly agree) the extent to which they were confident in performing the tasks mentioned in the items. The internal consistency of the scale was .811. The variable was then turned into a dichotomous variable using the median of the scale (3.95). Participants whose response was below the medium were categorized as individuals with low levels of entrepreneurial self-efficacy (coded as 0) and those with responses above the median were categorized as individuals with high levels of entrepreneurial self-efficacy (coded as 1).

Analysis and results

Before getting to the analysis, it is important to note that some of the hypotheses related to study one are null hypotheses. Given the theoretical support this research offered for the equality of venture creation intentions (stereotype protection), testing the null hypotheses is reasonable. Testing the null hypotheses is well established in psychology research (Grant, 1962). Null hypotheses have also been tested in management research published in management top tier journals (e.g. Hambrick, Cho, andChen, 1996; Hubbard, Vetter, and Little, 1998; Lawless and Anderson, 1996). In testing the null hypotheses, we followed previous research recommendations to improve the statistical power of the analysis. First, we established a beta level of .05 (Cohen, 1977), second, we reported the confidence intervals; and finally we reported power for every standard statistical test (Cashen and Geiger, 2004). In addition, an equivalency test was conducted to assess the probability of the null hypothesis being true when comparing groups. Equivalency testing is a statistical procedure "used to determine whether two groups are sufficiently near to each other to be considered equivalent" (Rogers, Howard, and Vessey, 1993: 553).

To test hypotheses one and two, data was split to high and low self-efficacy conditions. Then a 2 (gender) by 3 (stereotype condition) factorial analysis of variance (ANOVA) was conducted. Table 3.1 shows the means, standard deviation and 95 percent confidence intervals for venture creation intention and sample sizes for different conditions as they relate to high and low entrepreneurial self-efficacy conditions. In addition to comparing the mean differences, we examined whether means differed significantly across self-efficacy levels within each condition. We also examined whether the nullified condition means were statistically equivalent to the means in the other two conditions within each gender group.

The purpose of this analysis was to examine whether the effects of negative gender stereotype on venture creation intentions varied when entrepreneurial self-efficacy of men and women were high versus low. When negative gender stereotypes were activated, men with low entrepreneurial self-efficacy reported higher venture creation intentions (M = 3.56) than women with low entrepreneurial self-efficacy (M = 2.87). The mean difference (LSD) was .75 and significant (p <.01). Accordingly, women with low levels of entrepreneurial self-efficacy reported lower levels of venture creation intentions than men when the negative gender stereotypes are present. Thus, hypothesis one is supported.

When negative gender stereotypes were activated, men with high levels of entrepreneurial self-efficacy reported higher levels of venture creation intentions (M = 3.86) compared to women with high entrepreneurial self-efficacy (M = 3.55). The mean difference (LSD) was .32 but not significant. To explore the reasons behind this non-significant finding, I examined whether the sample size of the study differs from what the statistical power testing recommends. The statistical power analysis for the effect size of .15 and the power (1- β) of .75 indicate that the total sample size for each of the conditions needs to be 29. The sample sizes considered here are 34 for men and 36 for women. Accordingly, the non-significance is not the result of low statistical power. However, finding a non-significance result cannot establish that the null hypothesis is true. In addition, equivalency testing needs to be conducted to assess the equivalency between two groups. Two groups are considered to be equivalent if the mean difference between two groups is so small that one population mean is equivalent to a second population mean (Gupta et al., 2008). It has to be noted that since access to the population was not possible in this case, the whole sample was considered as the population, and the specific conditions under study was considered as the sample. In order to conduct the equivalency test, two one-sided z tests was conducted. If the lower z value was greater than 1.65, the groups were considered equivalent (Rogers et al., 1993).

Results of the analysis indicated no equivalency between men's and women's venture creation intentions ($z < 1.65$, $p > .05$) with high levels of entrepreneurial self-efficacy. Accordingly, while no significant difference was found between men's and women's venture creation intentions when entrepreneurial self-efficacy was high, the two groups were not found to be equivalent; thus, hypothesis 2 was not supported. While women's venture creation intentions was not found to be equal to men when entrepreneurial self-efficacy is high, unlike low entrepreneurial self-efficacy condition, men were not found to have significant higher intentions than women.

Study 2

The second study examined the interaction effects of stereotype reactance and entrepreneurial self-efficacy on venture growth intentions.

Table 3.1 Means, standard deviation and 95 percent confidence intervals for entrepreneurial intention and sample sizes for different conditions as they relate to entrepreneurial self-efficacy (ESE)

	Men					
	Negative gender stereotype		*Positive gender stereotype*		*Nullified condition*	
Parameters	High ESE	Low ESE	High ESE	Low ESE	High SE	Low ESE
M	3.86 i2	3.56 i2	3.67 e2	2.99 f2	3.98 a1	2.97 b1
95% CI	3.54–4.18	3.23–3.89	3.25–4.08	2.56–3.42	3.42–4.55	2.31–3.65
N	34	29	20	17	11	7
SD	0.16	0.16	0.21	0.22	0.29	0.34
	Women					
	Negative gender stereotype		*Positive gender stereotype*		*Nullified condition*	
Parameters	High ESE	Low ESE	High ESE	Low ESE	High ESE	Low ESE
M	3.54 j2	2.82 k2	3.72 g2	3.06 h2	3.94 c1	2.86 d1
95% CI	3.22–3.88	2.42–3.21	3.34–4.10	2.68–3.44	3.49–4.40	2.51–3.21
N	36	20	27	22	19	25
SD	0.17	0.2	0.19	0.19	0.23	0.18

Note: Means with different letter subscripts differ from each other across self-efficacy levels at the .05 alpha levels under each stereotype condition for the corresponding gender. Means with the first subscript 1 are statistically equivalent to the control group mean for the same gender whereas, the first subscript 2 indicates no statistical equivalence with the control group mean for the corresponding gender.

Sample and procedure

Email was sent to 914 women entrepreneurs across the United States. The entrepreneurs were randomly assigned to two different surveys, one measuring reactance to negative stereotypes and relative deprivation and another measuring vulnerability to positive gender stereotypes and relative gratification. The entrepreneurs were also asked to answer questions related to venture growth intentions. A total of 150 women entrepreneurs responded to the survey (16 percent response rate) and 105 of them completed the survey. Data was screened for outliers, normality, linearity, homoscedasticity and independence using IBM SPSS. Eventually, 92 responses were suitable for analysis. The majority of the respondents were white (88 percent) with average age of 54 years. 39 percent of the sample had graduate degrees, 13 percent took some graduate courses, 30 percent had bachelor degrees, 7 percent had associate degrees, 12 percent took some college courses and 2 percent had high school diplomas. The businesses were located in different states with the majority of the businesses (17 percent) located in California. The average business age was 14 years and the majority of businesses were in professional, scientific or technical services fields (26 percent).

Measures

STEREOTYPES REACTANCE

Four items were adopted from Spencer (1993) to measure women entrepreneur's vulnerability to negative gender stereotypes. The items were reversely coded to reflect stereotype reactance. The scale had been used in other studies, such as in von Hippel, Kalokerinos, and Henry (2013) and von Hippel, Walsh, and Zouroudis (2011). Sample items included "Some people feel that I am less willing to take business risks because I am a woman," and "Some people feel that my business can never become as big as a man's business because I prioritize maintaining relationships over focusing on business matters." The participants were asked to indicate their level of agreement with each item. Respondents rated on a 5-point Likert scale (1 = strongly disagree, 5 = strongly agree), the extent to which they agreed with the negative gender stereotypes related to women entrepreneurs. The internal consistency estimate for the scale was .870.

BEHAVIORAL GROWTH INTENTIONS

To measure the behavioral intention to grow a business, a scale with 3 items was adopted from Guimond and Dambrun (2002). The respondents were asked to indicate their willingness to carry out actions related to venture growth. Sample items included "Analyzing the market to identify growth opportunities," and "Attracting and hiring qualified employees to expand my business." Respondents rated on a 5-point Likert scale (1 = not interested at all, 5 = very much interested) to the extent to which they were willing to take the stated actions. The internal consistency estimate for the scale was .761.

ENTREPRENEURIAL SELF-EFFICACY

Six items developed by De Noble et al. (1999) was used to measure entrepreneurial self-efficacy. This measure was used in several other studies such as in Hmieleski and Corbett (2008) and Hmieleski and Baron (2008). Sample items included "I can originate new ideas and products," and "I can recruit and train key employees." The respondents rated on a 5-point Likert scale (1 = strongly disagree, 5 = strongly agree) the extent to which they were confident in the performing the tasks mentioned in the items. The internal consistency of the scale was .811.

Data analysis

Correlations and descriptive statistics for each variable in the model are provided in Table 3.2. Since there were no very high correlations (e.g., >.7) among the predictor variables, multicollinearity was not an issue.

To test the relationships proposed in hypotheses three and four, we used Hay's Process plug in SPSS. The overall model for the interaction effect of stereotype reactance and entrepreneurial self-efficacy on growth intentions is significant (F (3.89) = 4.92, p<.01, R^2 = .14). The independent variable stereotype reactance has a significant positive relationship with growth intentions (b = 1.37, t (92) = 2.74, p = .007). Thus hypothesis three is supported. The moderator *entrepreneurial self-efficacy* has a significant positive relationship with growth intentions (b = 1.30, t (92) = 3.41, p = .001). The interaction of stereotype reactance and entrepreneurial self-efficacy was also found to be significant (b = –.31, t (92) = –2.61, p = .01). After plotting the interaction effect (see Figure 3.1), we found that as stereotype reactance increases, individuals with high levels of self-efficacy have higher levels of growth intentions compared to those who had low self-efficacy. Accordingly, H4 is supported.

Table 3.2 Descriptive statistics and correlations

Variables	*Mean*	*S.D.*	*1*	*2*
1 Entrepreneurial Self-Efficacy	4.17	.50		
2 Stereotype Reactance	2.98	1.08	–.104	
3 Growth Intentions	4.46	.71	.252*	.086

Notes: n = 153. * p < .05, ** p < .01

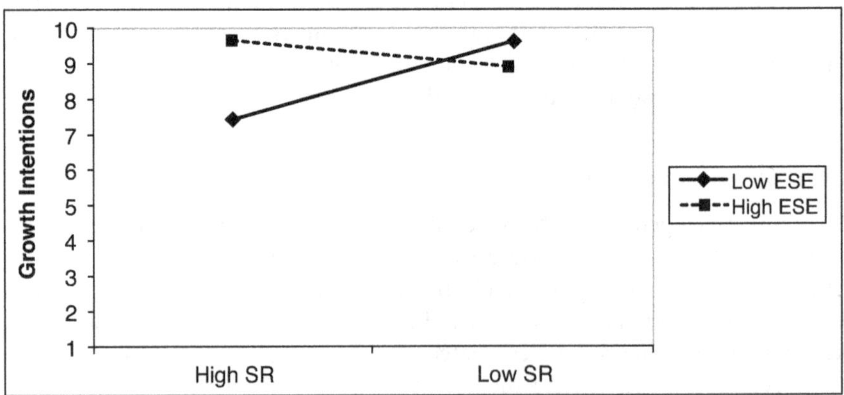

Figure 3.1 Interaction effect of entrepreneurial self-efficacy (ESE) and stereotype reactance (SR)

Discussion

The literature on women's entrepreneurship has mostly focused on problems and challenges, the causes and roots of such problems, and on offering explanations for these problems (James, 2012). This research attempted to show how women surmount the challenges they face and how they form intentions to build and grow ventures despite such challenges.

We found that when entrepreneurial self-efficacy is low, women experience stereotype threat and have lower venture creation intentions than men. When entrepreneurial self-efficacy was high, the stereotype threat was not evident. While women and men with high levels of entrepreneurial self-efficacy were not found to have equal venture creation intentions, no difference in their entrepreneurial intention was found. Accordingly, it can be argued that entrepreneurial self-efficacy cleared the threat in the air caused by negative gender stereotypes, and stereotype threat is only evident when entrepreneurial self-efficacy is low.

This research also attempted to respond to recent calls to extend the stereotype research to organizational settings. Our research was not limited to the laboratory setting and examined the effects of stereotype reactance in an entrepreneurial setting. Our analysis suggests a positive relationship between stereotype reactance and venture growth intentions. Also, as stereotype reactance increased, women with high entrepreneurial self-efficacy had higher levels of venture growth intentions compared to those with low entrepreneurial self-efficacy. Accordingly, stereotype reactance is more effective when accompanied by entrepreneurial self-efficacy.

Consequently, the question raised in this research in regards to increasing number of women-business-owned firms and their size, despite the existence of negative gender stereotypes, is answered through entrepreneurial self-efficacy. Women's entrepreneurial self-efficacy is helping them overcome the challenges related to stereotypical context of entrepreneurship.

This research is beneficial in practical terms since it offers an understanding of optimum functioning of women entrepreneurs. Showing that women entrepreneurs can actually overcome challenges in terms of starting and growing ventures can encourage other women to join the context. In addition, while entrepreneurial self-efficacy has been shown as important to individuals' entrepreneurial activities, the results of this study highlight the specific importance of entrepreneurial self-efficacy for women entrepreneurs. Policy makers and, especially, educators can play a crucial role in helping women improve entrepreneurial self-efficacy. Entrepreneurial education has been shown to be specifically important in this regard. Unfortunately, most of the entrepreneurship textbooks are fraught with the masculine models, which are mainly concerned with masculine characteristics of entrepreneurship. Moreover, the majority of entrepreneur examples mentioned in the textbooks are men (e.g. Steve Jobs, Mark Zuckerberg). Female entrepreneurs, such as Mary Ash and Coco Chanel, are rarely pointed out in entrepreneurship textbooks. We need to emphasize and highlight the feminine side of entrepreneurship and use more female examples in the textbooks. Taking such an approach will not only help women overcome negative gender stereotypes but will also help them realize their own advantages in starting and growing a business. This would hopefully contribute to the increasing numbers of women-owned firms and their growth.

Limitations and future study suggestions

It should be noted that there is a fine line between high entrepreneurial self-efficacy and overconfidence. The effects observed in this research as the result of high entrepreneurial self-efficacy might in fact be the result of overconfidence. Overconfidence, which is the individuals' tendency to exaggerate the extent of what they know is true, has negative implications for performance (Fischhoff, Slovic, and Lichtenstein, 1977). In the entrepreneurship context, it has been argued that overconfidence causes the entrepreneurs to misunderstand the potential for their venture, which leads to their failure (Singh, 2008). In the context of this study, if the observed effects are the result of overconfidence and not high entrepreneurial self-efficacy, the ultimate result may be venture failure. It is important to note that the likelihood of entrepreneurial success is at its optimum level when the confidence levels are at medium levels (Singh, 2008). If what was identified in this research as high levels of self-efficacy is overconfidence indeed, the likelihood of successful venture creation declines.

In addition, we measured entrepreneurial intentions and not entrepreneurial behavior. While entrepreneurial intentions are the main driver of entrepreneurial behavior, we encourage future research to also examine the impact of stereotype reactance on entrepreneurial behavior. This approach helps better understand the chronic effects of stereotypes on individuals' behavior. Moreover, this research only examined stereotype protection as one of the possible reactance responses to negative stereotypes. However, stereotype reactance may also lead stereotyped individuals to increase their efforts beyond normal performance levels and exceed performance expectations. For example, it may lead women to perform better than men, despite the existence of negative gender stereotypes. A more detailed examination and discussion of this phenomenon is both warranted and necessary, and we encourage future research to address this phenomenon.

The other limitation of the study is related to measuring business growth. Business growth intentions were measured through economic indicators. However, recent literature has criticized such an approach. It has been recommended that business growth and performance need to be measured though both social indicators as well. In doing so, we may actually find that men and women's businesses perform equally. Thus, we recommend future research to consider both financial and social indicators in measuring business growth intentions. Furthermore, future studies may also examine stereotypes as they relate to other minority groups, such as racial groups.

Finally, as this research showed, entrepreneurial self-efficacy contributed to women's overcoming of challenges. Future studies can actually look at women's improvements in regards to entrepreneurial self-efficacy using longitudinal studies. If such improvement exists, we may be able to better understand the recent increases in the entrepreneurial activities of women.

Conclusions

To date, much of women entrepreneurship has been focused on documenting the differences between male and female entrepreneurs and their ventures (Jennings and Brush, 2013). The literature on women's entrepreneurship has mostly focused on problems and challenges, the causes and roots of such problems and on offering explanations for these problems (James, 2012). Previous research has failed to provide an explanation for how women overcome such problems. This research explained how women entrepreneurs overcome the negative gender stereotypes through the implications of stereotype reactance/protection theory (Kray et al., 2001; Javadian and Zoogah, 2014) and entrepreneurial self-efficacy.

The results indicated that entrepreneurial self-efficacy helps women overcome the stereotype threat. Specifically, when negative gender stereotypes were present, women with high levels of entrepreneurial self-efficacy did not have lower venture creation intentions compared to men. Moreover, stereotype reactance among women entrepreneurs was found to positively impact their venture growth intentions. Women with high levels of entrepreneurial self-efficacy were found to have stronger venture growth intentions as stereotype reactance increased.

References

Ahl, H. (2006). Why research on women entrepreneurs needs new directions. *Entrepreneurship Theory and Practice*, 30, 595–621.

Ajzen, I. (2001). Nature and operation of attitudes. *Annual Review of Psychology*, 52, 27–58.

Arora, P., Haynie, J. M., and Laurence, G. A. (2011). Counterfactual thinking and entrepreneurial self-efficacy: The moderating role of self-esteem and dispositional affect. *Entrepreneurship Theory and Practice*, 37(2), 359–385.

Ashforth, B. E., and Mael, F. (1989). Social identity theory and the organization. *Academy of Management Review*, 14(1), 20–39.

Baron, R. A. (1999). *Perceptions of Entrepreneurs: Evidence for a Positive Stereotype.* Unpublished manuscript, Rensselaer Polytechnic Institute.

Baron, R. A., Markman, G. D., and Hirsa, A. (2001). Perceptions of women and men as entrepreneurs: Evidence for differential effects of attributional augmenting. *Journal of Applied Psychology*, 86(5), 923–929.

Bird, B. (1988). Implementing entrepreneurial ideas: The case for intention. *Academy of Management Review*, 13(3), 442–453.

Boyd, N. G., and Vozikis, G. S. (1994). The influence of self-efficacy on the development of entrepreneurial intentions and actions. *Entrepreneurship Theory and Practice*, 18, 63.

Brehm, J. W. (1966). A theory of psychological reactance. In W. Burke, D. Lake and J. Paine (Eds.), *Organization Change: A Comprehensive Read.* San Francisco, CA: Jossey-Bass.

Bromiley, P. (1991). Testing a causal model of corporate risk taking and performance. *Academy of Management Journal*, 34(1), 37–59.

Carter, S., and Rosa, P. (1998). The financing of male and female owned businesses. *Entrepreneurship and Regional Development*, 10(3), 225–241.

Cashen, L. H., and Geiger, S. W. (2004). Statistical power and the testing of null hypotheses: A review of contemporary management research and recommendations for future studies. *Organizational Research Methods*, 7(2), 151–167.

Chalabaev, A., Stone, J., Sarrazin, P., and Croizet, J. C. (2008). Investigating physiological and self-reported mediators of stereotype lift effects on a motor task. *Basic and Applied Social Psychology*, 30(1), 18–26.

Cohen, J. (1977). *Statistical Power Analysis for the Behavioral Sciences.* New York, NY: Lawrence Erlbaum Associates, Inc.

Coleman, S., and Robb, A. (2012). *A Rising Tide: Financing Strategies for Women-Owned Firms.* Stanford, CA: Stanford Press.

Cooper, A. (1993). Challenges in predicting new firm performance. *Journal of Business Venturing*, 8, 241–253.

Crisp, R. J., and Hewstone, M. (2007). Multiple social categorization. *Advances in Experimental Social Psychology*, 39, 163–254.

De Bruin, A., Brush, C. G., and Welter, F. (2006). Introduction to the special issue: Towards building cumulative knowledge on women's entrepreneurship. *Entrepreneurship Theory and Practice*, 30(5), 585–593.

De Noble, A. F., Jung, D., and Ehrlich, S. B. (1999). Entrepreneurial self-efficacy: The development of a measure and its relationship to entrepreneurial action. *Frontiers of Entrepreneurship Research*, 1, 73–87.

Devine, P. G. (1989). Stereotypes and prejudice: Their automatic and controlled components. *Journal of Personality and Social Psychology*, 56, 5–18.

Ellemers, N., Spears, R., and Doosje, B. (2002). Self and social identity. *Annual Review of Psychology*, 53(1), 161–186.

Fagenson, E., and Marcus, E. (1991). Perceptions of the sex-role stereotypic characteristics of entrepreneurs: Women's evaluations. *Entrepreneurship Theory and Practice*, 15(4), 33–47.

Fischer, E., Reuber, R., and Dyke, L. (1993). A theoretical overview and extension of research on sex, gender, and entrepreneurship. *Journal of Business Venturing*, 8, 151–168.

Fischhoff, B., Slovic, P., and Lichtenstein, S. (1977). Knowing with certainty: The appropriateness of extreme confidence. *Journal of Experimental Psychology: Human Perceptions and Performance*, 3, 552–564.

Fishbein, M., and Ajzen, I. (1975). *Belief, Attitude, Intention and Behavior: An Introduction to Theory and Research.* Reading, MA: Addison-Wesley.

Grant, D. A. (1962). Testing the null hypothesis and the strategy and tactics of investigating theoretical models. *Psychological Review*, 69(1), 54.

Guimond, S., and Dambrun, M. (2002). When prosperity breeds intergroup hostility: The effects of relative deprivation and relative gratification on prejudice. *Personality and Social Psychology Bulletin*, 28(7), 900–912.

Gupta, V. K., Goktan, A. B., and Gunay, G. (2014). Gender differences in evaluation of new business opportunity: A stereotype threat perspective. *Journal of Business Venturing*, 29(2), 273–288.

Gupta, V.K., and Turban, D. (2012). Evaluation of new business ideas: Do gender stereotypes play a role? *Journal of Managerial Issues*, 24, 14–156.

Gupta, V.K., Turban, D., and Bhawe, N.M. (2008). The effect of gender stereotype assimilation and reactance on entrepreneurial intentions. *Journal of Applied Psychology*, 93, 1053–1061.

Gupta, V. K., Turban, D. B., and Pareek, A. (2013). Differences between men and women in opportunity evaluation as a function of gender stereotypes and stereotype activation. *Entrepreneurship Theory and Practice*, 37(4), 771–778.

Gupta, V. K., Turban, D., Wasti, S., and Sikdar, A. (2009). The role of gender stereotypes in perceptions of entrepreneurs and intentions to become an entrepreneur. *Entrepreneurship Theory & Practice*, 33(2), 397–417.

Hambrick, D. C., Cho, T. S., and Chen, M. J. (1996). The influence of top management team heterogeneity on firms' competitive moves. *Administrative Science Quarterly*, 41, 659–684.

Haslam, S. A., and Turner, J. C. (1992). Context-dependent variation in social stereotyping: The relationship between frame of reference, self-categorization and accentuation. *European Journal of Social Psychology*, 22(3), 251–277.

Heilman, M. E., and Okimoto, T. G. (2007). Why are women penalized for success at male tasks? The implied communality deficit. *Journal of Applied Psychology*, 92, 81–92.

Heilman, M.E., Wallen, A.S., Fuchs, D., and Tamkins, M.M. (2004). Penalties for success: Reactions to women who succeed at male gender-typed tasks. *Journal of Applied Psychology*, 89, 416–427.

Hmieleski, K. M., and Baron, R. A. (2008). Regulatory focus and new venture performance: A study of entrepreneurial opportunity exploitation under conditions of risk versus uncertainty. *Strategic Entrepreneurship Journal*, 2(4), 285–299.

Hmieleski, K. M., and Corbett, A. C. (2008). The contrasting interaction effects of improvisational behavior with entrepreneurial self-efficacy on new venture performance and entrepreneur work satisfaction. *Journal of Business Venturing*, 23(4), 482–496.

Hoyt, C. L. (2005). The role of leadership efficacy and stereotype activation in women's identification with leadership. *Journal of Leadership and Organizational Studies*, 11(4), 2–14.

Hoyt, C. L., and Blascovich, J. (2007). Leadership efficacy and women leaders' responses to stereotype activation. *Group Processes and Intergroup Relations*, 10(4), 595–616.

Hoyt, C. L., Johnson, S. K., Murphy, S. E., and Skinnell, K. H. (2010). The impact of blatant stereotype activation and group sex-composition on female leaders. *The Leadership Quarterly*, 21(5), 716–732.

Hubbard, R., Vetter, D. E., and Little, E. L. (1998). Replication in strategic management: Scientific testing for validity, generalizability, and usefulness. *Strategic Management Journal*, 19(3), 243–254.

James, A.E. (2012). Conceptualizing 'woman' as an entrepreneurial advantage: A reflexive approach. In K.D. Hughes and J.E. Jennings (Eds.), *Global Women's Entrepreneurship Research: Diverse Settings, Questions and Approaches*. Cheltenham, MD: Edward Elgar.

Javadian, G., and Zoogah, D. B. (2014). Toward a comprehensive understanding of stereotype vulnerability and stereotype reactance in organizational settings: The contribution of relative deprivation theory. *Industrial and Organizational Psychology*, 7(3), 403–408.

Jennings, J. E., and Brush, C. G. (2013). Research on women entrepreneurs: Challenges to (and from) the broader entrepreneurship literature?. *The Academy of Management Annals*, 7(1), 661–713.

Kalleberg, A., and Leicht, K. (1991). Gender and organizational performance: Determinants of small business survival and success. *Academy of Management Journal*, 34(1), 136–161.

Kray, L. J., Thompson, L., and Galinsky, A. (2001). Battle of the sexes: Gender stereotype confirmation and reactance in negotiations. *Journal of Personality and Social Psychology*, 80(6), 942.

Krueger, N., and Dickson, P. R. (1994). How believing in ourselves increases risk taking: Perceived self-efficacy and opportunity recognition. *Decision Sciences*, 25(3), 385–400.

Lawless, M. W., and Anderson, P. C. (1996). Generational technological change: Effects of innovation and local rivalry on performance. *Academy of Management Journal*, 39(5), 1185–1217.

Markman, G.D., Balkin, D.B., and Baron, R.A. (2002). Inventors and new venture formation: The effects of general self-efficacy and regretful thinking. *Entrepreneurship Theory and Practice*, 27(2), 149–165.

Nosek, B. A., Banaji, M. R., and Greenwald, A. G. (2002). Math = male, me = female, therefore math = me. *Journal of Personality and Social Psychology*, 83, 44–59.

Oyserman, D., Harrison, K., and Bybee, D. (2001). Can racial identity be promotive of academic efficacy? *International Journal of Behavioral Development*, 25(4), 379–385.

Poon, J. M., Ainuddin, R. A., and Junit, S.O.H. (2006). Effects of self-concept traits and entrepreneurial orientation on firm performance. *International Small Business Journal*, 24(1), 61–82.

Powell, G.N., and Graves, L.M. (2003). *Women and Men in Management.* Thousand Oaks, CA: Sage.

Randel, A. E. (2002). Identity salience: A moderator of the relationship between group gender composition and work group conflict. *Journal of Organizational Behavior*, 23, 749–766.

Rogers, J. L., Howard, K. I., and Vessey, J. T. (1993). Using significance tests to evaluate equivalence between two experimental groups. *Psychological Bulletin*, 113(3), 553.

Singh, R. P. (2008). *Exploring Why So Many Entrepreneurs Fail: Is Entrepreneurial Overconfidence a Mental Defect?* Paper presented at Academy of Management Meeting, Anaheim, CA.

Smith, J. L., and White, P. H. (2002). An examination of implicitly activated, explicitly activated, and nullified stereotypes on mathematical performance: It's not just a woman's issue. *Sex Roles*, 47(3–4), 179–191.

Spencer, S. J. (1993). *The Effect of Stereotype Vulnerability on Women's Math Performance.* Unpublished doctoral dissertation, University of Michigan, Ann Arbor.

Steele, C. M. (1997). A threat in the air: How stereotypes shape intellectual identity and performance. *American Psychologist*, 52, 613–629.

Steele, C. M., and Aronson, J. (1995). Stereotype threat and the intellectual test performance of African Americans. *Journal of Personality and Social Psychology*, 69(5), 797.

Venkatraman, N., and Ramanujam, V. (1986). Measurement of business performance in strategy research: A comparison of approaches. *Academy of Management Review*, 11(4), 801–814.

von Hippel, C., Kalokerinos, E. K., and Henry, J. D. (2013). Stereotype threat among older employees: Relationship with job attitudes and turnover intentions. *Psychology and Aging*, 28(1), 17–27.

von Hippel, C., Walsh, A. M., and Zouroudis, A. (2011). Identity separation in response to stereotype threat. *Social Psychological and Personality Science*, 2(3), 317–324.

Wegener, D. T., Clark, J. K., and Petty, R. E. (2006). Not all stereotyping is created equal: Differential consequences of thoughtful versus non thoughtful stereotyping. *Journal of Personality and Social Psychology*, 90, 42–59.

Zhao, H., Seibert, S. E., and Hills, G. E. (2005). The mediating role of self-efficacy in the development of entrepreneurial intentions. *Journal of Applied Psychology*, 90(6), 1265.

4 Representations of gender

The media as the mirror of gender roles

Marlene Loureiro, Galvão Meirinhos, Carmem Leal and Vanessa Ratten

1. Introduction

Our society currently believes in the "equality" between Man and Woman; both have the same skills, attitudes, feelings and aptitudes. However, what has been proven is that, as far as their representation and role in society are concerned, there are still traces of stereotypes and traditional roles. In this sense, in this chapter we try to present a brief exploration on the role of the mass media in the communication and transmission of social ideas of gender and of gender roles.

The mass media are one of the social and political places of identity construction, and mass media also construct definitions and ideologies of the different age groups, ethnical and social classes, culture and sexual groups (Silveirinha, 2004). In this perspective, we postulate that the media function as a mirror of the society they portray, perpetuating their values, ideologies, laws and norms.

Thus, this work of reflection seeks to raise the main research topics related to gender presented in the mass media, with an initial focus on the role of gender in the "positioning" of the viewer. This includes the role of male and female images in the mass media (movies, television, photographs, publicity). Later, the subject of research turns out to be the role played by the mass media in the transmission of patriarchal ideology and the place of women in society. Nowadays, there are more connections between gender studies focusing on gender discourse and gender roles and identities presented and/or conveyed by the media.

The issue of gender touches almost every aspect of the relationship between the mass media, society, mass communication and the definition of gender. Therefore, this chapter will cover the following topics:

- the media and society;
- gender as social construction;
- studies of gender and feminism;
- the media as the mirror of gender roles.

2. The *media* and society

We are, by nature, social beings and, therefore, we need to communicate. We all communicate, even when we do not even talk. Communication is, therefore, a *sine qua non* condition of social life (Rego, 2007:25). Communication is a keyword in today's society because it is present and globalized in social, public and economic life (Beaudichon, 2001: 14). So what we are experiencing today is that communication is everywhere, being inseparable from the concepts of society and culture (Ferin, 2002: 99). We live in an era of "global communication", which is "[. . .] based on Information and Communication Technologies, expanding markets and consumption, massive daily bureaucratization and homogeneity of lifestyles"[1] (Ferin, 2002: 25). Consequently, we also live in the era of globalization, where communication is massified and global (McQuail, 2003: 241).

Thus, to speak of mass communication, we must speak of the mass media, underlining the preponderant role that those media have in society and in the world in general. Since the arising of the first mass media (Press, Radio and Television), we try to understand the possible consequences of these media in society and what is their role as opinion makers and transmitters of knowledge. For Sousa, "(. . .) books, newspapers and magazines have transformed civilization, since they shaped the modern public sphere, contributed to social, political and economic transformations, promoted education and the interest in the world, made circulated ideas and information and modified the culture"[2] (Sousa, 2006: 542).

According to Sousa (2006), the importance of the mass media is based on their ability to represent people, society and culture, since it is by the media that we know what is happening in the world, that we know and visualize other cultures, and that we know what exists, what is published or what is done. Thus, they play a role of social responsibility insofar as they produce and reproduce, construct and reconstruct social and cultural processes (Sousa, 2006: 539). That is, the mass media are developed taking into consideration the society in which they are set, but they also influence that same society through the contents that they disseminate. So, we can deduce that society and the mass media have a close relationship and frame or influence each other. Indeed, McQuail (2003: 65) even advocates interdependence between the mass media and society, interacting and influencing each other.

We also believe that through the history of the mass media, it is possible to follow the transformations of society, the changes of values and the changes of behaviour over time, since the mass media have a central role in the definition of acceptable and convenient behaviours and attitudes according to the social surrounding environment, "in establishing the parameters of normality, in the availability of information, in the promotion of knowledge and in the social offer of referents about reality"[3] (Sousa, 2006: 539). On the other hand, there is a very strong tendency of those who have authority to consider communication conveyed by mass media, at least as a tacit support for order maintenance (McQuail, 2003: 177).

For McQuail (2003), the mass media are in some way related to the prevailing structure of economic and political power:

- Firstly, because they have an economic cost and a value, being the object of competition for their control and access;
- secondly, they are subject to legal, political and economic regulations;
- and, thirdly, the mass media are usually regarded as effective instruments of power, with the potential to exert influence over their audiences.

Thus, discussions about media power are grouped into two paradigms: the paradigm of dominant media and the paradigm of pluralistic media (see Figure 4.1). The dominant media paradigm views the media as subservient to other institutions, being controlled by a small number of powerful and similar interests. In this sense, they spread a limited and undifferentiated worldview, shaped by dominant interests. In turn, audiences are conditioned to accept the view of the offered world. The result is the reinforcement and legitimation of the dominant structure and power, conditioning the change and alternatives. On the other hand, the pluralistic media paradigm is the opposite, defending diversity and unpredictability. The pluralist model believes that there is no unified and dominant elite and that change and democratic control are possible. Therefore, differentiated audiences are seen as indicating requirements, able to withstand persuasion and to react to what the media offer.

Figure 4.1 Two opposite models of the media power

	Dominant media paradigm	*Pluralist media paradigm*
Society source	Dominant or elite class	Groups of cultural, social and political interests in competition
Media	Under uniformly and centred property	Many and independent of each other
Production	Standardised, routinized and controlled	Creative, free and original
Contents and worldview	Selective and determined by power	Diverse and competitive points of view
Audience	Dependent, passive, organised on a large scale	Fragmented, selective, reactive and active
Effects	Strong and confirming the established social order	Numerous, without consistency or prediction of direction; sometimes no effect at all.

Source: McQuail (2003)

Although these two models are described as opposites, it is possible to consider the existence of mixed versions, in which the tendency for dominance of the masses are limited by opposing forces and find resistance in their audiences. In this sense, mass media are simultaneously vehicles of images of what is new and fashionable in terms of goods, ideas, techniques and values, from the city to the countryside and from the social top to the bottom (McQuail, 2003: 73). Thus, they present themselves with potential disseminators of alternative value systems and potentially weaken traditional values. Consequently, whenever the media exert influence, they also cause change. In other words, the mass media can simultaneously withstand and subvert social cohesion; that is, media can have effects in two directions: centrifugal or centripetal. The centrifugal effect concerns the stimulus for social change, freedom, individualism and fragmentation; the centripetal refers to the effects in the form of greater social unity, order, cohesion and integration.

Therefore, the mass media can be analysed as portraits of our society and as a way to understand the social transformations that occur throughout the ages, as well as to perceive the representations of gender and the questions of identity they convey.

3. Gender as a social construct

Gender is here understood as a concept of sociological order, distinguishing itself, therefore, from sex (the biological domain) since it concerns only the physical part that distinguishes individuals, namely differences in the reproductive apparatus. According to Julia T. Wood, "Sex is innate, but gender is socially created and learned by individuals" (Wood, 1996: 4). For Julia T. Wood, to be born man or woman does not necessarily imply that one thinks, one acts and one feels in the ways that the society believes that the man and the woman must act (Wood, 1996: 4). Thus, although gender is linked to sex to distinguish between feminine and masculine, gender is a more comprehensive term that goes beyond the purely biological domain and encompasses the psychological characteristics, the sociological and cultural formation of the individual. That is, gender is "socially constructed" (Rodrigues, 2003:16). According to this conception, the concept of gender is formed by socialization and culture and, therefore, Judith Butler affirms"[. . .] gender is neither the causal result of sex nor as seemingly fixed as sex" (Butler, 2007: 8). Thus, the notion of gender will be the main generator of the differences between men and women.

Nevertheless, the term sex can sometimes appear, but it will always be used in the sense of gender, since it implies the notions of gender identity and gender role. Often, as may be inferred, gender identity is mistaken for sexual identity. However, we are not talking about the same, although these two identities are interrelated. In fact, it is individuals who construct their gender identity by identifying themselves socially and culturally as male or female. Sexual identity is constructed through the experience of sexuality with partners of the same sex or the opposite sex. Thus, for example, for some homosexual men, gender identity is masculine, whereas sexual identity, in terms of fantasy and object choice, is feminine (Rodrigues, 2003: 18).

Therefore, this gender identity will lead to the existence of feminine and masculine gender roles, which reflect, in essence, "[. . .] arbitrary patterns or rules that a society establishes for its members, defining their behaviour, their clothes, their ways of relating"[4](Rodrigues, 2003: 18) and how they communicate. Therefore, from an early age, children are being socialized taking into account their different gender roles, starting with the biological part, sex. "Like age, sex is a biological category that serves as a fundamental basis for the differentiation of roles, norms and expectations [. . .]. It is these roles, norms and expectations that constitute gender, the social construct of sex" (Eckert, 1997: 213). In fact, there is certain determinism in the way gender is being constructed, since this construction is made from the natural/biological sex.

Thus, while sex can be considered as a biological categorization based primarily on its potential reproductive role, gender is the social elaboration of sex, which is biological. In fact, "[. . .] to whatever extent gender may be related to biology, it does not flow naturally ad directly from our bodies (Eckert and McConnel-Ginet, 2003: 13). Gender is thus a process of construction based on the biological sex, according to which individuals adopt and follow behaviours, attitudes and postures according to the expected gender roles. It is at this point that gender and sex converge, since

> [. . .] gendered performances are available to everyone, but with them come constraints on who can perform which personae with impunity. And this is where gender and sex come together, as society tries to match up ways of behaving with biological sex assignments
>
> (Eckert and McConnell-Ginet, 2003:10).

Although gender may be related to biology, it does not appear directly from our body. As Julia T. Wood said, we are asexual even before we are born, but we only acquire gender in the process of social interaction (Wood, 1996: 6). Gender is the process of creating the dichotomy between the sexes, erasing the similarities and stressing the differences, being always thought in terms of opposition. Thus, male and female, as two bipolar categories "[. . .] are behavioural constructs that are powerful regulators of human affairs" (Key, 1996: 14). Harriet Whitehead (1981) argues that when we talk about cultural construction of gender, we are giving meaning or social sense to the physical differences between the sexes, and, instead of speaking in masculine and feminine, it is spoken of man and woman:

> When I speak of cultural constructions of gender, I mean simply the ideas that give social meaning to physical differences between the sexes, rendering two biological classes, male and female, into two social classes, men and women, and making the social relationships in which men and women stand toward each other appear reasonable and appropriate.
>
> (Whitehead, 1981: 83)

In this way, the biological differences are reinforced and exaggerated to construct the idea of gender. That's why women polish nails, dye hair, depilate their bodies, etc., everything to differentiate their body from the masculine. In this sense, gender identity is built throughout life, since birth, through the attribution of a name: feminine or masculine. From then on, it is the parents who are responsible for the formation of the child's gender, since they are going to take care of the child according to whether it is a boy or a girl. Over the years, the child will also take part in the process, "[. . .] doing its own gender work and learning to support the gender work of others" (Eckert and McConnell-Ginet, 2003: 16). Holmes and Meyerhoff (2003) also reiterate that gender is a social construct, rather than a given social category, which is a product and result of social interaction. They stress that "[. . .] gender emerges over time in interaction with others" (Holmes and Meyerhoff, 2003: 11).

From another angle, gender, or the gender identity, is socially and culturally constructed, and gender differentiation can be understood as a product of socialization (Maccoby, 2003: 3). By socialization, Eleanor Maccoby (2003) understands the process or processes through which each generation of adults passes on to the next generation of children the set of knowledge, beliefs and aptitudes that constitute the culture of the group. The process of socializing in childhood can be seen as anticipatory, as it will prepare children for the roles they will play as adults. Adolescence, the period of peer support, provides exploration and consolidation of a gender identity that is established through a communicative system that is built up through the sharing of secrets and peer bonding. The communicative approach to adult social gender identity is rooted in children's critical experiences of girlhood and boyhood (Cook-Gumperz, 1995: 403–404).

Therefore, the child defines his/her gender identity according to the surrounding social environment. Fichtelius, Johansson, and Nordin (1980) argue that children construct their ideas of gender and gender roles according to what they observe of the differentiation of gender roles and through what has been and is communicated to them by adults, and, from there, they construct their gender models and standards to follow. In turn, Cordelia Fine (2010) even emphasizes that children are born in a world where gender is continually emphasized through conventions, present in clothing, appearance, language, colour and symbols, denouncing that differentiating the masculine from the feminine is of great importance:

> children are born into a world in which gender is continually emphasized through conventions of dress, appearance, language, colour, segregation, and symbols. Everything around the child indicates that whether one is male or female is a matter of great importance.
>
> (Fine, 2010: 227)

The development of gender does not end in adolescence; it continues when these young people enter to the labour market, when they play their roles in the family they constitute and throughout their lives. The development of gender behaviours in an individual continues after adolescence into their working and family life.

> As we age, we continue to learn new ways of being men and women: what's expected from a teenaged girl is rather different from expectations for a woman in her mid-forties and those expectations differ from those for a woman approaching eighty. [. . .]
>
> As we have seen above, learning to be male or female involves learning to look and act in particular ways, learning to participate in particular ways in relationships and communities, and learn to see the world from a particular perspective.
>
> (Eckert and McConnell-Ginet, 2003: 30)

Therefore, it can be affirmed that gender is not something that one has, but something one does, and it is not built in an individual way, but in a collaborative way through the interaction between individuals (Eckert and McConnell-Ginet, 2003: 31–32). Therefore, Eleanor Maccoby argues that gender, in addition to being constructed through socialization, is constructed and defended in context, that is, in a group context where individuals interact (Maccoby, 2003: 12), but she stresses that"[. . .] people behave differently depending on whether they are interacting with a member of their own sex or someone of the other sex" (Maccoby, 2003: 187). Joan Swann (2002) postulatesthe same, that gender, like language, is fluid, contingent and context-dependent (Swann, 2002: 47). Thus, gender roles are not entirely pre-determined by sex, but constructed and established through language and discourse. In fact, gender consists of a pattern of relationships that develops in time to define the masculine and the feminine, simultaneously structuring and regulating the relationship between individuals in society. For this reason, gender is in every aspect of life and society – in institutions and organizations, in public and private spaces, in the arts, in clothing, in games and child plays, in language, etc. The differentiation of masculine and feminine serves not only to guarantee biological breeding, but also to guarantee social reproduction, since society is organized in these two categories – masculine and feminine – which continually perpetuate social gender roles.

Thus, gender is supported by a set of ideologies and conventions that takes part of every aspect of our lives. Ideology refers to a set of beliefs through which people explain and justify their behaviour and interpret that of others. Therefore, ideology is present in the issue of gender because gender is constructed through what people believe to be the characteristic of one gender to the detriment of the other. In this way, the gender ideology establishes an order and an opposition, explaining and justifying the gender of individuals. Therefore, the dominant ideology does not simply prescribe that male and female should be different, but it also insists and believes they are simply different (Eckert and McConnell-Ginet, 2003: 35).

On the other hand, this gender differentiation also stands by in institutions and at work. Firstly, for physiological reasons, women have always been regarded as the weaker sex. In general, the woman is shorter, is lighter and has less muscle mass than the man; therefore, it is justifiable that women are seen as incapable of doing certain tasks or performing certain activities:

> Women have long been regarded as members of the weaker sex. As a group, they are shorter, lighter, and less muscular than men and are regarded in our society as generally unable to perform heavy manual work or to compete in certain stressful or potentially violent athletic events. These differences have been used as justification for keeping women out of certain jobs, such as construction, and such sports as weight lifting, football, and hockey.
>
> (Lips et al., 1978: 147)

Nevertheless, despite these differences, women have been able to occupy places and positions whose access has been hampered by these preconceived ideas. In Western societies, the division of labour by gender is still linked to different power and status. Men's activities are associated with a larger societal power. In most cultures, it is the man who has larger access to public positions of power and influence. This difference is the result of "[. . .] social structure that awards men higher status and stereotypes them as more competent than women" (Lips and Colwill, 1978: 241). Women, in turn, have influence in domestic situations and in private contexts. In this sense, we talk about discrimination, as "there is plentiful evidence that discrimination exists at all levels, and is a powerful force affecting women's opportunities for job training, for being hired, and for being promoted" (Maccoby, 2003: 227).

However, this perspective of the world of work seems outdated, as there are already many professional women who are part of great organizations – of doctors, of lawyers, of university departments – where men and women work together and have an equal status. On the other hand, also in other types of work, which formerly were considered unisex, they are already performed by both sexes; for example: clerk in a supermarket, taxi driver, judge, lorry driver, pilot, police, nurse, kindergarten teacher, etc. Consequently, the increasing number of women in the labour market has caused the change of some ideologies, namely gender segregation at work, to become gender integration.

Indeed, in contemporary times, although there is already a strong speculation and discussion about gender social roles and identities, gender identities are still relatively fixed, and there are still well-defined roles of mother, father, son, man, woman, etc. However, the change and/or evolution for some of these roles have been conveyed by the mass media, through which the individual constructs his/her identity. In fact, the mass media play a key role in the production and circulation of meanings that determine how individuals see gender

4. Gender studies and feminism

Initially gender studies was very close to feminism. However, not all those who address themselves to gender studies have a feminist position. Therefore, it is important to know what feminism is and how it relates to gender studies.

Historically, the feminist movement began in the nineteenth century and it had as an aim the establishment of equal rights between women and men in the social, political, legal and economic fields (AA.VV. 2006: 64). The vindication of the female vote was the first major goal. Although in 1791, Olympe de Gauges, with the *Declaration of the Rights of Woman and Woman Citizen*, and Mary Wollstonecraft, in 1792, with *Vindication of the Rights of the Women*, demanded the emancipation of women, only in the nineteenth century did the movement gain effective repercussion and come to light. Feminist associations and newspapers spread feminist ideals, such as the *English Women's Journal* (1870) and the *Women's Suffrage Journal* (1870). 1869 is also an important date, as Stuart Mill publishes the book *On the Subjection of Women*, which condemns the exploitation and discrimination of women, not only socially but also at the family level, and defends the equality of women's rights with regard to men, namely in the world of work and business:

> There is no country of Europe in which the ablest men have not frequently experienced, and keenly appreciated, the value of the advice and help of clever and experienced women of the world, in the attainment both of private and public objects; and there are important matters of public administration to which few men are equally competent with such women; [. . .] But what we are now discussing is not the need which society has of the services of women in public business, but the dull and hopeless life to which it so often condemns them, by forbidding them to exercise the practical abilities which many of them are conscious of, in any wider field than one which to some of the never was, and to others is no longer open.
>
> (Mill, 1986: 105)

However, feminist claims are being organized through collective demonstrations and hunger strikes, among others.

With World War I, feminist claims truly imposed themselves, because women, replacing men enlisted in war, played important roles that before they have never had access to. In fact, the power of man was at that moment called into question, since, while the male sex was dedicated to war and death, women were the source of life, since they cared for the children, the elderly and the wounded people. In this way, feminists showed the fundamental role of women in the society and the evolution of humankind (Pierson, 1987: 221 and following). However, it was only in 1928, in England, that the woman began to vote. As political objectives were reached, feminist attention turned to other fields, such as discrimination in salaries, access to culture and information, equality according to laws and maternity care.

In 1950, the feminist movement was influenced by the thinking and work of Simone de Beauvoir, who drew attention to the "objectification" of women, caused by male social domination, in which man views woman as the *other*, someone who is different from him, but who does not have the capacity to affirm and equate herself with him.

> Économiquement hommes et femmes constituent presque deux castes; toutes choses égales, les premiers ont des situations plus avantageuses, des salaires plus élevé, plus de chances de réussite de leurs concurrentes de fraîche date; ils occupent dans l'industrie, la politique, etc., un beaucoup plus grand nombre des places et ce sont eux qui détiennent les postes les plus importants.
>
> (Beauvoir, 1976: 23)

This idea will be accentuated itself by the 1960s with the pretension of sexual liberation, which has sometimes turned into a war against the dominant male order and which has given rise to a series of demonstrations and the emergence of a feminist literature.

For Deborah Cameron, feminism "[. . .] is a movement for the full humanity of women" (Cameron, 1992: 4). The linguist stresses that feminism does not speak of women's rights or equality between men and women, since this equality presupposes that the pattern is man. Therefore, "feminists are ultimately in pursuit of a more radical change, the creation of a world in which one gender does not set the standard of human value" (Cameron, 1992: 4). Obviously, in order to achieve these goals, there must be a change in values as a whole, in which woman is

> Liberated from their present subordinated position with its multiple restrictions, exclusions and oppressions (such as relative poverty, economic dependence, sexual exploitation and vulnerability to violence, poorer health, overwork, lack of civil and legal rights – the list goes on and on). But the transformation that will result from this liberation is envisaged as a profound one, affecting the whole humanity.
>
> (Cameron, 1992: 4)

Thus, feminism will seek firstly to understand how the current relationships between men and women are constructed, since they are not natural. It will be in the light of this understanding that we should pursue change. In this sense, feminism will focus on how women are represented by the various cultural products representative of society (Cameron, 1992: 6).

At the heart, what began to be questioned by feminists was what the gender issue, more than a matter of difference, has to do with hierarchy. Indeed, although the term gender applied to grammar had originated in Greece, with Protagoras, meaning class or type, the truth is that it has always been associated with sex. For a long time, the two concepts seem to be linked and, even today, they condition the perception of grammatical gender as well as social differences. And it is also in this order of ideas that it is also spoken of sexist language or sexism in language.

Conceição Nogueira (2001) analyses the history and the feminist struggle, trying to verify the extent to which feminism contributes to the construction of a more egalitarian society through language. Indeed, the feminist movement postulates that gender differentiation is not natural, but it arises from the interaction between individuals, hence the importance of language in the construction of gender. For this reason, Nogueira highlighted the role of many English feminists in order to make women more visible in the language (Nogueira, 2001: 218), since language was at the service of male power and domination. Therefore, as the feminist movement understood, it is not enough to change laws, it is necessary to change at all "[. . .] the subjacent conceptions of gender roles that created and sustained these laws"[5] (Nogueira, 2001: 242), that "[. . .] implies a reflexive, critical, and committed positioning, that is, the need for a new vocabulary of values"[6] (Nogueira, 2001: 245).

Therefore, we are currently at a time when we are looking for a more inclusive society, where gender is not a justification for social inequality. Indeed, although one of the great achievements of the last century has been, "[. . .] without a doubt, the transformation that took place in the social situation of women and, at the same time, in the social relations between the two sexes"[7] (Silva, 1999: 15), there are still discriminatory social practices arising from "the tyranny of preconceptions that continue to weigh negatively on women and the (male) way how human activity and social relations are organized"[8] (Silva, 1999: 18).

5. The *media* as the mirror of gender roles

The mass media have a great power of persuasion and convincing due to the space they occupy in the modern world. Most of their production has, therefore, a value of truth, which makes their representations seem real (Ghilardi-Lucena, 2008). That is why in understanding the history of the mass media we can understand the gender roles. In fact, the representations conveyed by the mass media, at the same time as they derive from the attitudes of the individuals and from the values that each social segment considers, also reinforce tendencies of behaviour or propitiate the establishment of new values, giving a kind of endorsement so that certain behavioural changes can be consolidated. Thus, the mass media construct the representations from the real world, as this is transformed, in large part, by the representations conveyed in the mass media. Media representations then become reality (Ghilardi-Lucena, 2008). In this sense, the mass media "played an important or perhaps decisive role in the emancipation of people from ignorance and in the construction of the ambience of "general knowledge" that characterizes our time"[9] (Sousa, 2006: 539). In fact, the mass media are a powerful weapon, either as a strategy/medium for building collective identities, or as vehicles of gender identity. Indeed, the mass media seem to be at the heart of identity issues.

In this order of ideas, several researches about gender representations in the mass media have appeared. For example, Goffman (1976) looked at more than 500 advertisements where women, men and children came along and concluded that advertisements represent the conventions and social roles of each gender in society. Also Kramarae (1981) studied the representation of the sexes in adolescent publications, from which she concluded that the interests of girls and boys differed according to the behaviours that are expected of them. On the other hand, Myra Macdonald (1995) looked more specifically at the representation of women in Western media, emphasizing the importance of discourse in the media, which is associated with the institutional structures of power and authority (Macdonald, 1995: 43). More recently, Rosalind Gill (2007) also addressed the issue of gender in the mass media today. For the author, the pertinence of the study of the relationship between gender and the media is that media are simultaneously disclosure agents of feminist ideas and, on the other hand, they still convey images and patterns alluding to a latent sexism (Gill, 2007: 2). On the other hand, for Meyers (1999), the mass media play a role of maintaining the hegemonic consensus or the *status quo* in which women, like the elderly, blacks, homosexuals, among others, appear as subordinate or inferior groups. In this way, the mass media appear as reproducing the dominant ideology of the reality:

> Subordinated groups – women, people of colour, the poor and working classes, lesbians and gay men, the elderly – are encouraged to "buy into" the dominant ideology which, in fact, maintains the status quo by keeping them subordinated. Thus, the ideological work of the media consists, in part, of presenting a reality that appears more natural or real than the material circumstances of subordinated people's lives.
>
> (Meyers, 1999: 7)

Nevertheless, the researcher also notes that many of the messages conveyed by the media go beyond the dominant ideology and are quite polysemic, depending on the interpretation of their audience (Meyers, 1999: 8).

Nonetheless, gender ideology and asymmetric power relations continue to be conveyed in the media, but in a more subtle way (Mills, 2008: 1). Therefore, the main goal is the social transformation. Effectively, society has changed dramatically in regards to women, largely due to the growing number of women working full-time away from home. Of course, this change entails changes in the way women are seen, but it can also be seen as a threat to those men who persist in having a stereotyped view of women and who continue to disprove the access women have to professional careers and to their professional promotion. Change also has an impact on how women behave and see themselves. Therefore, due to their growing financial independence and status in the labour market, "women are less likely to tolerate sexist comments and discrimination" (Mills, 2008: 19). However, we cannot forget that often it is women who adopt and have attitudes and behaviours based on stereotyped and sexist views.

In fact, the reform of the sexist mentality implies that it is accepted and promoted by those in power, as a "reform can only be effective if it is accepted and promoted by those in positions of influence" (Mills, 2008: 17), because the changes are always difficult to accept and, in this particular case, also found resistance on the part of many men.

In this sense, the integration of women into the public sphere has not been easily accepted, especially by men. Michelle Zimbalist Rosaldo (1974) considered it fundamental to differentiate between the public sphere and the domestic sphere and to understand the status of women in society. As long as a woman remains in the domestic and private sphere, she will always have a lower status than a man. On the other hand, she also argues that the more society differentiates between these spheres of activity, more differentiation will be between the status and value of masculine and feminine activities. For this reason, Rosaldo (1974) also advocates that women will achieve more status by entering in the public sphere, still a male domain. In this way, societies would become more egalitarian if there were not such a marked differentiation between the public sphere and the domestic sphere (Rosaldo, 1974: 36).

As women have been entering into the public sphere, there have, in fact, been a series of institutional and legal changes to eliminate many sexist expressions that feminists have never failed to denounce. However, this does not necessarily mean, as Susan Ehrlich and Ruth King (1998: 179) stressed, that language or speakers are no longer sexist. These researchers even suggest that more subtle sexist terms will replace those that have disappeared. In this line of ideas is Sara Mills (2008), who argues that these changes in language made open sexism disappear, but a sexism much more subtle and also discriminatory arises:

> It could be argued that these changes have meant that overt sexism has been 'driven underground' and that other more subtle forms of expression, which are equally pernicious and discriminatory, have been used instead.
> (Mills, 2008: 21)

Therefore, we can reiterate an evolution of sexism. Originally the term sexism implied an antagonistic relationship between the sexes as a result of a patriarchal society whose system favoured the man to the detriment of the woman. However, although sexism is the fruit of man, not all men are sexist. It is therefore necessary to continue this process of change that has already begun and which has as a condition *sine qua non* the ascension of women in society and in the labour market, demonstrating their value and power.

Calero Fernández (1999) argues that the genuine reform, in order to make sexism disappear, must go through two fundamental institutions – the school and the family – since they constitute themselves as modellers of personality and behaviours as well as transmitters of knowledge, essential for active participation in public and private life (Calero Fernández, 1999: 31). We also add the role of the mass media, which, today, are real socializing agents and formatters of individuals. In this sense, as the mirrors of society, the mass media increasingly provide patterns and representations of gender.

Gender representations in the mass media generate discussions and speculations on the identity of the individual nowadays. The concepts of identity and social gender involve very complex issues that have not always been seen in the same way, and they are changing. Therefore, it is important to distinguish between pre-modern and modern society. According to Kellner (2001), in pre-modern society individuals did not go through identity crises because it was fixed, solid and stable. There were no problems with social roles, as they were not subject to reflection or discussion. For this reason, the mass media perpetuated the dominant values of the established power, such as in soap operas. According to Fiske (1987: 197), the soap opera reflects a patriarchal society but legitimizes feminine values where women struggle to establish themselves and spread their values within the dominant patriarchy.

Nowadays – modernity – identity becomes more mobile, multiple, personal, reflective and subject to change and innovation. Nevertheless, identity is also social and related to the other, as if the identity of a person depends on the recognition of others in combination with the validation given by that person to that recognition (Kellner, 2001: 295). In fact, the impact of globalization has produced changes in the world, generating discontinuity, fragmentation, rupture and displacement, and forcing the construction of new identities, disseminated mostly by the mass media as disseminators of alternative values. Nonetheless, gender roles or traditional forms of identity still prevail.

In the age of consumerism and of the mass media dominance, individuals no longer identify with the collective; in modern age, they identify themselves as an individuality being increasingly linked to the production of an image, and the appearance has been widely valued. Therefore, although they are vehicles of social integration, the mass media also have a centrifugal effect, which concerns the stimulus for social change, freedom, individualism and fragmentation.

Indeed, as Gauntlet (2008) stresses, gender representations are now more complex and less stereotyped than they were in the past. In general, women and men are considered as equals, although limited by the vestiges of some traditional ideas. In fact, there is a decline of traditions, which has consequently transformed gender and gender identities, making them more diverse and malleable. Nevertheless, if we look at the current situation and the social changes that have taken place, we quickly realize that women are increasingly in the public and media sphere, but they are still absent from the positions of leadership and have to reconcile professional and family roles (Gill, 2007).

Thus, the mass media play a fundamental role in the production and circulation of the senses that determine the representations of gender – feminine and masculine – that are seen by individuals. Western contemporary societies are, according to Hall (2005), characterized by the difference and possibility of creation of new identities, of new subjects, and, consequently, of the restructuring composition of the social structure. In this sense, the mass media collaborate in new articulations and/or in the assimilation of new categories by providing a series of examples and models of behaviours and attitudes with which people can identify (Ghilardi-Lucena, 2008). In this way, the mass media will also expose the contradictions of gender and reveal the paradox of contemporaneity: on the one hand, by encouraging innovations/changes (men in the kitchen, taking care of their children and in the domestic space) and, on the other hand, by maintaining the *status quo* (men as holders of power and as the dominant gender). Examples of mass media products that provide a series of examples and models of behaviours and attitudes that people can identify are television soap operas and movies. In fact, although they still have ideas of the *status quo* and the division of social roles between genders, they also provoke reflection on more avant-garde themes that go against traditional standards, namely issues of homosexuality and transsexuality; same-sex marriage; abortion; terminal diseases; disabled individuals; racism and discrimination; feminism; female professional success and female entrepreneurship, etc.

Therefore, increasingly, the representation of the female and male roles in the mass media will depend on how each individual identifies himself/herself with the representations and/or gender identities present in the media texts. And obviously, this interpretation of the social roles of gender present in the mass media will also depend on the socio-economic and political context of the individual.

Therefore, research on gender in mass media and in media discourses is only one aspect of its importance for gender studies and for the relevance that gender has as an important research variable. Therefore, different types of mass media contents are associated with the expression of gender identity, as well as psychological differences between male and female. Another pertinent issue raised by gender studies is whether choice of contents and mass media interpretation is capable of providing a lever of change or a resistance element for women in a society still structured by inequality (McQuail, 2003).

In summary, we can say that the different representations of gender presented in the media culture, regardless of the causes and the ways in which they are presented, evoke different responses and that gender differences lead to alternative ways of getting meaning from the mass media, either through centripetal or centrifugal effects.

6. Conclusion

Since the moment ultrasound informs that it is a boy or a girl, the life of the children is defined according to the gender and, from there, through the socialization, they learn and gain a gender identity or role, masculine or feminine. Gender roles are the behaviours, attitudes, personality traits, emotions and social and cultural attitudes considered appropriate for men or women:

> Gender roles are culturally defined behaviours that are seen as appropriate for males and females, including the attitudes, personality traits, emotions, and even postures and body language that are considered fundamental to being male or female in a culture. Gender roles also extend into social behaviours, such as the occupations we choose, how we dress and wear our hair, how we walk (men traditionally walk on the street side, open doors, etc.), how we talk (men often interrupt more, women defer more), and the ways in which we interact with others.
>
> (Carroll and Wolpe, 1996: 163)

It is these gender roles that become stereotypes that will condition our way of thinking, influencing how we understand others and what we expect from others. In this way, stereotypes guide our behaviour by taking into account gender roles and outline the development of children's behaviour who learn to follow adults and their gender roles. According to Basow (1992), rather than reflecting on different behaviours, gender stereotypes originate opposite behaviours, functioning as a "rule" or "standard" that people learn.

Being extensions of man (McLuhan, 2008) and reflecting on what is happening in society, the mass media portray these differences of gender roles, whether postulating a more traditionalist view or appealing to fragmentation and change.

It is undeniable that gender roles are changing and the 21st century shows very different attitudes and different behaviours from past centuries (Loureiro, 2014). Interrogations about what is male or female, whether being male or female, have different responses from the traditional and stereotyped views that still exist in our society and are still seen in the mass media. However, mass media, especially the new media associated with new technology, increasingly appear as potential disseminators of alternative value systems, potentially weakening traditional values.

Overall then, the modern media has a more complex view of gender and gender roles than ever before. The images of women and men are not based on stereotypes but are equally valued. However, those images remain different and diverse. Like Castells (2007) affirms, the greatest challenge of contemporaneity, and of the current mass media, is the demand for active, critical and conscious participation of citizens so that they can tread their own personal paths and, thus, question the relations of power and the asymmetries, changing the society in which they live.

Notes

1 Translated form Portuguese: "[. . .] alicerçada nas Tecnologias da Informação e da Comunicação, na expansão dos mercados e dos consumos, na burocratização maciça do quotidiano e na homogeneidade dos estilos de vida" (Ferin, 2002: 25).

2 Translated from Portuguese: "(. . .) os livros, jornais e revistas transformaram a civilização, pois moldaram a esfera pública moderna, contribuíram para as transformações sociais, políticas e económicas, promoveram a educação e o interesse pelo mundo, fizeram circular ideias e informações, modificaram a cultura"(Sousa, 2006: 542).

3 Translated from Portuguese: "no estabelecimento dos parâmetros da normalidade, na disponibilização de informação, na promoção do conhecimento e na oferta social de referentes sobre a realidade" (Sousa, 2006: 539).

4 Translated from Portuguese: "[. . .] padrões ou regras arbitrárias que uma sociedade estabelece para os seus membros, definindo os seus comportamentos, as suas roupas, os seus modos de se relacionarem" (Rodrigues, 2003: 18).

5 Translated from Portuguese: "[. . .] as concepções subjacentes de papéis de género que criaram e sustentaram essas leis"(Nogueira, 2001: 242).

6 Translated from Portuguese: "[. . .] implica assumir um posicionamento reflexivo, crítico, e de comprometimento, isso é, a necessidade de um novo vocabulário de valores" (Nogueira, 2001: 245).

7 Translated from Portuguese: "[. . .] sem dúvida, a transformação que se operou na situação social das mulheres e, do mesmo passo, nas relações sociais entre os dois sexos" (Silva, 1999: 15).
8 Translated from Portuguese: da tirania dos preconceitos que continuam a pesar negativamente sobre as mulheres e do próprio modo (masculino) como a atividade humana e as relações sociais estão organizadas" (Silva, 1999: 18).
9 Translated from Portuguese: "tiveram um papel importante, talvez mesmo decisivo, na emancipação das pessoas face à ignorância e na construção do ambiente de "conhecimento geral" que caracteriza os nossos tempos" (Sousa, 2006: 539).

References

Basow, S.A. (1992). *Gender: Stereotypes and Roles* (3rd ed.). Pacific Grove, CA: Brooks/ Cole Publishing Company.

Beaudichon, J. (2001). *A Comunicação: Processos, Formas e Aplicações.* Porto, PT: Porto Editora.

Beauvoir, S. de (1976). *Le Deuxième Sexe* (Vol. I and II. 2nd ed.). Paris: Gallimard.

Butler, J. (2007). *Gender Trouble.* London: Routledge.

Calero Fernández, Mª Angeles (1999). *Sexismo Lingüístico.* Madrid: Narcea.

Cameron, D. (1992). *Feminism and Linguistic Theory* (2nd ed.). New York: Palgrave.

Carroll, J.L., and Wolpe, P. R. (1996). *Sexuality and Gender in Society.* New York: Harper and Collins Publishers Inc.

Castells, M. (2007). *O Poder da Identidade* (Vol. II). Lisboa, PT: Fundação Calouste Gulbenkian.

Cerqueira, C. (n.d.). *Os média, os públicos e os discursos de género: (in)visibilidades, linguagens e protagonistas* [online]. Retrieved from: https://repositorium.sdum.uminho.pt/bitstream/1822/38034/1/CC_Representa%C3%A7%C3%B5es-Sociais-G%C3%A9nero-Publicidade_capitulo.pdf

Cook-Gumperz, J. (1995). Reproducing the discourse of mothering: How gendered talk makes gendered lives. In Kira Halland Mary Bucholtz (Eds.), *Gender Articulated: Language and the Socially Constructed Self* (pp. 401–419). London: Routledge.

Eckert, P. (1997). The whole woman: Sex and gender differences in variation. In Nikolas Coupland and Adam Jaworski (Eds.), *Sociolinguistics: A Reader and a Coursebook* (pp. 212–228). London: Macmillan Press Ltd.

Eckert, P., and McConnell-Ginet, S. (2003). *Language and Gender.* Cambridge: Cambridge University Press.

Ehrlich, S., and King, R. (1998). Gender-based language reform and the (de)politicization of the lexicon. In Jenny Cheshire and Peter Trudgill (Eds.), *The Sociolinguistic Reader, Volume 2: Gender and Discourse* (pp. 178–194). London; New York; Sydney; Auckland: Arnold.

Ferin Cunha, I. (2002). *Comunicação e Culturas do Quotidiano.* Lisboa, PT: Editora Quimera.

Fichtelius, A., Johansson, I., and Nordin, K. (1980). Three investigations of sex-associated speech variations in day school. In C. Kramarae (Ed.), *The Voices and Words of Women and Men* (pp. 219–225). Oxford: Pergamon Press.

Fine, C. (2010). *Delusions of Gender.* New York; London: W.W. Norton & Company.

Fiske, J. (1987). *Television Culture.* London: Routledge.

Gauntlet, D. (2008). *Media, Gender and Identity.* London; New York: Routledge.

Ghilardi-Lucena, M. I. (2008). Representações de gênero social na mídia. *Web Revista Discursividade* [online]. Retrieved from: www.discursividade.cepad.net.br/EDICOES/06/Arquivos/LUCENA.pdf

Gill, R. (2007). *Gender and Media*. Cambridge: Polity Press.

Goffman, E. (1976). Gender advertisements. *Studies in the Anthropology of Visual Communication*, 3, 69–154.

Hall, S. (2005). *A Identidade Cultural na Pós-Modernidade* (10th ed.). Translated by Tomaz Tadeu da Silva and Guacira Lopes Louro. Rio de Janeiro: DP&A.

Holmes, J., and Meyerhoff, M. (2003). Different voices, different views: An introduction to current research in language and gender. In Janet Holmes and Miriam Meyerhoff (Eds.), *The Handbook of Language and Gender* (pp. 1–17). Oxford: Blackwell Publishing.

Kellner, D. (2001). *A Cultura da mídia – estudos culturais: identidade e política entre o moderno e o pós-moderno*. Bauru, SP: EDUSC.

Key, M. R. (1996). *Male/Female Language* (2nd ed.). Lanhan, Maryland; London: Scarecrow Press.

Kramarae, C. (1981). *Women and Men Speaking*. Rowley, MA: Newbury House.

Lips, H.M., and Colwill, N. L.(1978). The paradox of power. In Hilary M. Lips and Nina Lee Colwill (Eds.), *The Psychology of Sex Differences* (pp. 225–242). London; Sydney; Toronto; New Delhi; Tokyo; Singapore; New Zealand: Prentice Hall.

Lips, H.M. et al. (1978). Sex differences in ability: Do men and women have different strengths and weaknesses? In Hilary M. Lips and Nina Lee Colwill (Eds.), *The Psychology of Sex Differences* (pp. 145–171). London; Sydney; Toronto; New Delhi; Tokyo; Singapore; New Zealand: Prentice Hall.

Loureiro, M. (2014). *O Género no Discurso de Opinião na Imprensa portuguesa*. Covilhã, PT: Livros LabCom.

Maccoby, E.E. (2003). *The Two Sexes*. Cambridge, MA: Harvard University Press.

Macdonald, M. (1995). *Representing Women: Myths of Femininity in the Popular Media*. London; New York; Sydney; Auckland: Edward Arnold.

McLuhan, M. (2008). *Compreender os Meios de Comunicação*. Translated by José Miguel Silva. Lisbo, PT: Relógio d'Água Editores.

McQuail, D. (2003). *Teoria da Comunicação de Massas*. Lisboa, PT: Fundação Calouste Gulbenkian.

Meyers, M. (1999). Fracturing women. In Marian Meyers (Ed.), *Mediated Women: Representations in Popular Culture* (pp. 3–22). Cresskill, NJ: Hampton Press.

Mill, J. S. (1986). *The Subjection of Women*. New York: Prometheus Books.

Mills, S. (2008). *Language and Sexism*. Cambridge: Cambridge University Press.

Nogueira, C. (2001). *Um Novo Olhar sobre as Relações Sociais de Género: Feminismo e Perspectivas Críticas na Psicologia Social*. Braga, PT: Fundação Calouste Gulbenkian e Fundação para a Ciência e Tecnologia.

Pierson, R. R. (1987). 'Did your mother wear army boots?' Feminist theory and women's relation to war, peace and revolution. In Sharon Macdonaldet al.(Eds.), *Images of Women in Peace and War: Cross-Cultural and Historical Perspectives* (pp. 205–227). London: Macmillan Press Ltd.

Rego, A. (2007). *Comunicação Pessoal e Organizacional*. Lisboa, PT: Ed. Sílabo.

Rodrigues, P. (2003). *Questões de Género na Infância*. Lisboa, PT: Piaget.

Rosaldo, M. Z. (1974). Women, culture, and society: A theoretical overview. In M. Zimbalist Rosaldo and Louise Lamphere (Eds.), *Woman, Culture and Society* (pp. 17–42). Stanford: Stanford University Press.

Silva, M. (1999). *A Igualdade de Género. Caminhos e Atalhos para uma Sociedade Inclusiva.* Lisboa: Comissão para a Igualdade e para os Direitos das Mulheres.

Silveirinha, M. J. (2004). Representadas e representantes: As mulheres e os media. *As Mulheres e os Media*, 5(3), 9–30.

Sousa, J. P. (2006). *Elementos de Teoria e Pesquisa da Comunicação e dos Media* (2nd ed.) [online]. Retrieved from: http://bocc.unisinos.br/pag/sousa-jorge-pedro-elementos-teoria-pequisa-comunicacao-media.pdf

Swann, J. (2002). Yes, but is it gender? In LiaLitosselitiand Jane Sunderland (Eds.), *Gender Identity and Discourse Analysis* (pp. 43–67). Amsterdam: John Benjamins Publishing Company.

Whitehead, H. (1981). The bow and the burden strap: A new look at institutionalized homosexuality in native North America. In Sherry B. Ortner and Harriet Whitehead (Eds.), *Sexual Meanings: The Cultural Construction of Gender and Sexuality* (pp. 80–115). Cambridge; London; New York; New Rochelle; Melbourne; Sydney: Cambridge University Press.

Wood, J.T. (1996). Gender, relationships, and communication. In Julia T. Wood (Ed.), *Gendered Relationships* (pp. 3–19). Mountain View; London; Toronto: Mayfield Publishing Company.

5 Gendered perspectives in succession process of family businesses

A conceptual review

Anil Boz Semerci

1. Introduction

Family businesses represent the remarkable portion in many countries' economy. Gersick, Davis, Hampton, and Lansberg (1996) have stated that family businesses constitute two-thirds of economic activities in developed countries. Heck and Stafford (2001) have also demonstrated that the estimated percentage of family businesses in Europe and the Middle East is above 70 percent of all companies. They create job opportunities, produce gross domestic products, foster innovative activities and generate a high amount of gross revenue (Olson et al., 2003; Poza, 2013; Vera and Dean, 2005). Although these economic and social contributions might also be considered for non-family businesses, the main reason behind the specific focus on family businesses is their multi-faceted structures. The interaction of family and business, by family business nature, indicates its effect in several ways. While some family-related factors (such as siblings conflict, weak leadership, competing for personal values and interests) might be considered as obstacles to business growth or organizational change (Ward, 1997), some other family-based components (such as reduced agency costs, family assets, human capital) might be seen as substantial power of family-owned businesses (Dyer, 2006). All these interrelated dynamics render the complexity of family businesses and arouse the attention of researchers and practitioners.

The other crucial and challenging discussion in family business literature is the sustainability. Ward (2016) has reported that 40 percent of all firms are experiencing or going to come across a succession process. Even if the sustainability is an important issue for all kind of firms, it is particularly challenging for family businesses. It is important to note that most family businesses do not succeed sustainability after the founding generation and only about 12 percent of family businesses make transmission successfully to the third generation (Poza, 2013). There is recognition that the reciprocal relationship of families and businesses maintain its presence in the multigenerational transmission of family businesses (Olson et al., 2003). The transition process of the family businesses from one generation to another is defined as family business succession. The main actors of family business succession are incumbent and successors. Whatley

(2011) has defined incumbent as "the person who is leaving or retiring from the most senior position within the family owned business" and successor as "the person who has been identified as taking over the most senior position within the family business." Given the significance of family businesses and their survival for sustainability, the succession process and the factors that have roles in that process should be investigated in detail. The succession is considered as a certain event for family businesses and might be planned earlier (Lee, Jasper, and Goebel, 2003). However, the selection of successor is affected by many predictable and unpredictable psychological and cultural elements besides the family-based ones. Since there is a desire to hold management control in a certain family, the candidates' pool generally occurs from the family members and particularly from the child/children of the incumbent (Miller and Breton-Miller, 2006). Although family integrity, values and harmony commonly considered as having an important role in succession decision (Caykoylu, 2013), some other social and legal dynamics might also influence the successor selection, even within the family members.

In regards to demographic characteristics, gender represents a critical variable in succession processes. Dumas (1992) has noted that the gender of both incumbent and successors play a significant role in succession processes of family owned businesses. Although Dawley, Hoffman, and Smith (2004) have demonstrated that neither female nor male outperforms to each other, many researchershave pointed out the low rates of females in the managerial positions and appointment of successors (Dumas, 1989; Martin, 2001; Oakley, 2000). It is important to investigate the reasons and outcomes behind the exclusions of females from the succession processes to protect family businesses from wasting human capital. Moreover, having objective and integrative assessments criteria in succession processes would be constructive for both families and businesses (Wang, 2010). Although there are many valuable types of research related to family business succession processes, the number of papers that particularly concentrate on gender issues in succession is limited. Gender is generally considered in many papers as a descriptive factor but is not taken into account as the main research variable or a discussing matter. After the Dumas's studies, which were published in the 1990s, there are few studies conducted mainly related to gender and succession. In that point, it is important to review previous studies and reveal the gaps that should be filled by further researches.

This chapter provides the review of literature for the last 16 years with a specific focus on gender and succession in family business. Although there are existing studies on the succession process of family businesses (Barach and Ganitsky, 1995; Filser, Kraus, and Märk, 2013; Gilding, Gregory, and Cosson, 2015; Shepherd-Worrell, Alleyne, Holder, and Pierce, 2015; Stavrou, 1999; Thurman andNason, 2016) and the role of gender or gender stereotypes in the succession process (Harveston, Davis, and Lyden, 1997; Pyromalis, Vozikis, Kalkanteras, Rogdaki, and Sigalas, 2008; Vera and Dean, 2005), no previous studies have examined the current conceptual framework of family business succession literature in terms of gender. This chapter is the only study we are aware of that uses the qualitative data mining techniques and provides insight into thematic and relational situations of gender in the family business succession process. This longitudinal study investigates the evolution of the field through a bibliometric examination of articles published between 2000 and 2016 using the text analytic software Leximancer. Leximancer provides unbiased results and inter-relational conceptual maps automatically. The present chapter contributes to discussions in 'How has the field of family business succession literature evolved in regarding gender?' It also indicates the amount of consideration and structure that researchers had, which in turn state the required focuses in this field.

2. Literature review on family business succession and gender

2.1 Before 2000s

The literature on family businesses has developed over the last 30 years (Sharma, 2004). Since family businesses are closely related to both social (family) and economic (business) units, the perspectives of scholars and practitioners interested in family firms vary from sociology to economy. It enriches the domain and scope of the literature and provides a highly comprehensive field of study. Starting from the late 1980s, gender issues are an essential subject investigated in the family business field." Barnes (1988) has indicated the problems and obstacles that daughters and young sons have faced. According to Barnes's interviews and observations, parents and siblings seem to be more skeptic towards their daughters or sisters. Moreover, the younger sons generally encounter rival siblings and try to prove themselves in hierarchical order.

Although there are some studies that investigated the relationships between fathers and sons or between brothers as potential successors (Davis and Tagiuri, 1989; Friedman, 1991; Swagger, 1991),the presence of daughters in family businesses has been examined in limited research. It would not be wrong if Barnes (1988) and Dumas (1989) studies are considered as initial journal articles on gender issues in the family business succession process (Handler, 1994). Dumas (1989) has interviewed forty family members, consisting of daughters, mothers and fathers from eighteen family businesses and reported the findings related to challenges that daughters faced in a managerial position andin the succession process. Dumas (1989) used the term of 'invisible successor' that refers to daughters not being seen as potential managers or successors in businesses. In the same years, Salganicoff (1990) noted similar problems that women had and highlighted the role of stereotypes. She also reported the role of media in emphasizing the established assumptions towards women. Iannarelli (1992) has also revealed the differences between socialization processes of daughters and sons. While these varied approaches help develop managerial and leadership skills of sons and prepare them for being potential successors, they lead to keeping women as an invisible or unrecognized resource for family businesses (Handler, 1994).

Gender was discussed regarding its impact on the successors' decision and the choice of successors to take over the family farm (Dumas, Dupuis, Richer, and St. Cyr, 1995). It was reported that daughters encounter the problem of invisibility also in the succession process of family businesses in agriculture. Another stream of researcheshas revealed that women are well represented in family-ownedbusinesses, but they have obstacles in obtaining substantial ownerships (Dumas, 1998). More interestingly, even if both women and men agreed on the invisibility of women in family firms, some women willingly accept the forefront position of their husbands in the management of firms and take the back seat (Cole, 1997). Dumas (1992) has also reported that some mothers believe that daughters working in the family business is inappropriate and might cause problems in family members' relations. All these findings indicate that gendered-based biases are important discussion subjects in the family business domain until the 1990s. The reasons behind these biases vary. The socialization forms of girls and boys, traditional views of families or the role of media have been considered as triggers. Furthermore, women's acceptance of these stereotypical beliefs might also provide a favorable environment for maintaining these values.

Although there are some studies that have aimed to examine women's problems in family businesses empirically before the 2000s, they represent the initial steps in this context and suggest to conduct more researches related to women positions in new generations of family businesses (Cole, 1997; Dumas, 1998; Salganicoff, 1990). According to Wang (2010), the studies conducted after the Dumas's (1989, and 1992) have been few and have not demonstrated a comprehensive understanding.

2.2 Between 2000 and 2016

With the rise in a number of women in work life, the consideration of gender-based issues in family businesses has increased. However, it seems that while the number of studies regarding gender and succession has increased between 2000 and 2009, they are still few after 2009. Although some studies used quantitative analysis (Ahrens, Landmann, and Woywode, 2015), the dominant research method in the field seems to be qualitative methods (qualitative content analysis). Cadieux, Lorrain, and Hugron (2002) have indicated that qualitative research methods are appropriate in order to examine details of the succession process in family businesses. The studies differ regarding researchers' approaches, related concepts and countries' context examined. Santiago (2000) has had interviews on 'family business background,''family and business structure and relationships' and 'the succession process adopted by families' with nineteen family members from eight family businesses in the Philippines. The findings have indicated the importance of harmony between family and business values. Accordingly, family values shape the business culture, and the consistency between them provides a successful and acceptable transition from one generation to another. However, the traditional family values might present a preventer environment for women in succession processes of family businesses in the Philippines. Bennedsen, Nielsen, Pérez-González, and Wolfenzon

(2007) have pointed out that families whose first child is male are 32.7 percent more likely to succeed into the family business than ones whose first child is female in Denmark. Tatoglu, Kula, and Glaister (2008) have also reported daughters' low rate in consideration of potential successors in family businesses in Turkey. In that regard, from succession planning to action, more objective assessments that cover all family members are required in respect to countries' context.

In regarding to success in succession processes, Ibrahim, Soufani, and Lam (2001) have noted the need to predict and manage conflicts and to consider daughters in succession processes. It is particularly important to have inclusive and 'multiple stakeholder perspectives' in managerial transition processes. Therefore, family businesses will experience the low rate of resistance to change and conflict, which in turn provide more successful transition in the context of sustainability (Haberman and Danes, 2007).

Female members of families have been excluded from the succession process, even if they have more relevant competencies or educational background compared to their brothers (Howorth and Ali, 2001; Martin, 2001). García-Álvarez, López-Sintas, and Gonzalvo (2002) have reported that females are included in the succession processes when the founders' children are all female or when they are the first in birth-order. However, when they compared the potential successors' education level, it is noted that females have a higher formal education than the males. While this educational progress leads females' interest into the contemporary areas related to business competitiveness in the future, it might also cause delayed entry of daughters into the businesses. Further, Haddadj 's (2003) longitudinal study has revealed that a predecessor's decisions not to consider daughters as potential successors are still a case in family businesses, even though they started to take responsibilities in early ages (e.g. during school holidays).

On the other hand, Constantinidis and Nelson (2009), in their study of USA and Belgium family businesses, have discussed the succession in regards to the daughters' perspectives. They have explained their findings in two main categories: the daughters' challenges after having leadership positions and their push/pull motivations for working in family businesses. Pull motivations are described as daughters' willingness to participate in family businesses and take responsibilities whereas pushfactors refer to a family's pressures on daughters to be involved in family firms. Constantinidis and Nelson (2009) have stated that daughters' perceptions on these motivators are heavily related to interests and approaches of their families. Curimbaba (2002) has also categorized the motivations of daughters into three groups, which are 'needing a job,' 'recognizing opportunities' and 'spontaneity.' Families' consideration on daughters' potential as possible successor would help to improve females' skills and knowledge and prepare them for possible leadership positions. In that regard, family businesses would be more attractive for daughtersand they would enjoy working in their family businesses (pull motivations), which in turn would enhance their leadership performance and contribute to the family businesses' sustainability.

Since the succession process of the family business is not just contained to children, marriages and the role of wives should be considered in gendered perspectives. Although there is limited study related to the impact of mothers or wives in managerial issues of family businesses, Solomon et al. (2011) have stated both the exclusion of daughters and mothers/wives from family businesses' leadership positions. Traditional values and 'gender-rigid marriage' are considered as constraining factors in succession and result in theabsence of daughters and wives in the succession process.

Some researchers have taken different approaches to gender and succession issues by examining the succession process in women-owned family businesses. Although Sonfield and Lussier (2009) have not found any gender-based differences on ten management characteristics variables, including succession plans, Cadieux et al. (2002) have asserted some different points in succession planning of women-owned businesses. Their findings stated that the consideration of succession in women's minds occurred after a significant life event, such as the death of a husband, the involvement of successors into the business or graduation of successors. After the consideration of transferring a business, Cadieux et al. (2002) have highlighted some resistances caused by an owner's characteristics, the relationship between owners and potential successors, or organizational environment. However, they have not particularly focused on gender-based preferences that women have in their succession decisions. Vera and Dean (2005) have found similar results related to succession decisions of women-owned family businesses. They have conducted interviews with ten daughters who took over their families' businesses from their parents. The daughters who took over control of their companies from their mothers have expressed the reluctance of their mother in the succession of their businesses. They have reported that serious illnesses represent the turning points for their mothers' decisions about succession. In regarding potential successors, although the daughters have not stated any priorities for male or older siblings in succession process, they have reported their feelings on their low inclusion in the succession process compared to their brothers and the need to work hard and prove themselves (Vera and Dean, 2005).

Besides the empirical studies on one or numerous cases, there are also literature review papers related to gender and succession in family businesses. After the increased number of papers on family business succession and gender issues, the reviewsare neededto provide an overview and introduce the gaps that can be studied in further studies. Jimenez (2009) has conducted research based on a review of 48 articles, books and dissertations published between 1985 and 2008. The reviews of these publications have indicated two main groups, which are 1) obstacles and 2) positive aspects of women's participation in the family business. The publications classified as obstacles refer to women's invisibility, emotional leadership, and succession and primogeniture subjects whereas positive aspects present the professional career of women in family businesses and their contributions in running the family firms. The review of these publications has been concluded with directions for future researches. Similarly, but more specifically,Wang (2010) has carried out a literature review about daughters' exclusion from succession processes of family businesses. Although Wang's (2010) study is the most similar one to this chapter, the publications were grouped and analyzed by the author subjectively.

This chapter and its methodology contribute to the literature in several ways. First, as mentioned previously, the systematic literature review of certain subjects enables researchers to identify researched topics currently and define main directions for further researches. It would encourage researchers and policymakers to maintain investigations and implementations on deficient points. Second, the reviews of literature within specific time periods help to indicate the evolution of relevant issues respectively. Third, using Leximancer as a qualitative software tool provides a moreunbiased platform in obtaining and interpreting conceptual findings. Last but not least, the design and methodology used in this chapter might be useful for other studies in different specific domains.

3. Method

3.1 Data collection

The aim of this chapter is to demonstrate the conceptual structure of gender-related scientific articles in family business succession between 2000 and 2016. Accordingly, 'family business succession' literature is investigated with the focus on 'gender.' 'Gender,' 'gender stereotype,' 'daughter/son,' 'female/male,' and 'woman/man' were used as keywords in the searching process. In many studies gender was used as a demographic variable to demonstrate the profile of potential successors or the gender of the business owner/founder. Journal articles that indicate the main movement of gender issues in family business succession literature are included. In consideration of journals, indexation restrictions were not applied. However, books, book chapters, book reviews, conference papers, and editorials were excluded. After the gender-specific focus on journal articles, nineteen articles were obtained between 2000 and 2016. Appendix 5.1 demonstrates the descriptive information of selected articles.

If the study used Leximancer as a software tool, the abstracts and keywords of the articles were included for analyses (Cretchley, Rooney, and Gallois, 2010). However, considering only abstracts and keywords might cause one to miss the concepts that were not included in abstracts or keywords but were presented considerably in the rest of the text (Volery and Mazzarol, 2015). Therefore, the full articles were includedand analyzed in this study.

3.2 Leximancer in generating the conceptual structures

Leximancer is a statistical software tool that enables the researcher to identify themes, concepts, and the dominance of and the interrelationships among those concepts. Leximancer is a tool to conduct a content analysis of written data in the light of grounded theory (Corbin and Strauss, 1990). In grounded theory, the themes are discovered through mining the data, finding relational meaning and then compiling the concepts into the themes. Leximancer produces a conceptual map by using word frequencies and the interrelation of these words with each other. The words that often co-occur within the same or close sentences are presentedin close proximity in the conceptual map (Smith and Humphreys, 2006). Leximancer also generates size, brightness and centrality of each concept, which indicates its importance in relation to other concepts. Therefore, the obtained findings enable researchers to examine the dominance of a concept and its relationship with other ones within a related subject. The combined clusters generate a theme, which is named the same as an outstandingconcept in that theme. The software enables the researcher to change the theme name according to concepts it covers (Cretchley et al., 2010).

In recent years Leximancer is used in many studies as a qualitative analysis tool. It can be used for bibliometric research on one's journal articles (Cretchley et al., 2010; Volery and Mazzarol, 2015), or it makes the examination of one specific topic possible within the literature (Roeschke, 2015). In the end, Leximancer generates a colorful concept map that indicates the concepts, the clusters of concepts (themes), the interrelations and the importance of these concepts within the related context.

4. Results

The summaries of articles were presented in Appendix 5.1. As can be seen, the majority of articles were published in *Family Business Review*. The dominant research method was qualitative, in which interviews and qualitative content analysis were used prevalently.

Before running Leximancer, in order to have a clear and meaningful conceptual map, the common functional words (such as *and, or, but*) and general terms with low meaning to the concept map (such as *findings, results, examined, study, paper*) were excluded from the analysis. The singular and plural words such as family and families or business and businesses were merged in order to not have different findings on these words with the same meanings (Cretchley et al., 2010).

Figure 5.1 presents the overall map of themes, concepts and their interrelations. The twelve themes with many concepts are shown. The themes, starting with capital letters and written in bold, were shown as circles and the concepts within these themes as italic text. The importance of themes was numberedin rank order. The relations of concepts and themes can be seen with dashed lines, whereas the closeness and overlapping of circles also present the close relations of concepts within those themes. The size of the circles depends on the number of the concepts that it has. It can be seen that the most important themes were *Daughters, Management* and the *Founders*. The first most important theme was *Daughters*. This theme contained *gender, children, social* and *differences* as concepts. When the interrelations of concepts were checked, it has been found that *gender*is associated with *differences* and *social* concepts within the same (*Daughters*) theme and closely with the *Role* theme. It indicates the prevalence of researches that have revealed the gender-based differences in social roles and socialization.

The second major theme was *Management*. It comprised *control, transfer, change, decision* and *power* as concepts. The position of the theme (as a circle) asserts its relations with many other themes. The theme was located close to

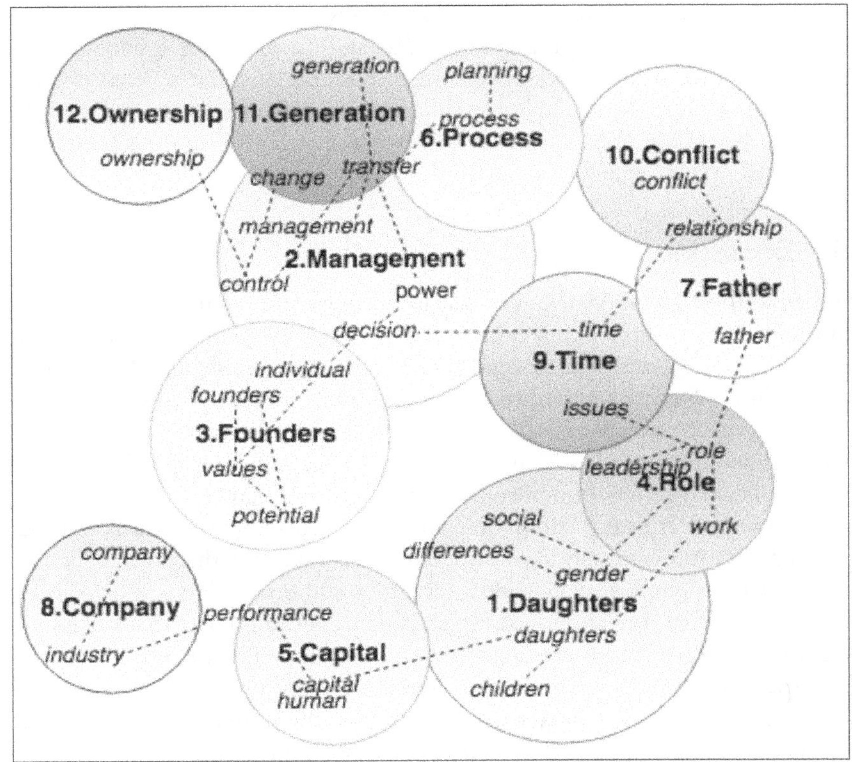

Figure 5.1 Articles conceptual map

Founders, Generation, Process and *Time* themes. Although the *Generation, Process*, and *Time* were less important themes, their positions were closer to the *Management* compared to where the *Founders* was. The importance of the founders, however, manifested itself as a third major theme (*Founders*) in our results. It contained *values, individual*, and *potential* as concepts, and these three concepts were highly interrelated. All these findings related to second and third themes; their concepts and their interrelations confirm the impact of founders' individual values in considering the potential successors. Moreover, these findings reflect the importance of founders on the decisions about when and how to transfer the power and control of businesses to next generations.

Although the *Role* theme was seen as a lesser theme, its interrelations with *Daughters, Conflict*, and *Father* have indicated outstanding studied areas in succession literature. It indicates the prevalence of researches that are not only related to different social roles of sons and daughters but also the role conflicts or work-family conflicts that women face during their work life. On the other hand, it also demonstrates the critical status of father and father-daughter relationships in the succession process of family businesses.

The interrelations of the theme *Capital* and *Company* have indicated the outputs of succession processes for family businesses within specific industry sectors. Also, some studies have examined the performance of companies by some financial indicators, such as return on asset or return on capital, after the succession process ended.

5. Discussion

Although there are limited studies that take gender as a main discussion subject in family business succession literature, it is clear that the number of these studies is increased after 2000. The conceptual map of articles suggests that the dominant themes in the literature related to gender and family business succession over the last 16 years are 'daughters' and 'management.' While it is not surprising, the concepts and interrelations of themes have presented more detailed frameworks.

The obtained results from mapping the themes, concepts and their interrelations provide several suggestions for forthcoming researches. First, the dominance of founders' role and the impact of individual values in this role reflect the needs of examinations in individual levels. In addition, there was a focus on father and daughter relationships, which is the result of the fact that the founders are male in general. Interestingly, despite a rise in studies using the daughter's perspective in the succession process, mothers are not prominent as a concept. The rise in the number of women employment and entrepreneurship provide the needs for a specific focus on mother-owned family businesses. Although there are limited studies related to mother ownerships and successions in those companies (Cadieux et al., 2002; Sonfield and Lussier, 2009), more researches are needed to demonstrate mother and daughter relationships and the mother's role in succession even if fathers own the companies.

Second, despite the relatively small number of studies dealing with different industry sectors (vera anddean, 2005; Ibrahim et al., 2001), the comparative studies not only within different sectors but also within various cultures are required. The interrelations of family and business differentiate family businesses from others. Undoubtedly, families are the small units of societies and are shaped by cultural values of the countries that they live in. Therefore, the examination of succession processes within different social contexts would be useful to see the impact of macro-level gender-based values (Constantinidis and Nelson, 2009). The other obtained finding was on the companies' performances. It is clear that many studies related to family businesses have used financial indicators in reporting the performance change of companies after the successions (for example Bennedsen et al., 2007). However, the transformation in managerial positions also affects the perceptional indicators, such as organizational culture, organizational commitment of employees or organizational justice related to the whole organization. In parallel with the succession process, the examination of perceptional factors within the organization would be useful in order to indicate successors' impacts.

The legal status of women is another concern that is not represented sufficiently. Legal rights of women after marriage vary in each country. The studies focusing on legal rights of women before and after marriage within different country contexts would be appropriate to reveal legal obstacles that women have. Although in many studies it is suggested that the presence of respect between family members regardless of generation, gender or birth order conclude with more successful and unproblematic successions, the legal protections of women might help them to experience an objective succession in a more egalitarian environment. In that manner, the detailed scientific researches might also provide practical directions and suggestions to policy makers and, in turn, help to protect women's rights.

Furthermore, the descriptive analysis of articles has revealed the dominancy of qualitative methods in researches (Appendix 5.1). Despite the several advantages of qualitative methods (such as in-depth interviews or document analysis) in understanding and tracking the issues in succession, it might be more comprehensive if these qualitative methods are diversified with others (such as observations or focus groups). Also, the increased effort of scholars is required to investigate the succession process from different viewpoints of actors (fathers, mothers, children, employees, nonfamily members in managerial positions, customers) simultaneously.

6. Conclusion

This chapter presents an integrative framework that draws on previous empirical researches and synthesizes the gendered perspective in succession of family businesses. The purpose of this chapter was to identify the conceptual profile of gender-based literature in succession and indicate the evolution of conceptual structure within the field between 2000 and 2016. This would enable us to see how the handling of gender-based issues related to family business succession was in the last 16 years. It also helps to increase readers' awareness on the gendered perspective in the succession process. Such an integrative framework is timely and useful because, within the gender and family business fields, there is not any bibliometric review that can support a common conceptual platform for both practitioners and researchers.

To sum up, it is clear that the development of the field of succession process of family businesses is still in progress. The gendered perspective through this field refers to one aspect of this development. I hope this work will help to encourage scholars and policy makers to conduct researches with gendered perspectives in family business successions.

This study has a number of limitations. Although Leximancer is an appropriate and comprehensive software tool for bibliometric analysis, it may not have demonstrated all the concepts that the studies had. The time scope of this chapter was between 2000 and 2016. The analysis of literature within a broader period might be more comprehensive. However, the researches conducting this analysis within different and certain time periods would help to see how the conceptual map of gendered perspectives in family business succession literature has changed.

Appendix

Table 5.1 Summaries of articles included in analysis (2000–2016)

*Year**	*Authors***	*Journal*	*Title*	*Major Focus*	*Methodology*	*Findings****
2000	Santiago, A.L.	*Family Business Review*	Succession Experiences in the Philippines Family Businesses	Succession process	**Sample:** Family members of 8 family businesses in the Philippines. **Data collection:** In depth interviews	Successful succession highly depends on family values.
2001	Ibrahim, A. B., et al.	*Family Business Review*	A Study of Succession in a Family Firm	Succession process	**Sample:** Family members of 1 family business in the communication sector. **Data collection:** Docum ent analysis	Conflicts, reluctance, lack of planning and exclusion of daughters in the succession process.
2001	Howorth, C. & Ali, Z. A.	*Family Business Review*	Family Business Succession in Portugal: An Examination of Case Studies in the Furniture Industry	Succession process	**Sample:** Family members of 3 family firms in the furniture industry in Portugal. **Data collection:** In depth interviews	The impact of family values, reluctance, sons' priority even if the daughters have higher education level.
2001	Martin, L.	*Women in Management Review*	More jobs for the boys? Succession planning in SMEs	Succession process	**Sample:** Family members of 128 small-medium sized companies. **Data collection:** In depth interviews	Lack of succession planning and exclusion of daughters.

2002	García-Álvarez, E., et al.	*Family Business Review*	Socialization Patterns of Successors in First- to Second-Generation Family Businesses	Socialization of potential successors	**Sample:** 13 male Spanish firm founders. **Data collection:** In depth interviews	Founders' dominant role in building the family and business values.
2002	Cadieux, L., et al.	*Family Business Review*	Succession in Women-Owned Family Businesses: A Case Study	Succession process in women-owned family businesses	**Sample:** Family members of 4 women-owned family businesses from the manu-facturing sector in Canada. **Data collection:** In depth interviews	Lack of succession planning and importance of parent-child relationships in decreasing the resistance to succession.
2002	Curimbaba, F.	*Family Business Review*	The Dynamics of Women's Roles as Family Business Managers	Daughters' experiences in family businesses	**Sample:** 12 daughters who are working in management positions in family businesses in Brazil. **Data collection:** In depth interviews	Daughters' positions were grouped as 'invisible,' 'professional' and 'anchor.'
2003	Haddadj, S.	*Journal of Organizational Change Management*	Organization change and the complexity of succession: A longitudinal case study from France	Succession within an organizational change perspective	**Sample:** Family members and other management employees of 1 family business in France. **Data collection:** In depth interviews (longitudinal)	The appropriateness of multi-level approaches in succession processes. Exclusion of the daughter as a potential successor (from daughters' perspective).

(*Continued*)

Table 5.1 (Continued)

*Year**	*Authors***	*Journal*	*Title*	*Major Focus*	*Methodology*	*Findings****
2005	Vera, C. F. & Dean, M.C.	*Family Business Review*	An Examination of the Challenges Daughters Face in family Business	The obstacles that daughters had before and after the succession process	**Sample:** 10 daughters who had taken over their families' businesses that are in four different sectors. **Data collection:** In depth interviews	Reasons for joining the family business challenges that they had before and during the succession, work-family conflict and stereotyping from outsiders.
2007	Haberman, H. & Danes, M. S.	*Family Business Review*	Father-Daughter and Father-Son Family Business Management Transfer Comparison: Family FIRO Model	Succession process with the examination of father-son and father-daughter relationships	**Sample:** Family members of 2 family businesses from farm sector **Data collection:** In depth interviews	The impacts of family values on succession processes. The invisibility of daughters until their request.
2007	Bennedson, M., et al.	*The Quarterly Journal of Economics*	Inside The Family Firm: The Role of Families in Succession Decisions and Performance	The performances of family and nonfamily CEOs. Firm financial performance after the succession	**Sample:** succession processes in family businesses in Denmark. **Data collection:** Data bases (secondary data)	The preferences towards sons in succession processes compared to daughters.
2008	Tatoglu, E., et al.	*International Small Business Journal*	Succession Planning in Family-owned Businesses: Evidence from Turkey	Succession process	**Sample:** The predecessors of 408 family businesses in Turkey in the manufacturing sector. **Data collection:** Self-administered survey	The role of predecessors on selecting succession criteria, exclusion of daughters as a potential successor, and the ignorance of work experiences of a successor in other firms.

2009	Sonfield, M. C. & Lussier R. N.	*International Journal of Gender and Entrepreneurship*	Gender in family business ownership and management: A six-country analysis	Gender-based differences in ten management characteristics (including succession) of family businesses	**Sample:** The owners of 593 family businesses in Croatia, Egypt, France, India, Kuwait and the USA. **Data collection:** Self-administrated survey	There were not any significant differences between men and women in ten management characteristics (including succession planning).
2009	Constantinidis, C. & Nelson, T.	*Management International*	Integrating Succession and Gender Issues from the Perspective of the Daughter of Family Enterprise: A Cross-National Investigation	The challenges and willingness daughters have in the succession process of family businesses	**Sample:** 11 daughters of family firms in Belgium and 138 daughters of family firms in the USA. **Data collection:** In depth interviews and self-administrated survey	The challenges that daughters have in family businesses and other businesses. The advantages and disadvantages of working in family business.
2009	Jimenez, R. M.	*Family Business Review*	Research on Women in Family Firms: Current Status and Future Directions	Literature review on women in family businesses	Forty-eight articles, twenty-three books and three doctoral dissertations related to women in family firms and published between 1985 and 2008.	Women working in family businesses were examined in two terms (obstacles and positive aspects). The invisibility of women in the succession process refers one of the main obstacles.
2010	Wang, C.	*Journal of Family and Economic Issues*	Daughter Exclusion in Family Business Succession: A Review of the Literature	Literature review on daughters in succession process of family businesses	Researches related to daughters in succession in academic refereed journals.	The invisibility of daughters and obstacles in succession processes were explained with micro and macro factors.

(*Continued*)

Table 5.1 (Continued)

*Year**	*Authors***	*Journal*	*Title*	*Major Focus*	*Methodology*	*Findings****
2011	Soloman, A., et al.	*Family Process*	"Don't Lock Me Out": Life-Story Interviews of Family Business Owners Facing Succession	Succession process	**Sample:** Ten family business owners. **Data collection:** In depth interviews	The findings from life-story interviews were grouped into two groups, which are facilitating and constraining factors on succession. Gendered approaches presented as one of the matters in constraining factors.
2014	Avlonito, A., et al.	*International Entrepreneurship and Management Journal*	Sibling rivalry: Implications for the family business succession process	Sibling rivalry and its effect on satisfaction with and effectiveness of succession	Theoretical study.	The antecedents of sibling relationship-rivalry in adulthood and its impact on succession outcome were examined. Gender was represented as one of the sibling characteristics, which has an impact on the rivalry.
2015	Ahrens, J., et al.	*Journal of Family Business Strategy*	Gender preferences in the CEO successions of family firms: Family characteristics and human capital of the successor	Succession process	**Sample:** 804 CEO successions in family businesses between 2002 and 2008 in Germany. **Data collection:** Interviews and data bases (secondary data)	Families characteristics and successors human capital were examined. Gender preferences that favor males in succession process of family businesses were indicated.

* The papers were sorted according to years they have published.
** Due to the limited space, the authors' names were presented as '*et al.*' if there were more than two authors.
*** Due to the limited space, only the findings related to our chapter were presented shortly.

References

Ahrens, J. P., Landmann, A., and Woywode, M. (2015). Gender preferences in the CEO successions of family firms: Family characteristics and human capital of the successor. *Journal of Family Business Strategy*, 6(2), 86–103.

Barach, J. A., and Ganitsky, J. B. (1995). Successful succession in family business. *Family Business Review*, 8(2), 131–155.

Barnes, L. B. (1988). Incongruent hierarchies: Daughters and younger sons as company CEOs. *Family Business Review*, 1(1), 9–21.

Bennedsen, M., Nielsen, K. M., Pérez-González, F., and Wolfenzon, D. (2007). Inside the family firm: The role of families in succession decisions and performance. *The Quarterly Journal of Economics*, 122(2), 647–691.

Cadieux, L., Lorrain, J., and Hugron, P. (2002). Succession in women-owned family businesses: A case study. *Family Business Review*, 15(1), 17–30.

Caykoylu, S. (2013). *Post-Succession Predecessor-Successor Interactions and their Relational and Organizational Outcomes*. Doctoral dissertation, Beedie School of Business Faculty: Segal Graduate School.

Cole, P. M. (1997). Women in family business. *Family Business Review*, 10(4), 353–371.

Constantinidis, C., and Nelson, T. (2009). Integrating succession and gender issues from the perspective of the daughter of family enterprise: A cross-national investigation. *Management International*, 14(1), 43.

Corbin, J. M., and Strauss, A. (1990). Grounded theory research: Procedures, canons, and evaluative criteria. *Qualitative Sociology*, 13(1), 3–21.

Cretchley, J., Rooney, D., and Gallois, C. (2010). Mapping a 40-year history with Leximancer: Themes and concepts in the journal of cross-cultural psychology. *Journal of Cross-Cultural Psychology*, 41(3), 318–328.

Curimbaba, F. (2002). The dynamics of women's roles as family business managers. *Family Business Review*, 15(3), 239–252.

Davis, J. A., and Tagiuri, R. (1989). The influence of life stage on father-son work relationships in family companies. *Family Business Review*, 2(1), 47–74.

Dawley, D., Hoffman, J., and Smith, A. (2004). Leader succession: Does gender matter? *The Leadership and Organisation Development Journal*, 25(8), 678–690.

Dumas, C. (1989). Understanding of father-daughter and father-son dyads in family-owned businesses. *Family Business Review*, 2(1), 31–46.

Dumas, C. (1992). Integrating the daughter into family business management. *Entrepreneurship: Theory and Practice*, 16(4), 41–56.

Dumas, C. (1998). Women's pathways to participation and leadership in the family-owned firm. *Family Business Review*, 11(3), 219–228.

Dumas, C., Dupuis, J. P., Richer, F., and St. Cyr, L. (1995). Factors that influence the next generation's decision to take over the family farm. *Family Business Review*, 8(2), 99–120.

Dyer, W. G. (2006). Examining the 'family effect' on firm performance. *Family Business Review*, 19(4), 253–273.

Filser, M., Kraus, S., and Märk, S. (2013). Psychological aspects of succession in family business management. *Management Research Review*, 36(3), 256–277.

Friedman, S. D. (1991). Sibling relationships and intergenerational succession in family firms. *Family Business Review*, 4(1), 3–20.

García-Álvarez, E., López-Sintas, J., and Gonzalvo, P. S. (2002). Socialization patterns of successors in first-to second-generation family businesses. *Family Business Review*, 15(3), 189–203.

Gersick, K. E., Davis, J., Hampton, M., and Lansberg, I. (1996). *Generation to Generation: Life Cycles of the Family Business.* Boston: Harvard Business School Press.

Gilding, M., Gregory, S., and Cosson, B. (2015). Motives and outcomes in family business succession planning. *Entrepreneurship Theory and Practice*, 39(2), 299–312.

Haberman, H., and Danes, S. M. (2007). Father-daughter and father-son family business management transfer comparison: Family FIRO model application. *Family Business Review*, 20(2), 163–184.

Haddadj, S. (2003). Organization change and the complexity of succession: A longitudinal case study from France. *Journal of Organizational Change Management*, 16(2), 135–153.

Handler, W. C. (1994). Succession in family business: A review of the research. *Family Business Review*, 7(2), 133–157.

Harveston, P. D., Davis, P. S., and Lyden, J. A. (1997). Succession planning in family business: The impact of owner gender. *Family Business Review*, 10(4), 373–396.

Heck, R. K., and Stafford, K. (2001). The vital institution of family business: Economic benefits hidden in plain sight. *Destroying Myths and Creating Value in Family Business*, 9–17.

Howorth, C., and Ali, Z. A. (2001). Family business succession in Portugal: An examination of case studies in the furniture industry. *Family Business Review*, 14(3), 231–244.

Iannarelli, C. L. (1992). *The Socialization of Leaders: A Study of Gender in Family Business.* Unpublished doctoral dissertation, University of Pittsburgh.

Ibrahim, A. B., Soufani, K., and Lam, J. (2001). A study of succession in a family firm. *Family Business Review*, 14(3), 245–258.

Jimenez, M. R. (2009). Research on women in family firms: Current status and future directions. *Family Business Review*, 22(1), 53–64.

Lee, Y. G., Jasper, C. R., and Goebel, K. P. (2003). A profile of succession planning among family business owners. *Financial Counseling and Planning*, 14(2), 31–41.

Martin, H. F. (2001). Is family governance an oxymoron? *Family Business Review*, 14(2), 91–96.

Miller, D., and Breton-Miller, L. (2006). Family governance and firm performance: Agency, stewardship, and capabilities. *Family Business Review*, 19(1), 73–87.

Oakley, J.G. (2000). Gender-based barriers to senior management positions: Understanding the scarcity of female CEOs. *Journal of Business Ethics*, 27(4): 321-334.

Olson, P. D., Zuiker, V. S., Danes, S. M., Stafford, K., Heck, R. K., and Duncan, K. A. (2003). The impact of the family and the business on family business sustainability. *Journal of Business Venturing*, 18(5), 639–666.

Poza, E. J. (2013). *Family Business.* Cengage Learning.

Pyromalis, V. D., Vozikis, G. S., Kalkanteras, T. A., Rogdaki, M. E., and Sigalas, G. P. (2008). An integrated framework for testing the success of the family business succession process according to gender specificity. In Poutziouris, P., Smyrnios, K. and Klein, S. (Eds) *Handbook of Research on Family Business*, Edward Elgar, Cheltenham (pp. 422–442).

Roeschke, A. (2015). *The Concept and Evolution of Entrepreneurial Leadership: A Bibliometric Analysis.* Academy of Management Proceedings (Vol. 2015, No. 1, p. 18007). Academy of Management.

Salganicoff, M. (1990). Women in family businesses: Challenges and opportunities. *Family Business Review*, 3(2), 125–137.

Santiago, A. L. (2000). Succession experiences in Philippine family businesses. *Family Business Review*, 13(1), 15–35.

Sharma, P. (2004). An overview of the field of family business studies: Current status and directions for the future. *Family Business Review*, 17(1), 1–36.

Shepherd-Worrell, M. N., Alleyne, P., Holder, M. K., and Pierce, M. A. (2015). Family business succession among entrepreneurs: Evidence from prominent family businesses in Barbados. *The Journal of Public Sector Policy Analysis*, 1: 24-51.

Smith, A. E., and Humphreys, M. S. (2006). Evaluation of unsupervised semantic mapping of natural language with Leximancer concept mapping. *Behavior Research Methods*, 38(2), 262–279.

Solomon, A., Breunlin, D., Panattoni, K., Gustafson, M., Ransburg, D., Ryan, C., . . . Terrien, J. (2011). 'Don't lock me out': Life-story interviews of family business owners facing succession. *FamilyProcess*, 50(2), 149–166.

Sonfield, M. C., and Lussier, R. N. (2009). Gender in family business ownership and management: A six-country analysis. *International Journal of Gender and Entrepreneurship*, 1(2), 96–117.

Stavrou, E. T. (1999). Succession in family businesses: Exploring the effects of demographic factors on offspring intentions to join and take over the business. *Journal of Small Business Management*, 37(3), 43.

Swagger, G. (1991). Assessing the successor generation in family businesses. *Family Business Review*, 4(4), 397–411.

Tatoglu, E., Kula, V., and Glaister, K. W. (2008). Succession planning in family-owned businesses: Evidence from Turkey. *International Small Business Journal*, 26(2), 155–180.

Thurman, P. W., and Nason, R. S. (2016). *Father-Daughter Succession in Family Business: A Cross-Cultural Perspective*. CRC Press.

Vera, C. F., and Dean, M. A. (2005). An examination of the challenges daughters face in family business succession. *Family Business Review*, 18(4), 321–345.

Volery, T., and Mazzarol, T. (2015). The evolution of the small business and entrepreneurship field: A bibliometric investigation of articles published in the International Small Business Journal. *International Small Business Journal*, 33(4), 374–396.

Wang, C. (2010). Daughter exclusion in family business succession: A review of the literature. *Journal of Family and Economic Issues*, 31(4), 475–484.

Ward, J. L. (1997). Growing the family business: Special challenges and best practices. *Family Business Review*, 10(4), 323–337.

Ward, J. L. (2016). *Perpetuating the Family Business: 50 Lessons Learned From Long Lasting, Successful Families in Business*. New York: Springer.

Whatley, L. (2011). A new model for family owned business succession. *Organization Development Journal*, 29(4), 21.

6 Family embeddedness and gendered professional entrepreneurship

Evidence from the self-employment of female lawyers in the U.S.

Sang-Joon Kim and So Young Choi

Introduction

The prior literature focusing on women's entrepreneurship highlights that discrimination in and around traditional organizations, or structural barriers in the society, drives women to consider entrepreneurship (e.g. Ramadani, Gërguri, Dana, and Tašaminova, 2013; Patrick, Stephens, and Weinstein, 2016; Budig, 2006a). As such, women entrepreneurship has been largely understood in terms of small businesses or family businesses (e.g. Ramadani et al., 2013). Specifically, given that women have been structurally disadvantageous in the society (Kanter, 1977; Morrison and Von Glinow, 1990; Riger and Galligan, 1980), factors for women entrepreneurship have been mainly associated with such structural aspects, such as a glass ceiling, childcare, work-family balance, etc. (e.g. Budig, 2006a; Carr, 1996; Hughes, 2003). Dominated by the structural barrier issues in understanding women entrepreneurship, we may not fully understand how women take the initiatives to create a new business or found a new organization. What would happen if women entrepreneurs often avoided such structural barriers? Would women professionals (such as lawyers, doctors, professors, and so forth) who are accredited by society, if they intend to run their own business, still be critically affected by the structural barriers?

In this chapter, we are inspired to touch upon this unexplored context of entrepreneurship of professional women. Since professional women, compared to women with other occupations, may have more leeway to avoid the structural barriers, the conventional theories related to women entrepreneurship may not fully explain the phenomena of professional entrepreneurship. This will help us further understand how the structural barriers affect women entrepreneurship. To explore factors to motivate such women-specific entrepreneurship, we take two aspects into account. First, we attempt to figure out a particular pattern of gendered entrepreneurship. Specifically, we consider self-employment as an evidence to illustrate the process of gendered entrepreneurship. As professional entrepreneurship is defined as "self-employment to join professional partnerships and establish a professional practice" (Dawson, Henley, and Latreille, 2009: 12), self-employment, which comes up with opening an independent business or being a freelancer, can be a type of entrepreneurship (Douglas and Shepherd, 2002; Budig, 2006a; Dawson et al., 2009). Besides, in the sense that one of the motives for self-employment of women is the experience of discrimination or dissatisfaction with the traditional organizations (e.g. Gilad and Levine, 1986), the process of self-employment makes sure how a gender-specific type of entrepreneurship unfolds (Budig, 2006a; Patrick et al., 2016). Based on this, we posit that professional women's self-employment is a significant phenomenon in understanding the process of women entrepreneurship.

Second, assuming that people are not atomized, but rather are "embedded" in their social relations (Granovetter, 1985), we claim that various characteristics of family structure can influence the processes involved in women-specific entrepreneurship (Aldrich and Cliff, 2003). The prior literature on family embeddedness is related to how entrepreneurs can attain critical resources to mobilize the processes involved in the creation of new organization (Mari and Poggesi, 2016; Azmat and Fujimoto, 2016; Aldrich and Cliff, 2003). For example, Aldrich and Cliff (2003) specify how the behavioral patterns of venture creation based on family embeddedness bring opportunity recognition, the launch decision, resource mobilization, and the implementation of founding strategies, processes, and structures.

Taken together, this chapter examines how family embeddedness can influence professional women's initiatives for entrepreneurship. Since professionals, accredited by academic degrees, certificates, or other credentials, can secure their jobs at the traditional organizations, the structural-barrier thesis on women entrepreneurship may not be necessarily applicable for the professional entrepreneurship, or self-motivation of women professionals. That is, if we can find out certain factors for women professionals to consider being self-employed by leaving traditional organizations, the factors will indicate the conditions women are likely to engage in entrepreneurship. In this setting, we specify the characteristics of family embeddedness, which can foster professional entrepreneurship, or self-employment of women professionals. For the empirical settings, we focus on women in the legal professions, i.e. female lawyers, and trace their career choice of self-employment (such as becoming a solo practitioner or running an independent legal office). With a sample of 1,076female lawyers in the U.S, we examine how family embeddedness affects the women professionals' career choice of self-employment.

Theory and hypotheses

Professional entrepreneurship of women

Professional entrepreneurship, which is defined as "self-employment to join professional partnerships and establish a professional practice" (Dawson et al., 2009: 12), can be understood as the foundation of a business-oriented organization driven by professionals. Based on Leicht and Fennell (2008), professionals are people who conduct professional practices characterized with (a) the application of theoretical and scientific knowledge to tasks tied to core social knowledge or to tasks tied to core societal values (health, justice, financial status, etc.), (b) considerable autonomy and freedom from oversight, except by peer representatives of the professional occupation, and (c) exclusive or nearly exclusive control over a task domain linked to the application of the knowledge imparted to professionals as part of their training. As such, professionals include physicians, lawyers, and university professors as well as accountants, pharmacists, engineers, and scientists.

Given that the most significant driver of entrepreneurship is the hope to achieve autonomy, or desire for independence (Rindova, Barry, and Ketchen, 2009), professional entrepreneurship comes up with the form of freelancing or self-employment. The factors to motivate self-employment of women have been studied in two ways: pull and push. The pull factors are related to individual capabilities to accomplish their professional works, including job achievements (Le, 1999; Parker, 2004), recognition of business opportunities (Reynolds, Camp, Bygrave, Autio, and Hay, 2002; Gatewood, Shaver, and Gartner, 1995), expected earnings (Taylor, 1996; Clark and Drinkwater, 2010), and the aspiration for job autonomy and independence (Hughes, 2003; Dawson and Henley, 2012). On the other hand, the push factors refer to "negative situational factors such as dissatisfaction with existing employment, loss of employment, and career setback" (Gilad and Levine, 1986: 46). As such, the dissatisfaction with existing employment, loss of employment and career setback will foster self-employment participation.

We acknowledge that the push-related motivation of self-employment can distinguish gender differences. One major push factor is the presence of social barriers, such as the glass ceiling (e.g. Masurel, Nijkamp, and Vindigni, 2004; Budig, 2006a, 2006b). The glass ceiling reflects a barrier that prevents minorities (including women) from professionally advancing into high levels of an organization. Since the glass ceiling effect is closely related to an individual's career embedded in traditional organizations, the professional entrepreneurship of women would be influenced by the social barriers. In this sense, professional entrepreneurship, particularly self-employment of women, can be a gender-specific type of entrepreneurship. In fact, the form of self-employment has been studied around women in the prior literature (e.g. Sanders and Nee, 1996; Budig, 2006a, 2006b; Patrick et al., 2016). And it has been understood that female professionals take the form of self-employment as a type entrepreneurship in order to gain autonomy or seek for better earnings (Budig, 2006b).

In addition to the pull and push factors, family can be another critical factor of women's self-employment (Aldrich and Cliff, 2003). Given that gender roles have been constructed across generations, which are consciously or unconsciously accepted in the society, women's roles in the family may influence the career choice in their life courses (e.g. Kanter, 1977; Sharma, 2004; Fitzgerald and Muske, 2002). The gender roles can also be influenced in the context of entrepreneurship. Since women entrepreneurs or sole proprietors can benefit from enhanced autonomy, the conventional gender roles can be prevented from entrepreneurship (e.g. Presser, 1995). Also, as women entrepreneurs spend less time on housework, some of the family members can take the household roles (Aldrich and Cliff, 2003). Hence, family-related factors play a critical role in professional entrepreneurship of women. We will specify the family-related factors in terms of family embeddedness as follows.

Family embeddedness and professional entrepreneurship of women

Since the seminal work of Aldrich and Cliff (2003), family embeddedness has been illuminated as a perspective for entrepreneurship, indicating that families and business are not separate, but inextricably intertwined (Aldrich and Cliff, 2003; Azmat and Fujimoto, 2016; Mari and Poggesi, 2016). In particular, family embeddedness emphasizes that the family dynamics can affect the career decision of women entrepreneurship (Jennings and McDougald, 2007; Carr, 1996; Patrick et al., 2016).

Based on the concept of family embeddedness, we discern family-related origins of professional entrepreneurship. First, one of the most important family-embedded characteristics of women is work-family conflicts (Shelton, 2006; Noor, 2004). Given that, conventionally, women take on the primary responsibility for the household and child-caring tasks (Sharma, 2004; Fitzgerald and Muske, 2002; Aldrich and Cliff, 2003), women should take care of their careers or businesses as well as their families when they take the critical role in running a business. Since their energies, time, and attention are limited, it is impossible to satisfy the needs from both family and work simultaneously. For example, childcare is costly in terms of time spending, which can bring a certain type of discrimination (e.g. Patrick et al., 2016; Noseleit, 2014). To reconcile work-family conflicts, women will be likely to consider entrepreneurship, including self-employment (Aldrich and Cliff, 2003; Azmat and Fujimoto, 2016).

Likewise, female professionals would have to cope with the family-work conflicts (Shelton, 2006; Noor, 2004). According to Budig (2006a), for married professionals the adverse treatment by the organization can occur because the organization can perceive that the married professionals may not spend sufficient time for their jobs than single professionals. That is, female professionals who need to reconcile family obligations will regard self-employment as a reasonable option (Carr, 1996; Patrick et al., 2016). From this standpoint, we form a hypothesis speculating the relationship between perceived work-family conflicts and the likelihood of female professionals' self-employment:

Hypothesis 1: Female professionals who perceive work-family conflicts will be likely to become self-employed.

Second, situational aspects related to family embeddedness can help female professionals decide self-employment (e.g. Budig, 2006b). In the life course of women, the role of a woman in her family varies, which might open an opportunity for entrepreneurship. In particular, women's roles in a family are developmentally structured in the life course. For example, a family is originated by the practice of marriage; then the first child makes the family go to another phase; then as the child (or children) live no longer with their parents, the family composition is made by only two; then the family has transformed into the family led by children. In this life course of a family, we can specify the roles of women into wifehood and motherhood. These punctuated gender roles may influence the motivation of self-employment (e.g. Danes and Olson, 2003; Ekinsmyth, 2013).

In fact, previous studies showed that marriage encourages women rather than men to consider self-employment (e.g. Patrick et al., 2016; Carr, 1996). Wifehood, thus, will lead to self-employment of female professionals. However, motherhood has an ambivalent meaning for female professionals. As Patrick et al. (2016) pointed out, since childcare is "the higher burden placed on women's time as a care giver" (p. 369), motherhood may motivate women to consider self-employment. Yet, some studies claim that childcare may not force women to consider leaving the traditional salary-based employment. In general, self-employment as a type of entrepreneurship is riskier than salary-based employment. Since women tend to be more risk averse, self-employment may not be perceived as an alternative to salary-based employment (e.g. Fossen, 2012). Rather, salary-based employment may be advantageous in taking care of their children for professionals. Taken together we can understand that childcare is a burden placed on women's time, but self-employment can be a higher burden placed on women's income. In this time-income tradeoff, women will choose not to be self-employed. Therefore, we hypothesize regarding the relationship between motherhood and self-employment:

Hypothesis 2: For female professionals, wifehood will increase the likelihood of self-employment.

Hypothesis 3: For female professionals, motherhood will decrease the likelihood of self-employment.

Third, generational pressures of family members may influence women's entrepreneurship. Family members in former generations (i.e. parents or grandparents) who work in the same field can share their "know-hows" through having informal conversations or vicariously teach how they work. For example, if family members were also lawyers, they could share social norms, set of values, and work ethic. This will let the next generation in the family consider the same profession or types of work. In terms of professional work (Leicht and Fennell, 2008), generational transcendence can be more likely to occur than other occupations because these professional works can bring them higher social statuses (e.g. Freidson, 1988). Therefore, if former generations in the family have the same professions, the next generation can benefit from family members. This also implies that as a critical social capital, these familial relationships can be a gatekeeper for career advancement at traditional organizations (e.g. Ibarra, 1993). In other words, the family legacy will motivate female professionals to keep salary-based employment rather than transitioning to self-employment. Since entrepreneurship requires adapting to unfamiliar environments and overcoming lack of experiences (Stinchcombe, 1965), self-employment is riskier than salary-based employment in terms of survival. For professionals, their jobs at the traditional organizations may be secured; thereby, they can sustain their career. To succeed in self-employment, they need to take considerable costs beyond the advantages from family legacy. As such, female professionals would utilize their family legacy by staying at the traditional organizations rather than self-employment. Therefore, in selecting the career choice of self-employment, family legacy will not be helpful for female professionals, which forms the last hypothesis:

Hypothesis 4: Female professionals whose parents or grandparents have same professions will be demotivated to be self-employed.

Methods

Data and population

To test how family embeddedness affects self-employment of female professionals, we consider the career choice of self-employment from female lawyers in the U.S. After earning a JD degree, lawyers usually enter law firms or legal department of an organization. Or they can directly open their own legal office, i.e. self-employment. Given that the career choice of self-employment will be followed by the operational processes of entrepreneurship (such as obtaining human and financial capital, opening a legal office, and so on), the career choice of self-employment can indicate how lawyers can get through the entrepreneurship processes. To capture such a career choice, we collect the relevant data from *After the JD*. *After the JD*, a longitudinal study of lawyers in the U.S. administered and published by the American Bar Foundation,[1] includes the data of the professional life of 5,353 lawyers. Specifically, the *After the JD* data has six subcomponents: (1) current professional employment; (2) professional employment history; (3) current employment and career transition; (4) training, education, and debt; (5) social, political, and community participation; and (6) other background information. Further, the database provides each individual lawyer's employment status, including when they started working for their current employer, the organizational type, and their position within the organization as well as demographical attributes.

The first survey (Wave I) was launched in May 2002 and the second survey (Wave II) was conducted from 2007–2008 as a follow up of Wave I (Plickert and Park, 2010). According to *After the JD*, the sample selection was two-fold. First, selection of geographic areas was made based on lawyer population distributions. Then lawyers in these areas who met the individual eligibility criteria were sampled (Plickert and Park, 2010). Through the two waves of surveys between 2003 and 2006, a series of individual information and career history was traced and collected from 5,353 lawyers in the U.S. To focus on the self-employment of female lawyers, we consider female lawyers as a sample of our study. After removing cases with missing or inconsistent responses on their family, we have a total sample of 1,076 female lawyers. There might be a potential for selection bias if those who responded to the questionnaires were systematically different from those in the original sample who chose not to participate in the survey. However, demographic characteristics of *After the JD* respondents were shown to closely match those of young lawyers in the 2000 Census, both in terms of composition of race and sex. Table 6.1 presents the sample distribution by region.

Estimation model

To test our hypotheses in the empirical setting, we employ a logistic regression model as we deal with the career choice of whether a female lawyer becomes self-employed. Specifically, by using a logit model, we estimate the probability of a female lawyer's self-employment with respect to the family-related variables, i.e. perceived work-life balance, wifehood and motherhood, and generational pressure. In constructing the estimation models, we control the possible reverse causality by separating the data for independent variables from those for the dependent variable. That is, for the dependent variable, i.e. the probability of self-employment, we use the second wave of the survey, conducted in 2006. Meanwhile, for the independent variables and control variables, we use the Wave I survey data, collected in 2003. This will avoid the cases where the dependent variable can influence the independent variables. In addition, to control for the potential selection bias that is introduced by identifying female lawyers in the given geographic areas, we consider clustered standard errors at the state level in all analyses.

Measures

Dependent variable

As we are seeking to understand how female lawyers pursue self-employment as a career choice, the dependent variable is a probability of female lawyer's self-employment. From the *After the JD* database, we obtain data about the female lawyer's job transition year and type of organization and identify whether the given female lawyer made a choice on self-employment. In this sense, *self-employment* is operationally defined as the state where the given female lawyer has engaged in a solo practice or runs her own legal office. From Wave II of *After the JD*, we code whether the female lawyer opens her own legal office or whether she identifies herself as being self-employed on the survey. Over the

Table 6.1 Sample distribution

State	*Frequency*	*Percentage (%) (Sample)*	*Percentage (%)(Whole)*	*State*	*Frequency*	*Percentage (%) (Sample)*	*Percentage (%) (Whole)*
Alabama	2	.19	.1	Mississippi	2	.19	.1
Alaska	1	.09	.1	Missouri	44	4.09	3.7
Arizona	4	.37	.4	Montana	1	.09	.1
California	169	15.71	15.3	Nevada	4	.37	.3
Colorado	4	.37	.4	New Jersey	32	2.97	2.7
Connecticut	31	2.88	2.9	New Mexico	1	.09	.1
District of Columbia	59	5.48	6.2	New York	99	9.20	8.6
Florida	51	4.74	5.3	North Carolina	4	.37	.6
Georgia	60	5.58	5.1	Ohio	5	.46	.3
Hawaii	5	.46	.2	Oklahoma	42	3.90	3.4
Illinois	96	8.92	8.6	Oregon	61	5.67	4.6
Indiana	42	3.90	4.2	Pennsylvania	6	.56	.3
Iowa	3	.28	.2	Rhode Island	1	.09	.1
Kansas	1	.09	.1	South Carolina	1	.09	.2
Kentucky	3	.28	.4	Tennessee	26	2.42	3.7
Louisiana	1	.09	.1	Texas	46	4.28	4.5
Maine	1	.09	.1	Utah	20	1.86	3.1
Maryland	17	1.58	1.2	Virginia	27	2.51	2.1
Massachusetts	24	2.23	2.7	Washington	6	.56	.5
Michigan	3	.28	.3	Wisconsin	6	.56	.3
Minnesota	55	5.11	4.8	Foreign Nations	10	.93	1.2

Note: # of female lawyers: 1,076

observation period, it is found that 7.43 percent of the female lawyers became solo practitioners or self-employed.

Independent variables

PERCEIVED WORK-LIFE BALANCE

As a family-related variable, we consider the extent to which a female lawyer recognizes the work-life conflicts. Operationally, perceived work-life balance is measured with the assessment of the given female lawyer on the survey item with a 7 point Likert scale, that included this question "In taking your current job, how important was each of the following factors in making your choice? l. Potential to balance work and personal life." According to the scale, the greater value of this variable indicates that the female lawyers are more conscious of work-life balance for choosing their career. This variable ranges from 1 to 7.

WIFEHOOD AND MOTHERHOOD

We define ***wifehood*** as the state where the given female lawyer gets married before having a child. To measure wifehood, first we consider whether the given female lawyer is a couple or not. The survey item asked the lawyers to choose their marital status among (1) Never married or never in a domestic partnership, (2) Married first time, (3) Remarried after divorce annulment or being widowed, (4) Domestic partnership, (5) Divorced or separated, (6) Widowed, and (7) Other. Based on this survey scheme, we code 1 if the given lawyer answered her marital status as "married first time", "remarried after divorce annulment or being widowed", or "domestic partnership". That is, wifehood is measured as whether a female lawyer lives with her spouse or domestic partner. Then we exclude the cases where the female lawyers have at least one child. This signifies that female lawyers in wifehood are those who have a spouse or domestic partner but no child (Spence and Lonner, 1979).

Meanwhile, ***motherhood*** is defined as the state where the given female lawyer takes responsibility to take care of more than one child (Spence and Lonner, 1979). To measure this, we trace whether a female lawyer takes care of her children. Then we code 1 if the given female lawyer has at least one child regardless of marriage. For both wifehood and motherhood, we exclude the cases where the female lawyer got married before earning the JD. In our dataset, 52.5 percent of the female lawyers are situated in wifehood and 35.1 percent in motherhood.

FAMILY LEGACY

Family legacy identifies whether family members, especially parents or grandparents, are lawyers. We count the number of family members in former generations (i.e. parents and grandparents) who are lawyers. If both parents and grandparents are lawyers, it can be understood the given female lawyer would have strong family legacy. In our dataset, this variable ranges from 0 to 2.

Control variables

In estimating the probability of a female lawyer's career choice of self-employment, we control for (a) race, (b) prior salary, (c) number of turnovers, (d) employment by law firms, (e) experienced discrimination, (f) legal practice experience, and (g) large firm experience. Race is used as the respondents answered. Following the categories determined by *After the JD*, race consists of 6 racial groups: African, Hispanic, Native, Asian, White, and Others. In the original database, each racial group is measured as a dummy variable. To include the race variable (or a set of dummy variables) in the regression model, we set the base racial group as White. Accordingly, the coefficient of each racial group indicates the mean difference between the racial group and White. *Prior salary* is defined as the maximum dollar amount of pay for work that the given lawyer earned from prior organizations. To measure the variable, we first collect the all the salary information of each female lawyer and find the maximum level of salaries she has made in her employment history. For *the number of turnovers*, we count the number of companies the given female lawyer has left before having the current employer. Then we take the logarithm of the count number as the distributions of the variable is skewed. *Employment by law firms* considers the probability that the given female lawyer has worked at the traditional law firms. To measure this variable, first we create a dichotomous variable indicating whether the given female lawyer previously worked at a law firm. Then, we use a probit model to estimate this dichotomous variable with respect to race, location (state), age, the ranking of law school from which the given female lawyer graduated, and the number of other accredited or certificate degrees (such as Master of Laws (LLM), other Master's degree, doctoral degree, MBA, and others). The estimated value is converted to the ratio of the probability density function (i.e. pdf) to the cumulative distribution function (i.e. cdf).

Experienced discrimination is measured with the contingencies where the given female lawyer left her former job because of discrimination. We trace all the career history of each female lawyer and code 1 if the given female lawyer answered that she left her former job due to discrimination. Then we sum up all the binary codes throughout the career history of the given female lawyer. *Legal practice experience* indicates with time duration in which the given lawyer works as a legal professional. The variable is measured as the time difference between the year of bar admission and the year of 2006, the year for the second wave of *After the JD*. Lastly, *large firm experience* refers to working experience at large firms (or firms with more than 100 employees). Based on this, we measure the variable as whether the given lawyer has worked in at least one firm that has more than 100 lawyers employed.

Table 6.2 presents the descriptive statistics and correlations for the analyses predicting female lawyers' career choice of self-employment.

Table 6.2 Descriptive statistics and correlations

N = 1076	*Mean*	*SD*	*Min*	*Max*	*1*	*2*	*3*	*4*	*5*	*6*	*7*	*8*	*9*	*10*	*11*	*12*	*13*	*14*	*15*
1 Self-employment	0.07	0.26	0	1															
2 Perceived work-life balance	5.98	1.48	1	7	012***														
3 Wifehood	0.53	0.50	0	1	.06*	.08*													
4 Motherhood	0.35	0.48	0	1	–.04	.09**	.37***												
5 Family legacy	0.16	0.41	0	2	–.06†	–.01	.01	.08**											
6 Race (African)	0.11	0.31	0	1	–.03	–.03	–.17***	–.09**	–.10**										
7 Race (Hispanic)	0.08	0.28	0	1	.02	.02	–.06†	–.04	–.07*	–.10***									
8 Race (Native)	0.01	0.11	0	1	.07*	.03	.05	.03	–.02	–.04	–.03								
9 Race (Asian)	0.10	0.30	0	1	–.06*	–.05†	–.04	–.03	–.08**	–.12***	–.10***	–.04							
10 Race (Others)	0.02	0.14	0	1	.01	.00	–.01	–.02	–.04	–.05	–.04	–.02	–.05						
11 Prior salary (in thousands)	96.14	53.67	6	750	–.11***	–.04	–.02	–.05	.04	–.02	.00	–.05	.11***	–.01					
12 ln # turnovers	1.21	1.10	0	5	.07*	.10***	–.01	–.12***	–.02	.00	.06*	.01	.01	.03	.15***				
13 Employment by law firms	0.76	0.24	0.00	5.25	.09**	–.01	.02	–.03	.01	.09**	.10**	.04	–.15***	.00	–.18***	–.09**			
14 Experienced discrimination	0.04	0.21	0	2	.05	.07*	.03	–.01	.02	.04	.01	–.02	.01	.04	.08**	.17***	–.02		
15 Legal practice experience	7.38	0.57	5	9	.04	–.06†	–.05†	–.04	.00	.10**	.03	–.01	.01	.03	.06*	.04	.00	.02	
16 Large firm experience	0.24	0.43	0	1	–.07*	.01	–.02	–.01	.06†	–.02	–.01	–.04	.06†	.00	.51***	.22***	–.18***	.01	.00

†p<.1 *p<.05 **p<.01 ***p<.001; two-tailed tests

Results

The effects of family embeddedness on self-employment of female lawyers

Table 6.3 shows the results of the logit models estimating the probability of selecting self-employment with respect to variables drawn from the perspective of family embeddedness (i.e. perceived work-life balance, wifehood and motherhood, and family legacy) and control variables (i.e. race, prior salary, turnovers, employment by law firms, experienced discrimination, legal practice experience, and large firm experience).

Model 1 of Table 6.3 includes only control variables. In Models 2 through 5, the effects of family-based variables on the career choice of self-employment are respectively tested. And Model 6 includes all the independent variables and control variables as a full model. From the estimation results in Model 6, we find that perceived work-life balance and wifehood can motivate the career choice of self-employment (β = .490; $p < .01$, β = .530; $p < .05$ respectively) while motherhood and family legacy hamper female lawyers' decision on self-employment (β = –.586; $p < .01$, β = –.753; $p < .05$ respectively).

In terms that family embeddedness is instantiated by the perception on work-life balance, the positive effect of perceived work-life balance on self-employment indicates that for female lawyers, family embeddedness in a cognitive sense, or awareness of work-family conflicts, can help themselves pursue self-employment. Meanwhile, the impact of family embeddedness on self-employment can be bifurcated depending on the life courses in which female lawyers are situated: wifehood and motherhood. We find that while wifehood enhances self-employment of female lawyers as a career choice, motherhood prevents them from being self-employed. In the prior literature, childcare has been understood as a critical factor for women's self-employment in the context of family businesses or small businesses (e.g. Patrick et al., 2016; Carr, 1996), but for female lawyers, childcare can be treated as a demotivating factor for self-employment. This suggests that salary-based employment, rather than self-employment, is a better option for female lawyers to cope with the family-work conflicts. Related to this, family legacy also shows a negative effect on self-employment for female lawyers. While family resources from former generations can be useful for career advancement, these resources, for female lawyers, would likely be utilized at the traditional organizations rather than at independent legal offices.

Gender difference of self-employment with respect to family embeddedness

To check how different these findings are shown in male lawyers, we sample a population of male lawyers from the *After the JD* database. We collect 1,168 male lawyers, showing overall 9.2 percent of the male population engaged in self-employment. With the sample, we perform the same logistic regression analyses.

In Table 6.4, we find only a significant, negative effect of motherhood (i.e. fatherhood) on self-employment (β = –.709; $p < .001$), which is consistent to

Table 6.3 Logistic estimations of female lawyers' self-employment

	Model 1	*Model 2*	*Model 3*	*Model 4*	*Model 5*	*Model 6*
Constant	–4.299**	–7.725***	–4.596**	–4.101**	–4.326**	–7.928***
	(1.425)	(1.907)	(1.453)	(1.429)	(1.421)	(1.974)
CONTROLS						
Race (African)	–.579	–.538	–.442	–.631†	–.681†	–.550
	(.368)	(.392)	(.402)	(.362)	(.373)	(.433)
Race (Hispanic)	.060	.028	.132	.030	–.042	–.026
	(.386)	(.435)	(.379)	(.377)	(.402)	(.428)
Race (Native)	1.110	1.030	1.059	1.176†	1.054	1.019
	(.695)	(.681)	(.691)	(.677)	(.681)	(.622)
Race (Asian)	–.953	–.896	–.920	–.972	–1.037	–.959
	(.650)	(.637)	(.660)	(.660)	(.660)	(.682)
Race (Others)	.017	–.021	.090	–.001	–.080	–.037
	(.964)	(.963)	(.961)	(.958)	(.956)	(.938)
Prior Salary (in thousands)	–.015*	–.015*	–.015**	–.016**	–.015*	–.014*
	(.006)	(.006)	(.006)	(.006)	(.006)	(.006)
ln#Turnovers	.277**	.247*	.278**	.263*	.271*	.214*
	(.106)	(.111)	(.107)	(.104)	(.105)	(.106)
Employment by Law Firms	.558†	.629*	.562†	.552†	.687*	.722*
	(.304)	(.309)	(.317)	(.286)	(.287)	(.281)
Experienced Discrimination	.579*	.484†	.540†	.590*	.607*	.499†
	(.282)	(.265)	(.293)	(.289)	(.293)	(.291)

	Model 1	*Model 2*	*Model 3*	*Model 4*	*Model 5*	*Model 6*
Legal Practice Experience	.301	.333†	.303	.295	.303	.345†
	(.190)	(.199)	(.193)	(.191)	(.189)	(.206)
Large Firm Experience	.130	.088	.117	.142	.148	.091
	(.528)	(.577)	(.530)	(.521)	(.520)	(.572)
HYPOTHESIZED EFFECTS						
Perceived Work-Life Balance		.492**				.490**
		(.147)				(.144)
Wifehood			.407†			.530*
			(.233)			(.269)
Motherhood				–.342*		–.586**
				(.156)		(.189)
Family Legacy					–.878*	–.753*
					(.399)	(.380)
Log-likelihood	–263.43	–254.73	–262.10	–262.58	–260.87	–249.35
AIC	550.86	535.46	550.21	551.16	547.73	530.70
Deviance (χ2)	–	17.4***	2.66	1.7	5.12*	28.16***

# of Female Lawyers: 1,076,State-based clustered standard errors in parentheses
†p<.1 *p<.05 **p<.01 ***p<.001; two-tailed tests

Table 6.4 Logistic estimations of male lawyers' self-employment

	Model 1	*Model 2*	*Model 3*	*Model 4*	*Model 5*	*Model 6*
Constant	–3.615***	–4.259***	–3.494**	–3.218**	–3.600**	–3.973***
	(1.032)	(1.181)	(1.006)	(1.020)	(1.048)	(1.135)
CONTROLS						
Race (African)	.395	.392	.367	.375	.394	.372
	(.534)	(.538)	(.525)	(.542)	(.535)	(.533)
Race (Hispanic)	.195	.172	.167	.166	.191	.135
	(.409)	(.416)	(.417)	(.390)	(.421)	(.432)
Race (Native)	.825	.991	.850	.897	.823	1.076
	(.863)	(.824)	(.878)	(.908)	(.867)	(.876)
Race (Asian)	–.899	–.851	–.931	–1.013†	–.902	–.971†
	(.569)	(.565)	(.587)	(.569)	(.578)	(.587)
Race (Others)	.759	.732	.729	.674	.757	.640
	(.634)	(.656)	(.639)	(.628)	(.625)	(.647)
Prior Salary (in thousands)	–.008*	–.008*	–.008*	–.008*	–.008*	–.008*
	(.004)	(.004)	(.004)	(.004)	(.004)	(.004)
ln # Turnovers	.078	.082	.080	.063	.078	.066
	(.078)	(.079)	(.077)	(.077)	(.078)	(.076)
Employment by Law Firms	–.130	–.111	–.125	–.193	–.132	–.182
	(.223)	(.223)	(.220)	(.223)	(.225)	(.226)
Experienced Discrimination	.751	.709	.731	.652	.748	.602
	(.609)	(.588)	(.606)	(.602)	(.610)	(.580)

	Model 1	*Model 2*	*Model 3*	*Model 4*	*Model 5*	*Model 6*
Legal Practice Experience	.287*	.290*	.284*	.271*	.286*	.278*
	(.127)	(.129)	(.128)	(.130)	(.128)	(.136)
Large Firm Experience	–.601	–.619	–.597	–.578	–.602	–.593
	(.368)	(.377)	(.366)	(.367)	(.368)	(.374)
HYPOTHESIZED EFFECTS						
Perceived Work-Life Balance		.110				.128
		(.079)				(.081)
Husbandhood			–.172			.029
			(.247)			(.242)
Fatherhood				–.655**		–.709***
				(.220)		(.194)
Family Legacy					–.037	–.035
					(.236)	(.238)
Log-likelihood	–339.90	–338.38	–339.57	–335.69	–339.89	–333.60
AIC	703.79	702.75	705.14	697.37	705.77	699.20
Deviance ($\chi 2$)	–	3.04†	.66	8.42**	.02	12.6*

# of Female Lawyers: 1,168,State-based clustered standard errors in parentheses
†p<.1 *p<.05 **p<.01 ***p<.001; two-tailed tests

the result from the female-lawyer sample. This finding reveals that having a child is still a burden for males. In other words, for the professionals, childcare is not a gender-specific factor for self-employment. Other than that, we find that there are no significant effects of other family-related variables for male lawyers. These findings reveal that family embeddedness is more significantly related to female's career choice of self-employment.

In addition, to make the gender comparison regarding the impact of family embeddedness on self-employment more comprehensive, we compile the datasets of the female sample and the male sample and run the logit models and figure out whether gender moderation is significantly found in the compiled data. Table 6.5 presents the logit models with the gender moderation terms.

Model 2 presents that self-employment itself is more likely to be pursued by male lawyers than by females as the main effect of gender is shown negative ($\beta = -.474$; $p < .001$). Based on this, we find that perceived work-life balance and motherhood only have significant interaction effects ($\beta = .218$; $p < .01$ and $\beta = -.657$; $p < .001$). That is, perceived work-life balance and motherhood are critical for both male and female lawyers to make a career choice of leaving traditional organizations or conventional salary-based employment. Specifically, if lawyers were conscious to work-life balance in their career development, self-employment would be a salient option for them. Yet, ironically, the situations where lawyers have responsibilities for childcare would not motivate them to pursue self-employment. Those divergent effects of family embeddedness appear commonly for both female and male lawyers.

When we take a close look at the coefficients of the interaction effects in Models 3 through 6, we can figure out gender difference further. First, for perceived work-life balance, female lawyers are more sensitive than male lawyers in engaging in self-employment ($\beta = .390$; $p < .01$ in Model 3). That is, female lawyers who perceive work-life balance for their career development are more likely than male lawyers to becoming self-employed. Second, as Model 5 shows, wifehood is more critical for self-employment than "husband-hood" ($\beta = .686$; $p < .10$ in Model 4). Given that self-employment can be motivated when one needs more flexible time for their family (e.g. Patrick et al., 2016; Carr, 1996), this result suggests that females tend to concentrate on their roles in their family so that they are more likely than males to change their career paths toward self-employment. As such, for female lawyers, self-employment can be regarded as a breakthrough to reconcile the family-work conflicts. However, the results show that for motherhood, there was a smaller effect on the results ($\beta = .343$; $p = .120$ in Model 5). This finding can be understood as indicating that both female and male lawyers consider self-employment as a way to enable more flexibility for childcare responsibilities. Last, in utilizing family resources for self-employment (i.e. for family legacy), male lawyers are more salient than females ($\beta = -.652$; $p < .10$ in Model 6). Although resources from family members can be a good source for both male and female lawyers, the actual utilization of these resources unfolds asymmetrically between male and female lawyers (e.g. Ibarra, 1993). As family legacy for self-employment is likely to be

Table 6.5 Gender moderation of lawyers' self-employment with respect to family embeddedness

	Model 1	*Model 2*	*Model 3*	*Model 4*	*Model 5*	*Model 6*
Constant	–3.990***	–4.839***	–4.364***	–4.686***	–4.798***	–4.918***
	(.917)	(1.008)	(1.003)	(1.016)	(1.001)	(1.019)
CONTROLS						
Race (African)	–.148	–.112	–.087	–.061	–.099	–.134
	(.312)	(.327)	(.324)	(.349)	(.328)	(.326)
Race (Hispanic)	.118	.084	.084	.083	.090	.071
	(.330)	(.350)	(.361)	(.343)	(.351)	(.352)
Race (Native)	.968	1.148†	1.057	1.154†	1.139†	1.141†
	(.664)	(.649)	(.653)	(.654)	(.653)	(.646)
Race (Asian)	–.963†	–.949	–.952†	–.963	–.956†	–.959†
	(.541)	(.578)	(.575)	(.588)	(.575)	(.576)
Race (Others)	.493	.394	.397	.383	.387	.384
	(.600)	(.576)	(.570)	(.572)	(.578)	(.578)
Prior Salary (in thousands)	–.010*	–.010*	–.010*	–.010*	–.010*	–.010*
	(.004)	(.004)	(.004)	(.004)	(.004)	(.004)
ln#Turnovers	.158**	.135*	.128*	.137*	.137*	.134*
	(.060)	(.062)	(.061)	(.063)	(.063)	(.063)
Employment by Law Firms	.159	.109	.097	.108	.105	.123
	(.182)	(.192)	(.194)	(.194)	(.192)	(.198)
Experienced Discrimination	.555*	.562*	.520*	.534*	.556*	.578*
	(.235)	(.232)	(.233)	(.228)	(.226)	(.237)
Legal Practice Experience	.295*	.294*	.299*	.294*	.293*	.299*
	(.118)	(.126)	(.127)	(.129)	(.126)	(.127)
Large Firm Experience	–.339	–.303	–.311	–.308	–.303	–.386
	(.320)	(.330)	(.332)	(.330)	(.330)	(.329)

(*Continued*)

Table 6.5 (Continued)

	Model 1	*Model 2*	*Model 3*	*Model 4*	*Model 5*	*Model 6*
HYPOTHESIZED EFFECTS						
Perceived Work-Life Balance		.218**	.127	.220**	.218**	.217**
		(.081)	(.078)	(.082)	(.081)	(.080)
Wifehood (Husbandhood)		.249	.251	–.048	.247	.246
		(.163)	(.164)	(.247)	(.163)	(.161)
Motherhood (Fatherhood)		–.657***	–.664***	–.655***	–.803***	–.652***
		(.157)	(.156)	(.159)	(.221)	(.155)
Family Legacy		–.243	–.232	–.246	–.247	–.013
		(.200)	(.201)	(.203)	(.199)	(.236)
Gender (Female = 1)		–.474***	–2.912***	–.883***	–.572***	–.399**
		(.113)	(.823)	(.239)	(.141)	(.127)
INTERACTION EFFECTS						
Female*Perceived Work-Life Balance			.390**			
			(.127)			
Female*Wifehood				.686†		
				(.382)		
Female*Motherhood					.343	
					(.220)	
Female*Family Legacy						–.652†
						(.387)
Log-likelihood	–610.41	–593.75	–590.08	–591.51	–593.27	–592.79
AIC	1244.83	1221.49	1216.17	1219.01	1222.54	1221.58
Deviance ($\chi 2$)	–	33.32***	7.34**	4.48*	.96	1.92

# of Lawyers: 2,244, State-based clustered standard errors in parentheses
†p<.1 *p<.05 **p<.01 ***p<.001; two-tailed tests

left to male lawyers more than females, the gendered structure can be reinforced. This will make male lawyers much more willing to take the advantages whereas female lawyers will not. As a result, appropriating family resources will not lead to self-employment of female lawyers.

Discussion and conclusion

In this chapter, by adopting a family-embeddedness perspective, we illuminate a process of women entrepreneurship, i.e. self-employment of women professionals. And we provide a further understanding of how professional women consider entrepreneurship. Specifically, based on the perspective of family embeddedness, we discern three aspects of family-related origins of professional entrepreneurship: perceived work-life balance, wifehood and motherhood, and family legacy. With the family-related aspects, this chapter illustrates how professional entrepreneurship can take place in the context of the legal profession. With a sample of 1,076 female lawyers in the U.S., we examine the effects of the family-related variables on the career choice of self-employment. As a result, we find that female lawyers who crucially perceive work-life balance for their career paths or who are situated in wifehood are likely to consider self-employment as a career choice. On the other hand, if a given female lawyer has responsibilities for childcare or her parents or grandparents are also lawyers, she is reluctant to become self-employed. We find that these results are distinguished from those of male lawyers.

Our findings show three implications. First, professional entrepreneurship can be gendered when we consider family embeddedness. Conscious to their family, female lawyers tend to consider being self-employed. The family-conscious family lawyer may not always accept self-employment because it involves the creation of an independent, new business (or organization)."For legal professions as a relatively secured career, we find salary-based employment may be more beneficial than self-employment professionals in coping with the family-work conflicts. This suggests that female lawyers who can take any risks entailed by leaving the traditional organizations or practices, rather than by those who are deeply situated in family embeddedness may make the career choice of self-employment.

Second, the impact of family embeddedness on self-employment provides a supplementary understanding of our knowledge on under what conditions women professionals can leave the traditional organizations to become an entrepreneur. In other words, we need to figure out what actions individuals take in managing family-work conflicts impact their later choices to remain in the framework of traditional organizational advancement versus entrepreneurship outside of the organization. At the traditional organizations, where males dominate the management hierarchy, females who do not take their leadership behavior based on traditional, white male styles of management will not be as successful in the workplace (Frankforter, 1996; Bartol, Martin, and Kromkowski, 2003). In this sense, prior literature mainly deals with the phenomena of women's self-selection as an alternative to overcome social barriers engendering themselves (e.g. Gilad and Levine, 1986; Rindova et al., 2009; Mari and Poggesi, 2016).

That is, women tend to be pushed toward (or self-select) outside traditional organizations to reconcile the discrepancies between the expected and actual treatment from the traditional organizations. In contrast, our findings reveal that women, even though they are assumed as structurally disadvantaged, can take initiatives for self-selecting staying at traditional organization, especially when family embeddedness is strongly involved in developing their career paths (such as motherhood for female professionals). This will be a different view on self-selection of women in their career development processes.

Last, the hypothesis on family legacy can give a hint for how family-based professions can be achieved. In general, by taking family resources from former generations regarding a certain occupation, family members can pursue common goals, which could help form a new organizational form. This suggests that by identifying various family-oriented occupations, we can specify various kinds of family-based organizations. However, many prior studies on family business have paid attention to retail businesses (e.g. Aldrich andCliff, 2003; Greene, Brush, and Gatewood, 2006; Danes and Olson, 2003; Sharma, 2004). Taking a different view, we can expand our understanding of family businesses by diversifying family-oriented occupations. In particular, we contend that family businesses also can be constructed through professional works, even though its motivation and process may be different from what we know on family businesses. For example, law firms partnered with family members can be understood as a type of family-based organization. Our finding that female lawyers who have family legacy are less likely to become self-employed may be understood as indicating that there is a possibility that female lawyers with family legacy are likely to belong to the family business owned by former generations. Thus, future research will specify how female professionals can participate in constructing a family business. This will be another career choice female lawyers can make to overcome the structural barriers in career development in male-oriented organizations.

Overall, this chapter proposes that the perspective of family embeddedness can be a theoretical foundation for the structuration of women entrepreneurship. Through the perspective of family embeddedness, which brings ideas on how women are rooted in familial relationships and how they can utilize the resources available within their family capital, we can figure out the possibilities that women have distinctive characteristics, which are clearly distinguished from men's in creating new career paths (e.g. self-employment). Furthermore, by investigating the family-related characteristics, we can further understand how women can take initiative for starting a business or creating a new organization.

Acknowledgement

The Ewha Womans University Research Grant of 2016 supported this work.

Note

1 www.americanbarfoundation.org/publications/afterthejd.html

References

Aldrich, H. E., and Cliff, J. E. (2003). The pervasive effects of family on entrepreneurship: Toward a family embeddedness perspective. *Journal of Business Venturing*, 18, 573–596.

Azmat, F., and Fujimoto, Y. (2016). Family embeddedness and entrepreneurship experience: A study of Indian migrant women entrepreneurs in Australia. *Entrepreneurship & Regional Development*, 28(9–10), 630–656.

Bartol, K. M., Martin, D. C., and Kromkowski, J. A. (2003). Leadership and the glass ceiling: Gender and ethnic group influences on leader behaviors at middle and executive managerial levels. *Journal of Leadership & Organizational Studies*, 9(3), 8–19.

Budig, M. (2006a). Intersections on the road to self-employment: Gender, family, and occupational class. *Social Forces*, 84(4), 2223–2239.

Budig, M. (2006b). Gender, self-employment, and earnings: The interlocking structures of family and professional status. *Gender and Society*, 20(6), 725–753.

Carr, D. (1996). Two paths to self-employment? Women's and men's self-employment in the United States, 1980. *Work and Occupations*, 23, 26–53.

Clark, K., and Drinkwater, S. (2010). Recent trends in minority ethnic entrepreneurship in Britain. *International Small Business Journal*, 28(2), 136–146.

Danes, S. M., and Olson, P. D. (2003). Women's role involvement in family businesses, business tensions, and business success. *Family Business Review*, XVI, 53–68.

Dawson, C., and Henley, A. (2012). 'Push' versus 'pull' entrepreneurship: An ambiguous distinction? *International Journal of Entrepreneurial Behaviour & Research*, 18(6), 697–719.

Dawson, C., Henley, A., and Latreille, P. (2009). *Why Do Individuals Choose Self-Employment?* IZA DP No. 3974.

Douglas, E., and Shepherd, D. (2002). Self-employment as a career choice: Attitudes, entrepreneurial intentions, and utility maximization. *Entrepreneurial Theory and Practice*, 26(3), 81–90.

Ekinsmyth, C. (2013). Managing the business of everyday life: The roles of space and place in 'mumpreneurship'. *International Journal of Entrepreneurial Behaviour & Research*, 19(5), 525–546.

Fitzgerald, M. A., and Muske, G. (2002). Copreneurs: An exploration and comparison to other family businesses. *Family Business Review*, XV, 1–15.

Fossen, F. (2012). Gender differences in entrepreneurial choice and risk aversion: A decomposition based on a microeconometric model. *Applied Economics*, 44(14), 1795–1812.

Frankforter, S. A. (1996). The progression of women beyond the glass ceiling. *Journal of Social Behavior and Personality*, 11, 121–132.

Freidson, E. (1988). *Professional Powers: A Study of the Institutionalization of Formal Knowledge*. Chicago: University of Chicago Press.

Gatewood, E. J., Shaver, K. G., and Gartner, W. B. (1995). A longitudinal study of cognitive factors influencing start-up behaviors and success at venture creation. *Journal of Business Venturing*, 10, 372–390.

Gilad, B., and Levine, P. (1986). A behavioral model of entrepreneurial supply. *Journal of Small Business Management*, 4, 45–53.

Granovetter, M. (1985). Economic action and social structure: The problem of embeddedness. *American Journal of Sociology*, 91(3), 481–510.

Greene, P. G., Brush, C. G., and Gatewood, E. J. (2006). Perspectives on women entrepreneurs: Past findings and new directions. In M. Minitti (Ed.), *Entrepreneurship: The Engine of Growth, Vol. 1. People* (pp. 181–204). New York: Praeger Publishing.

Hughes, K. (2003). Pushed or pulled? Women's entry into self-employment and small business ownership. *Gender, Work and Organization*, 10(4), 433–454.

Ibarra, H. (1993). Personal networks of women and minorities in management: A conceptual framework. *Academy of Management Review*, 18(1), 56–87.

Jennings, J. E., and McDougald, M. S. (2007). Work-family interface experiences and coping strategies: Implications for entrepreneurship research and practice. *Academy of Management Review*, 32, 747–760.

Kanter, R.M. (1977). *Men and Women of the Corporation*. New York: Basic Books.

Le, A.T. (1999). Empirical studies of self-employment. *Journal of Economic Surveys*, 13(4), 381–416.

Leicht, K. T., and Fennell, M. L. (2008). Institutionalism and the professions. In R. Greenwood, C. Oliver, K. Sahlin and R. Suddaby (Eds.), *The Sage Handbook of Organizational Institutionalism* (pp. 431–448). Los Angeles: Sage Publications.

Mari, M., and Poggesi, S. (2016). Family embeddedness and business performance: Evidences from women-owned firms. *Management Decision*, 54(2), 476–500.

Masurel, E., Nijkamp, P., and Vindigni, G. (2004). Breeding places for ethnic entrepreneurs: A comparative marketing approach. *Entrepreneurship and Regional Development*, 16(1), 77–86.

Morrison, A. M., and von Glinow, M. A. (1990). Women and minorities in management. *American Psychologist*, 45, 200–208.

Noor, N. (2004). Work-family conflict, work- and family-role salience and women's well-being. *Journal of Social Psychology*, 144, 389–405.

Noseleit, F. (2014). Female self-employment and children. *Small Business Economics*, 43(3), 549–569.

Parker, S. (2004). *The Economics of Self-Employment and Entrepreneurship*. Cambridge: Cambridge University Press.

Patrick, C., Stephens, H., and Weinstein, A. (2016). Where are all the self-employed women? Push and pull factors influencing female labor market decisions. *Small Business Economics*, 46(3), 365–390.

Plickert, G., and Park, J. (2010). *After the JD: A Longitudinal Study of Legal Careers in Transition*. American Bar Foundation (ABF).

Presser, H. (1995). Job, family, and gender: Determinants of nonstandard work schedules among employed Americans in 1991. *Demography*, 32, 577–598.

Ramadani, V., Gërguri, S., Dana, L. P., and Tašaminova, T. (2013). Women entrepreneurs in the Republic of Macedonia: Waiting for directions. *International Journal of Entrepreneurship and Small Business*, 19(1), 95–121.

Reynolds, P.D., Camp, S.M., Bygrave, W.D., Autio, E., and Hay, M. (2002).*Global Entrepreneurship Monitor 2001 Executive Report*. Babson Park, MA; London: Babson College; London Business School.

Riger, S., and Galligan, P. (1980). Women in management: An exploration of competing paradigms. *American Psychologist*, 35, 902–910.

Rindova, V., Barry, D., and Ketchen, J. D. (2009). Entrepreneuring as emancipation. *Academy of Management Review*, 34(3), 477–491.

Sanders, J. M., and Nee, V. (1996). Immigrant self-employment: The family social capital and the value of human capital. *American Sociological Review*, 61(2), 231–249.

Sharma, P. (2004). An overview of the field of family business studies: Current status and directions for the future. *Family Business Review*, 17, 1–36.

Shelton, L. M. (2006). Female entrepreneurs, work-family conflict, and venture performance: New insights into the work-family interface. *Journal of Small Business Management*, 44, 285–297.

Spence, D.L., and Lonner, T.D. (1979). Career set: A resource through transitions and crises. *The International Journal of Aging and Human Development*, 9(1), 51–65.

Stinchcombe, A. L. (1965). Organizations and social structure. In J. G. March (Ed.), *Handbook of Organizations* (pp. 153–193). Chicago: Rand McNally.

Taylor, M. (1996). Earnings, independence or unemployment: Why become self-employed? *Oxford Bulletin of Economics and Statistics*, 58(2), 253–266.

7 Could women ex-offenders reinvent their future? An entrepreneurial approach

Isabel Novo-Corti, María Ramil-Díaz, Nuria Calvo and María Barreiro-Gen

Introduction

Entrepreneurship can be an option to illegal means of income, such as selling drugs or prostitution, which ex-offenders often use when they leave prison and cannot get a job or other sources of revenue. This gendered analysis provides evidence as to the capacity of correctional institutions to integrate women who have been released from prison back into society and, in doing so, circumvent the dynamics of criminal recidivism (Brown and Ross, 2010; Richie, Freudenberg, and Page, 2001).

The model of Spanish prison, based on social reintegration (Wilson, Gallagher, and Mackenzie, 2000) incorporates gender specific training programming and is aimed to promote the integration of individuals within the labour market after completing a custodial sentence, but this model has no specific guidelines to be self-employed.

Public employment is a traditional refuge for women who want to participate in the labour market. According to the Spanish Labour Force Survey, in the last quarter of 2012, for instance, 54.76 percent of employed people in the public sector were women, as in previous periods (INE, 2013). However, the personnel and recruitment systems adopted by public institutions prohibit the incorporation of candidates with a criminal record. The adverse effects of disqualification constitute a two-fold punishment for the inmate. Public employment is inaccessible for prisoners. In spite of serving their full sentence, those released from prison suffer, as do all inmates, the stigma of their criminal record (Barreiro-Gen, 2012; Jensen and Giegold, 1976). This situation reinforces the idea that legal fact finders are more interested in guilt confirmation than in exoneration (Rassin, Eerland, and Kuijpers, 2010). The institutions extend this behaviour to the inmates' life after prison.

In addition, these inmates (both male and female) have difficulties in obtaining employment in the private sector. Employment policy in most private companies includes the screening of candidates. The existence of any factors that undermine the employer´s confidence, such as being an ex-inmate, is likely to exclude a candidate from the selection (Eisenhardt, 1989; Fama and Jensen,

1983; Hatch and Dyer, 2004; Hitt, Bierman, Shimizu, and Kochar, 2001; Koch and McGrath, 1996).

Gender, which is an additional factor that gives rise to exclusion, makes it even more difficult to integrate women ex-offenders. Therefore, people are influenced by their initial hypothesis regarding a crime when processing subsequent crime-related information (Ask and Anders Granhag, 2005; Hackett, 2013). When women leave prison they must deal with the problems that arise both from having been imprisoned and from being a woman (Opsal and Foley, 2013). According to with Sciulli (2013), conviction reduces the employment probability of females more than that of comparable males. While men recover a part of the disadvantage by increasing self-employment, conviction results in a strong labour market marginalization for females. Moreover, Opsal (2012) has shown that women use employment to begin to construct pro-social replacement selves and serious employment instability often corresponds with a re-emergence into criminal activity.

This situation, combined with the obstacles that exist in attaining employment in both the public and private sectors, means that, unless women become involved in specific labour reintegration programs supported by public institutions, the only path to the social inclusion of women ex-offenders has to be self-employment. Otherwise, options are narrowed and most of them are not legal alternatives, such as selling drugs.

However, there has been little real progress in studies connected to the prison population and entrepreneurship since the first exploratory research carried out in the '80s and '90s (Goodman, 1982; Rieple, 1998), with the one notable exception of (Downing, 2012) in respect to Bolivian prisons.

Thus, the goal of this research is to analyse the entrepreneurial potential of women released from prison in the Autonomous Region of Galicia, in the Northwest of Spain and to propose employment counselling aimed at increasing the entrepreneurial capacity of this group. A further objective of the work is to explore new ways of promoting the integration of this collective into the labour market. In other words, it should be possible to obtain certain generalizations from the main results of this research, making the conclusions applicable to other regions or countries, since the main characteristics of inmate populations might be deemed to be comparable, at least in those countries whose levels of development are similar (Sciulli, 2013).

It was carried out as a statistical analysis using a difference-of-means T-test and ANOVA. The object of these tests was to discover differences in male and female responses to the questionnaire and identify gender differences in entrepreneurial attitudes using a comparative analysis. The results of this analysis allowed us to put forward a set of proposals aimed at stimulating the entrepreneurial capacity of this group. This programming must be considered even with a lack of resources because the cost of this option is similar to giving a subsidy, but supporting self-employment is an investment whereas giving subsidies is an expense.

1. Preliminary diagnosis of the difficulties of the integration of women released from prison within the labour market

1.1 The situation of women on the labour market

Traditionally, the growing participation of women within the labour force has been perceived as problematic (Grundey and Sarvutyte, 2007). Political initiatives have promoted measures that reduce labour inequality between men and women in different European countries, such as Spain (Klemkaite and Monterrubio, 2010) or Lithuania, because women's and men's states in the labour market depends on the decisions taken by authorities (Kiausiene and Streimikiene, 2013) and on public policies carried out (Richie, 2001). However, many of the policies that have been created are superficial, do not strategically tackle the roots of inequality and consequently fail to integrate women on all of the labour force's levels. Measures that facilitate maternity leave, the promotion of part time jobs, and preferential access to training courses or fiscal incentives for women are certainly good for a government´s image and help companies to come across as socially responsible. However, it is not clear these measures solve the problem of labour gender inequality or the barriers to access for women in the labour market in practice (Alemagno and Dickie, 2005; Flabbi, 2010).

The exclusion of these people from the labour market will lead them, at least some of them, to the option of setting up a new company as an alternative. Prior research shows that women perceive the entrepreneurial requirements as more difficult than those for men (Fairlie and Robb, 2009; Zhao, Scott, and Hills, 2005). In this sense, entrepreneurship is not vocational for these women but simply a last resource, since the barriers to paid employment are, in the main, insuperable. Unobservable factors, such as different preferences, discrimination or risk aversion, may be responsible for a lower level of female entrepreneurship and lower economic returns for this activity (Langowitz and Minniti, 2007).

1.2 Entrepreneurship and influence factors

Studies on entrepreneurship carried out in many countries during the last twenty years have agreed that the factors that influence whether or not an individual tries to set up a business rather than being an employee can be divided into different kinds of factors: contextual, socio-demographic and cognitive (Langowitz and Minniti, 2007; Reynolds, Bygrave, and Hay, 2003).

For *contextual factors*, the authors include social and economic environment: employment, laws, financial structure, public policy, education system and household income (Wennekers, Van Wennekers, Thurik, and Reynolds, 2005).

For *social and demographic factors*, some authors have studied the relationship between variables, such as gender, age, marital status, situation of the family, health, characteristics of current employment and whether the individual has

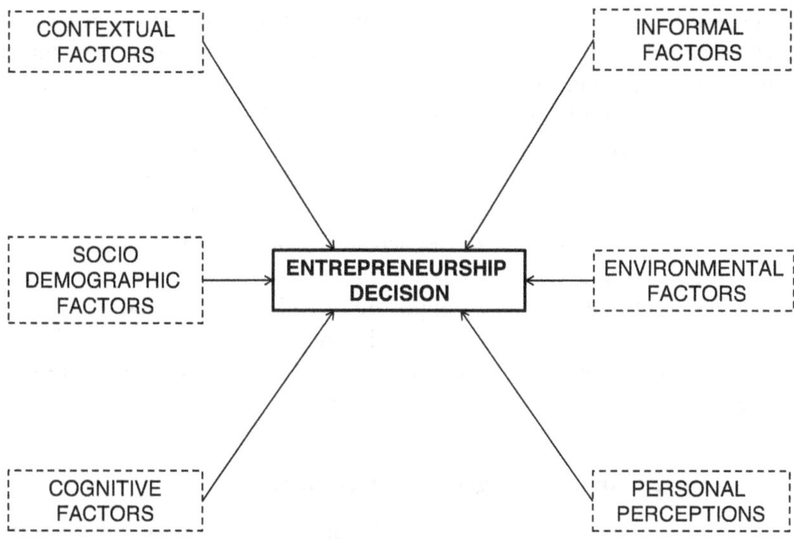

Figure 7.1 Factors of entrepreneurship decision

Source: Authors' own

skills or previous work experience. In recent years, certain authors have raised the importance of social support networks for entrepreneurial activity (Koellinger, Minniti, and Schade, 2013; Manolova, Eunni, and Gyoshev, 2008; Newbert, Tornikoski, and Quigley, 2013). In this sense, there are some proposals to create support networks involving all of the participants in stimulating entrepreneurship (public institutions, entrepreneurs, investors, financial organizations).

In line with this approach, some researchers have studied *cognitive factors* and their influence on the psychological characteristics of attitudes towards entrepreneurial initiatives (McClelland, 1961).

Shabbir and Di Gregorio (1996) have focused on certain structural issues that might influence company start-ups. They divide these issues into three sets related to internal resources (qualifications and/or their labour experience), external resources (financial capacity or the business location), and the relational resources (family support, or alliances with employees, suppliers or customers). However, they were unable to glean any conclusive results with respect to their research which analysed the capacity of female entrepreneurs to set up a new business in Pakistan.

In a quantitative study using the data offered by the Global Entrepreneurship Monitor set up 2010, Álvarez, Noguera, and Urbano (2012) concluded that *informal factors* (perception of entrepreneurial skills, social networks and the role of the family) had a significant effect on the probability of being a female entrepreneur, whereas *environmental factors* (financing, support policies and training) reinforced the entrepreneurial motivation of men and women equally. This study confirms the results of previous analyses carried out in other countries (Welter and Smallbone, 2008). Following this approach, Baughn, Chua, and Neupertke (2006) and Langowitz and Minniti (2007) affirmed that, in societies where the role of women is strongly linked to the household and family, women perceived entrepreneurial activity to be less desirable than men. These authors found that women tend to perceive themselves and the entrepreneurial environment as less favourable than men did across all countries studied in the GEM Project. In this study, a strong positive and significant correlation exists between self-confidence, the perception of opportunity and the likelihood of starting a new business. In fact, the perception of having sufficient skills is a dominant variable that seems to have an effect, which is independent of institutional characteristics, culture and the overall level of entrepreneurial activity.

1.3 Entrepreneurship and gender differences

The fact that women are less likely to undertake entrepreneurial initiatives than men might be explained by the fact that gender differences in business performance tend to be fairly discouraging for women. Fairlie and Robb (2009) found that female-owned businesses are often less successful than male-owned businesses because women have less start-up, business and human capital than their male counterparts because men tend to have enjoyed similar work experience in like businesses and prior work experience in family businesses. However, these results are inconclusive. In this sense, William (2004) observed that when women dedicated more time to their children, the duration and success of their businesses declined. In this line, the work of Justo and Díaz (2012) concludes that women entrepreneurs with dependent children tend to emphasize independence as a measure of business success, unlike men. Having to take on family responsibilities and dealing with an environment perceived as hostile to the figure of the entrepreneur reduces their participation in the social networks within the industry they belong to, thus lessening the chances that their business survives and grows (Baughn et al., 2006).

The GEM Project has examined entrepreneurial activity in more than 70 countries from the year 1999, and it shows that in all countries the percentage of female entrepreneurs is significantly lower than for men (Minniti, 2004). However, these differences do not mean that women take a back seat when it comes to entrepreneurship. The data (GEM, 2011) does not provide the characteristics and quality of business activities. It is clear that developing countries have higher rates of entrepreneurial activity than developed countries because the former have hardly any public employment, a traditional place of refuge for female workers and, in addition, a lack of small- and medium-sized businesses. In developing countries, the multinationals are those responsible for providing employment for the most highly qualified members of the population, and entrepreneurship is the only labour alternative for the rest (self-employment motivation).

However, in developed countries, gender appears to matter less than market opportunity. In fact, market opportunity is a more influential factor than the motivation to become self-employed. This result was obtained in a study carried out in 2009 by researchers from the GEM project. The results indicated that most entrepreneurial initiatives were due to a perception that there was an opportunity in the market, and this did not depend on gender: although in general terms, the rate of entrepreneurship for women was lower than for men in most countries, but there is not a big difference. In Spain, there were five times more companies created because male entrepreneurs believed there was a market opportunity than companies set up due to the need for self-employment. In the case of women, there were four and a half times as many (GEM, 2011).

Thus, most entrepreneurial initiatives only provide the entrepreneur with employment or perhaps a very low number of jobs as well (Ruiz Navarro, Camelo, De la Vega García-Pastor, Corduras Martínez, and Justo, 2010). More than 80 percent of businesses have fewer than five employees. This is independent of whether the entrepreneur is a man or a woman, and it is not key to this research, in which the main goal to create self-employment through entrepreneurship. Nevertheless, the analyses carried out by the GEM Observatory in the group of developed countries indicate that there is a significant number of differences in behaviour between female and male entrepreneurs.

The degree of competition that faces both male and female entrepreneurs is fairly similar in developed countries. In general, more than 50 percent of entrepreneurial activity, both male and female, has to face a lot of competition, this being the norm in most countries. The development of innovation and the capacity to diversify and expand internationally are the key factors when it comes to being more competitive. Hence, the countries that are intent on improving these factors are those that are most likely to generate entrepreneurial initiatives that are sustainable.

Geographically, the effects of the economic crisis (Table 7.1) mean that the percentage of entrepreneurial initiatives with no or negative expectations of growth is high and, in many countries, exceeds 50 percent of all the businesses set up, and this is the same for both men and women.

This is true for Germany, The United States, Slovenia, Spain, Finland, Greece, Italy, Netherlands, The United Kingdom and Switzerland.

1.4 Entrepreneurship and women ex-offenders

However, the mean data for entrepreneurial activity provided by the GEM Observatory does not faithfully reflect the real world situation for the members of the collective that are the object of this study. Women released from prison are forced to set up new businesses out of necessity since this is the only way they can gain employment. Fear of failure, the absence of entrepreneurial role models nearby or knowledge of previous entrepreneurial efforts experienced by other women ex-prisoners are not as important as incentive to undertake entrepreneurial initiatives as they are for women as a whole (Justo and Díaz, 2012).

Table 7.1 Percentage of entrepreneurial initiatives by men and women in terms of the type of expectation of growth

Country	*TEA Without expansion*		*TEA With some expansion and without NT*		*TEA Some expansion with NT*		*TEA 20 In-depth expansion*	
	M	*F*	*M*	*F*	*M*	*F*	*M*	*F*
Germany	62.6%	67.6%	29.5%	27.8%	3.6%	3.7%	4.3%	.9%
Belgium	51.7%	44.9%	24.7%	36.7%	20.2%	16.3%	3.4%	2.0%
Denmark	46.9%	60.0%	42.9%	36.0%	2.0%	4.0%	8.2%	.0%
USA	69.4%	64.6%	26.0%	31.3%	4.0%	1.0%	0.6%	3.0%
UAE	39.0%	30.3%	42.4%	45.5%	16.5%	21.2%	2.2%	3.0%
Slovenia	56.9%	60.5%	31.7%	31.6%	8.9%	.0%	2.4%	7.9%
Spain	60.8%	54.3%	26.0%	29.0%	9.6%	12.1%	3.7%	4.5%
Finland	61.3%	63.4%	29.0%	29.3%	8.1%	7.3%	1.6%	.0%
France	40.0%	56.3%	34.5%	31.3%	23.6%	6.3%	1.8%	6.3%
Greece	54.3%	65.0%	32.8%	30.0%	8.6%	5.0%	4.3%	.0%
Hong-Kong	58.0%	66.7%	28.0%	16.7%	12.0%	12.5%	2.0%	4.2%
Island	49.6%	50.7%	34.4%	29.0%	6.9%	7.2%	9.2%	13.0%
Israel	42.5%	51.3%	23.3%	28.2%	23.3%	17.9%	11.0%	2.6%
Italy	60.7%	70.4%	34.5%	22.2%	2.4%	7.4%	2.4%	.0%
Japan	42.5%	69.2%	35.0%	23.1%	20.0%	7.7%	2.5%	.0%
Norway	56.1%	52.6%	31.8%	44.7%	5.6%	2.6%	6.5%	.0%
Netherlands	50.0%	58.1%	43.5%	35.5%	5.4%	4.8%	1.1%	1.6%
South of Korea	56.1%	67.6%	35.5%	29.4%	6.5%	2.9%	1.9%	.0%
United Kingdom	67.6%	58.9%	26.7%	33.3%	4.4%	3.1%	1.3%	4.6%
Switzerland	58.0%	58.8%	30.4%	33.3%	5.8%	5.9%	5.8%	2.0%
Average	58.9%	57.8%	29.7%	31.2%	8.3%	7.3%	3.1%	3.7%

Source: prepared by the authors based on Ruiz Navarroet al. (2010)

With regard to women released from prison, some of the most important barriers to entrepreneurship are the negative ones such as a hostile environment, a lack of training and professional qualifications, and the absence of role models. In this sense, self-employment is more commonly a substitute for part-time work and labour market inactivity for women than it is for men. Moreover, entrepreneurship can be a response to illegal means of income, such as selling drugs or prostitution, which this group often uses.

At this point, it might be useful to explain the problems that women have with respect to models of reference in more depth. According to Justo and Díaz (2012), women do not have many models of reference, that is, there is a lack of women entrepreneurs that could provide a guide for the collective analysed in this study. This deficit is likely to hamper the creation of companies by this group. Other studies, such as Staniewski and Szopinski (2013), show the importance of having an example of entrepreneurship among family or friends in creating a business and in being self-employed.

However, the existence of such models is not strictly linked to a real individual but to *personal perceptions* of people, skewed by the differential importance of some characteristics (Eriksson-Zetterquist, 2008). In this sense, the lack of female ex-prisoners involved in entrepreneurial activity who might be role models is not, in itself, what discourages the entrepreneurial motivation of this community. Rather, this is because of the groups′ perception of the success and skills possessed by entrepreneurs with similar characteristics. In the same line, Minniti (2004) has analysed how an individual's confidence increases when there are precedents and models that can be copied or adhered to, and the effect that this knowledge has on making the business environment seem less ambiguous for the potential entrepreneur. The results also confirm that the lack of models of reference among these women tend to impinge negatively upon the rates of entrepreneurship (Justo and Díaz, 2012).

Furthermore, as García and Lane (2010) previously discussed, training and work within the prison may help women gain self-confidence and be better prepared to face the challenges of creating a business.

Finally, it should be stated that the creation of a company is very closely linked to the entrepreneur′s perception of his capacity to create a new business and to his capacity to tolerate the risk that is inherent in the process. These potential barriers cannot be surmounted easily through exogenous interventions, such as institutional incentive programs (Minniti and Nardoni, 2007). In order to discover how institutions can influence and support the entrepreneurial initiatives of women released from prison, it is necessary to identify the main factors that influence how individual perceptions are generated.

Finally, it can be concluded that there has been little real progress in studies connected to the prison population and entrepreneurship since the first exploratory research carried out in the '80s and '90s (Goodman, 1982; Rieple, 1998). The one notable exception is the recent study by Downing (2012), which proved entrepreneurship is a successful mechanism for prisoner rehabilitation with respect to Bolivian prisons, for which the author found that there were low levels of recidivism. It encourages the field of entrepreneurship and small business enterprise to think about possible contexts and benefits of successful entrepreneurial ventures.

2. The context of Spain's prisons and policies

According to Spanish Ministry of Home Affairs, there are 70.392 prisoners in Spain (Ministry of Home Affairs, 2013). Female prison population represents 7.61 percent of the total. This percentage has kept constant in the last few years. Therefore, women in prison are a minority group that do not have some benefits men have as the possibility of living in a special module for good behaviour because there is usually only one female module in prisons.

The philosophy of imprisonment that exists in Spain is rehabilitative. In fact, the Article 25 of the Spanish Constitution states that prison sentences and the holding of offenders in custody should aim at re-education and social rehabilitation and may not require forced labour.

In recent years, there have been various actions undertaken in Spanish public policy to make real this constitutional objective and to achieve the social inclusion of ex-inmates. One of the most notable measures carried out is the creation of Centres for Social Integration (CIS), which provide a midway point between prison and outright release. These centres and the provision of conditional release status help promote inmates' autonomy and responsibility, foster social ties and reduce the control exercised over the inmate population. Inmates can start to look for a job or other options while they are still serving their sentence in these centres.

When people leave prison in Spain, if they meet some requirements,[1] the State pays a subsidy similar to unemployment benefits. This aid represents an added expense to the State. From the authors' point of view, it would be recommended that aid should be granted to entrepreneurship. In this way, this expense could become an investment, both for the former inmate population as for the rest of society.

3. Self-employment as an option to avoid illegal sources of income

The initial thesis of this research is entrepreneurship can be an option to women released from prison to avoid illegal sources of income, alternatives that, in most cases, involve recidivism and re-incarceration. However, according to literature review that has been done, women have more problems being an entrepreneur because they do not have the same social networks than men.

Therefore, the null hypotheses that will be contrasted are:

H_{01}: *There are no differences between the female and male prison population about their level of entrepreneurial motivation.*

H_{02}: *There are no differences between the female and male prison population about the social support they have.*

4. Methodology

4.1 Participants

The sample consisted of inmates from the five prisons in Galicia (Northwest of Spain). These prisons are in spread out among different Galician provinces. They are situated in Teixeiro (A Coruña), Bonxe and Monterroso (Lugo), Pereiro of Aguiar (Ourense) and A Lama (Pontevedra). Likewise, there are also two institutions dedicated to social integration working with the imprisoned

Table 7.2 Description of the sample

VARIABLE	*CATEGORY*	*FREQUENCY*	*PERCENTAGE*
Sex	Men	352	74.4
	Women	121	25.6
	Total	473	100
Studies	No education	47	9.9
	Primary School	190	40.2
	High School	151	31.9
	Training	45	9.5
	College	27	5.7
	Total	460	97.3
Age	18–30	130	29.1
	31–50	284	63.5
	>50	33	7.4
	Total	447	94.5

population on grade 3 (semi-freedom) situated in A Coruña and Vigo (Pontevedra), the biggest cities in the region.

Since the aim was to study the potential entrepreneurial differences between men and women, a mixed gender sample was used. The sample is formed by473 inmates, 352 men and 121 women. It represents 12.75 percent of the Galician prison population (Ministry of Home Affairs, 2011). Questionnaires were collected in proportion to the number of inmates in each Centre or prison: Teixeiro (33.2 percent), Bonxe (9.2 percent), Monterroso (9.4 percent), Pereiro de Aguiar (9.2 percent), A Lama (35.5 percent) and CIS of A Coruña (3.5 percent).

Table 7.2 shows the most representative classification variables as age or their level of education.

All prisoners participated in this work voluntarily after signing the corresponding authorization to disseminate the results of the research.

4.2 Instruments

The questionnaire consisted of two parts: one part included classification questions that allowed us to know the personal characteristics of participants, and the other part was composed of issues about opinion or attitude, focusing on the different areas with some influence on social inclusion, according to scientific literature, as employment or training (Barreiro Gen, Novo Corti, and Ramil Díaz, 2013). In this section, prisoners reflected their level of agreement or disagreement with a series of affirmations or issues, on a 5-point Likert scale, where 1 is total disagreement and 5 total agreement.

4.3 Procedure

Secretariat General for Penitentiary Institutions gave the nominal required authorizations to the members of the research team and, after that, the fieldwork was initiated.

The questionnaire was evaluated by experts in social exclusion from University of A Coruña and specialised consultants, in particular Gaela Consultora S.C., and was revised, corrected and validated through a pre-test to 50 inmates. After that, it proceeded to the purification of the questionnaire, eliminating redundant questions and wrong understanding.

The final survey was translated into Arabic with support from the Official School of Languages in A Coruña due to the presence of prisoners of Arabic origin with whom the research team had some communication problems (they were specially concentrated in the high security prison Monterroso in Lugo).

After collecting the data, the averages of the two groups was compared using a difference-of-means T-test. The classification variable was gender.

Once the hypotheses had been tested (H_{01}: *There are no differences between the female and male prison population about their level of entrepreneurial motivation.* H_{02}: *There are no differences between the female and male prison population about the social support they have*), the potential differences were analysed by considering gender and looking at prisoners' opinions and attitudes with respect to integration within the labour market, training and family support.

The next phase involved carrying out an ANOVA test and looking at the entrepreneurial attitudes of women inmates as a factor. This section only uses data corresponding to the female inmate population.

5. Results

5.1 Comparing men and women's answers: independent sample t-test

There were no significant differences according to gender with respect to the T-test and responses to the item *If I had some help, when I left prison I would feel capable of working on my own, as an entrepreneur.* As a result, the first null hypothesis (H_{01}: *There are no differences between the female and male prison population about their level of entrepreneurial motivation*) cannot be rejected. The mean obtained for the male sample is 3.93 compared to 4.09 for women. Therefore, the mean answer is roughly 4 for both groups, which is equivalent to "almost positive that the answer is yes". The opinions of both groups are very positive with respect to entrepreneurial activity, within the institutions that provide this kind of support (Table 7.3).

With regard to one of the items related to what Subirats (2005) refer to as the pillars of social integration – social support networks – there are significant differences in the means for both sets of answers. As seen in Table 7.3, the significant differences correspond to statements related to networks: a) *I have*

Table 7.3 T-test for equality of means

Question	*Sex*	*N*	*Mean*	*Statistic t*	*Sig.*	*Differences in averages*
If I had some help, when I leave prison, I would feel able to work on my own, as an entrepreneur	Man	328	3.933	–0.953	.341	–.153
	Woman	116	4.086			
I have some friends who I will work for when I get out of prison	Man	330	3.076	3,061	*	.563
	Woman	117	2.513			
When I leave, my family will be waiting for me to come home	Man	324	4.512	1,993	*	.295
	Woman	115	4.217			
Courses and professions that I have learned in prison will help me find a job	Man	325	2.655	–2,104	*	–.381
	Woman	111	3.036			

* p < .05

some friends who I will work for when I get out of prison and b) *When I leave, my family will be waiting for me to come home.* The first assertion concerns the potential contacts prisoners have in order to obtain work when they get released from the penal institution. In this case, the average of the men's answers was 3.08 and 2.51 for women. With regard to the second proposition, the mean of the men was 4.51 and 4.21 for women. Hence, the second hypothesis (H_{02}: *There are no differences between the female and male prison population about the social support they have*) must be rejected.

According to Subirats (2005), education and training is the other area to avoid social exclusion. Knowledge gained in prison appeared to be more important for women. The mean for women in respect to what they were able to learn in prison (*Courses and professions that I have learned in prison will help me find a job*) was 3.04, while for men it was 2.66.

5.2 ANOVA for a single factor

ANOVA test was carried out to analyse entrepreneurial attitudes in regards to the sample of women only. An attempt was made to find a specific "profile of woman entrepreneur", but, as shown in Table 7.4, having children, the level of qualifications, age and country of birth, the severity of the crime committed and length of sentence all fail to produce significant differences in the mean answers at a confidence level over 95 percent.

Any of these factors might be deemed to be a significant characteristic of the entrepreneurial woman, but they are not conclusive in this sample (p>.05). The only relevant classification variable at a confidence level of 97 percent was whether or not these women had a job prior to their incarceration: women who

Table 7.4 ANOVA Test

		Sum of square	*Quadratic mean*	**F*	**Sig.*
Age	*Inter-Groups	183.849	45.962	.418	.795
	*Intra-Groups	11430.188	109.906		
	Total	11614.037			
Country of Birth	*Inter-Groups	1.194	.298	.24	.915
	*Intra-Groups	129.393	1.244		
	Total	130.587			
Civil state	*Inter-Groups	1.391	.348	.396	.811
	*Intra-Groups	94.038	.879		
	Total	95.429			
Children	*Inter-Groups	8.272	2.068	.466	.761
	*Intra-Groups	457.395	4.441		
	Total	465.667			
Studies/Qualification	*Inter-Groups	6.928	1.732	1.619	.175
	*Intra-Groups	114.501	1.07		
	Total	121.429			
Prior job	*Inter-Groups	1.969	.492	2.287	.065
	*Intra-Groups	23.252	.215		
	Total	25.221			

had prior employment perceived themselves as having greater entrepreneurial potential.

Discussion and conclusions

When a woman leaves prison and looks for a job, she usually has some non-socially desirable options to obtain incomes, such as selling drugs, crime or prostitution. Even if they cannot get enough resources to live, sometimes they become homeless.

However, there are three desirable labour alternatives: public employment, private employment or self-employment. Although public employment has been a traditional refuge for women who want to participate in the labour market, this is not a future option for women inmates because they have a criminal record that excludes them from this type of job, a dynamic that is just the reverse of what happens in society in general, which is a public job being the traditional refuge for women who want to participate in the labour market. Gaining private employment is problematic due to distrust and stigmatization. Hence, women prisoners may choose the path of entrepreneurship, being motivated by necessity. According to scientific literature (Álvarezet al., 2012), social networks are a very important informal factor when it comes to entrepreneurial motivation.

Our results have shown that women inmates perceive they receive less support than men. One reason for this is almost certainly because, historically, women have been the main providers of this kind of support for the family, and when they are incarcerated, it disappears. Hence, this is less common when the prisoners are men.

Therefore, while it was asserted initially that there are no significant differences in the attitudes of male and female prisoners with respect to entrepreneurial motivation, this finding might be overturned by looking at the results obtained in the last two questions of the survey. Women are more highly motivated in an entrepreneurial sense since they have much weaker social support networks, and yet they retain the same entrepreneurial attitude as men.

Women value what they can learn in prison more positively than men and this opens a window of opportunity to help boost potential female self-employment through the training provided in prison. Likewise, women who had prior employment believed they had greater entrepreneurial potential, according to García and Lane (2010). In fact, the female inmates who highlight sewing or the hospitality sector as the main activities they would choose to start a business, these businesses are more related to the training received in prison (sewing courses) than with previous work experience.

This study suggests that women inmates have less social support (from their family or acquaintances) for setting up new companies but have the same entrepreneurial attitudes as their male counterparts. Therefore, it may be concluded that, although the entrepreneurial motivation of women released from prison is not usually related to the exploitation of a market opportunity but rather to the motivation to become self-employed, penal institutions should guide these women in order to take advantage of the knowledge that they acquire in prison to set up new businesses. In this sense, employment counselling in penal institutions should be addressed to guide prisoners through this process whilst focusing the training they receive on the real-life contexts that women inmates face when they complete the terms of their sentence. This would allow them to familiarize themselves with this option and to assimilate this possibility as a real way of gaining employment, while at the same time generating a business plan as a nexus between the two environments. The main implications point in two directions: first, in the prison, the staff should manage vocational training in trades that may be of interest to entrepreneurship and also promote entrepreneurial attitudes and skills among the inmates. Secondly, the integration procedure of the prisoners into society (already released or in third grade should be based on access to credit and accompaniment in the early stages of new business creation.

Currently, employment counselling in penal institutions is usually aimed at attaining paid employment for this collective or giving a subsidy, which is generally a more expensive and less productive option. The cost of the entrepreneurial support provided by the Government could be the same amount of the current subsidy for social reinsertion, but in this case, this amount could be considered investment instead of expense and the starting point of a future employment option for future ex-prisoners.

Since women imprisoned and released from prison are, frequently, the breadwinners for their families, it was proposed that measures should be designed to complement the procedures adopted that specifically deal with entrepreneurship. In this sense, we proposed additional measures aimed to facilitate the personal and professional balance. Penal institutions could also, as part of their employment counselling, promote entrepreneurial networks and encourage the emergence of alliances with related groups to help substitute the lack of social support experienced by many female ex-prisoners.

As a limitation of this study, we have to mention that it has not been able to track women once they leave the prison, which is really difficult due to the Spanish law of data protection. Once they are released, ex-inmates often try to erase any ties to their prison setting. There is not a database with former prisoners for research use. Another limitation is that the participation in this study was voluntary and it could be a cause of bias. However, this limitation was assumed in order to avoid the risk of false answers.

The novelty of this study lies in the context used, something very difficult to access, as well as its organizational impact on penal institutions, which are often neglected by scholars. The social importance of the results is aligned with the idea of entrepreneurship as an option for women ex-offenders to avoid illegal sources of income and to overcome the barriers of the labour market.

Finally, future lines of research could be related to study the influence of financial support in the form of micro-credits to reduce the difficulties of the women ex-offenders when trying to access funding.

Note

1 For more information about that issue, see: www.sepe.es/contenido/prestaciones/ag00d02.html

References

Alemagno, S., and Dickie, J. (2005). Employment issues of women in jail. *Journal of Employment Counseling*, 42(2), 67–74.

Álvarez, C., Noguera, M., and Urbano, D. (2012). Determining factors and female entrepreneurship environment: A quantitative study in Spain. *Economía Industrial*, 383(1), 43–52.

Ask, K., and Anders Granhag, P. (2005). Motivational sources of confirmation bias in criminal investigations: The need for cognitive closure. *Journal of Investigative Psychology and Offender Profiling*, 2, 43–63.

Barreiro-Gen, M. (2012). La inclusión sociolaboral de la población reclusa de Galicia, España: Principales obstáculos y propuestas para su superación. *Atlantic Economic Review*, 1, 1–23.

Barreiro-Gen, M., Novo Corti, I., and Ramil Díaz, M. (2013). Mercado de trabajo, formación y exclusión social: Análisis de la situación de la población reclusa de Galicia. *Revista Galega de Economía*, 22 (Special Issue), 225–244.

Baughn, C.C., Chua, B., and Neupertke, K. E. (2006). The normative context for women's participation in entrepreneurship: A multi-country study. *Entrepreneurship Theory & Practice*, 30(5), 687–708.

Brown, M., and Ross, S. (2010). Mentoring, social capital and desistance: A study of women released from prison. *Australian and New Zealand Journal of Criminology*, 43(1), 31–50.

Downing, C. (2012). Bolivian prison entrepreneurship: An unexpectedly successful rehabilitation method? *Journal of Enterprising Communities*, 6(4), 339–349.

Eisenhardt, K. M. (1989). Agency theory: An assessment and review. *Academy of Management Review*, 14(1), 57–74.

Eriksson-Zetterquist, U. (2008). Gendered role modeling: A paradoxical construction process. *Scandinavian Journal of Management*, 24(3), 259–270.

Fairlie, R., and Robb, A. (2009). Gender differences in business performance: Evidence from the characteristics of business owner's survey. *Small Business Economics*, 33(4), 375–395.

Fama, E., and Jensen, M. (1983). Separation of ownership and control. *Journal of Law and Economics*, 26, 301–325.

Flabbi, L. (2010). Gender discrimination estimation in a search model with matching and bargaining. *International Economic Review*, 51(3), 745–783.

García, C.A., and Lane, J. (2010). Looking in the rearview mirror: What incarcerated women girls need from the system? *Feminist Criminology*, 5(3), 227–243.

Global Entrepreneurship Monitor, GEM. (2011). *Spanish Report.* Cáceres: Fundación Xavier de Salas.

Goodman, S. (1982). Prisoners as entrepreneurs – Developing a model for prisoner-run industry. *Boston University Law Review*, 62(5), 1163–1195.

Grundey, D., and Sarvutyte, M. (2007). Women entrepreneurship in the European labour market: Time to go online. *Transformations in Business and Economics*, 6(2), 197–218.

Hackett, C. (2013). Transformative visions: Governing through alternative practices and therapeutic interventions at women's reentry center. *Feminist Criminology*, 8(3), 221–242.

Hatch, N. W., and Dyer, J. H. (2004). Human capital and learning as a source of sustainable competitive advantage. *Strategic Management Journal*, 25(1), 1155–1178.

Hitt, M. A., Bierman, L., Shimizu, K., and Kochar, R. (2001). Direct and moderating effects of human capital on strategy and performance in professional service firms: A resource-based perspective. *Academy of Management Journal*, 44(1), 13–22.

Jensen, W., and Giegold, W. C. (1976). Finding jobs for ex-offenders – Study of employers attitudes. *American Business Law Journal*, 14(2), 195–225.

Justo, R., and Díaz, C. (2012). Incidence of reference models in business creation: Mediators and gender effects. *Economía Industrial*, 383(1), 111–123.

Kiausiene, I., and Streimikiene, D. (2013). The assessment of differences of women's and men's status in the labour market. *Transformations in Business and Economics*, 12(2), 125–137.

Klemkaite, L., and Monterrubio, L. (2010). *E-chance 2.0 for Women Entrepreneurship.* Edited by L. G. Chova, D. M. Belenguer and I. C. Torres, 3rd International Conference of Education, Research and Innovation (ICERI), Madrid.

Koch, M. J., and McGrath, R. (1996). Improving labor productivity: Human resource management policies do matter. *Strategic Management Journal*, 17(5), 335–354.

Koellinger, P., Minniti, M., and Schade, C. (2013). Gender differences in entrepreneurial propensity. *Oxford Bulletin of Economics and Statistics*, 75(2), 213–234.

Langowitz, N., and Minniti, M. (2007). The entrepreneurial propensity of women. *Entrepreneurship Theory and Practice*, 31(3), 341–364.

Manolova, T. S., Eunni, R. V., and Gyoshev, B. S. (2008). Institutional environments for entrepreneurship: Evidence from emerging economies in Eastern Europe. *Entrepreneurship: Theory & Practice*, 32(1), 203–218.

McClelland, D. C. (1961). *The Achieving Society*. Princeton, NJ: VanNostrand.

Ministry of Home Affairs. (2011). *Anuario estadístico del Ministerio del Interior, 2011*. Retrieved May 14, 2013 from: www.interior.gob.es/file/58/58114/58114.pdf

Ministry of Home Affairs. (2013). *Estadística penitenciaria, 2012*. Retrieved September 20, 2013 from: www.institucionpenitenciaria.es/web/portal/documentos/estadisticas.html?r=m&adm=TES&am=2012&mm=1&tm=GENE&tm2=GENE

Minniti, M. (2004). Entrepreneurial alertness and asymmetric information in a spin-glass model. *Journal of Business Venturing*, 19(5), 637–658.

Minniti, M., and Nardoni, C. (2007). Being in someone else's shoes: The role of gender in nascent entrepreneurship. *Small Business Economics*, 28, 223–238.

Newbert, S. L., Tornikoski, E. T., and Quigley, N. R. (2013). Exploring the evolution of supporter networks in the creation of new organizations. *Journal of Business Venturing*, 28(2), 281–298.

Opsal, T. (2012). 'Livin' on the straights': Identity, desistance, and work among women post-incarceration. *Sociological Inquiry*, 82(3), 378–403.

Opsal, T., and Foley, A. (2013). Making it on the outside: Understanding barriers to women's post-incarceration reintegration. *Sociology Compass*, 7(4), 265–277.

Rassin, E., Eerland, A., and Kuijpers, I. (2010). Let's find the evidence: An analogue study of confirmation bias in criminal investigations. *Journal of Investigative Psychology and Offender Profiling*, 7(2), 231–246.

Reynolds, P. D., Bygrave, B., and Hay, M. (2003). *Global Entrepreneurship Monitor Report*. Kansas City, MO: E. M. Kauffmann Foundation.

Richie, B. E. (2001). Challenges incarcerated women face as they return to their communities: Findings from life history interviews. *Crime & Delinquency*, 47(3), 368–389.

Richie, B. E., Freudenberg, N., and Page, J. (2001). Reintegrating women leaving jail into urban communities: A description of a model program. *Journal of Urban Health-Bulletin of the New York Academy of Medicine*, 78(2), 290–303.

Rieple, A. (1998). Offenders and entrepreneurship. *European Journal on Criminal Policy and Research*, 6(2), 235–256.

Ruiz Navarro, J., Camelo, C., De la Vega García-Pastor, I., Corduras Martínez, A., and Justo, R. (2010). *Women and Entrepreneurial Challenge in Spain*. Cádiz: Business School Press, Universidad de Cádiz-Instituto de Empresa.

Sciulli, D. (2013). Conviction, gender and labour market status. *Applied Economics Letters*, 20(11), 1113–1120.

Shabbir, A. S., and Di Gregorio, S. (1996). An examination of the relationship between women's personal goals and structural factors influencing their decision to start a business: The case of Pakistan. *Journal of Business Venturing*, 11, 507–529.

Spanish National Institute of Statistics (INE). (2013). Public sector employees by sex. *Labor Force Survey*. Retrieved February 14, 2013 from: www.ine.es/jaxiBD/menu.do?divi=EPA&his=1&type=db&L=0

Staniewski, M.W., and Szopinski, T. (2013). Influence of socioeconomic factors on the entrepreneurship of polish students. Transformations in Business and Economics, 12(3), 152–167.

Subirats, J. (2005). Social exclusion and devolution among Spanish autonomous communities. *Regional and Federal Studies*, 15(4), 471–483.

Welter, F., and Smallbone, D. (2008). Women's entrepreneurship from an institutional perspective: The case of Uzbekistan. *International Entrepreneurship and Management Journal*, 4(4), 505–520.

Wennekers, S., Van Wennekers, A., Thurik, R., and Reynolds, P. (2005). Nascent entrepreneurship and the level of economic development. *Small Business Economics*, 24(3), 293–309.

William, D.R. (2004). Effects of childcare activities on the duration of self-employment in Europe. *Entrepreneurship Theory & Practice*, 28(5), 467–485.

Wilson, D. B., Gallagher, C. A., and MacKenzie, D. L. (2000). A meta-analysis of corrections-based education, vocation, and work programs for adult offenders. *Journal of Research in Crime and Delinquency*, 37(4), 347–368.

Zhao, H., Scott, E.S., and Hills, G.E. (2005). The mediating role of self-efficacy in the development of entrepreneurial intentions. *Journal of Applied Psychology*, 90(6), 1265–1272.

8 Exploring the drivers of gender entrepreneurship

Focus on the motivational perspectives in USA, Italy and France

Vahid Jafari Sadeghi and Paolo Pietro Biancone

1. Introduction

Entrepreneurship is referred to as the recognition and chase of opportunity irrespective of the organisation's current resources (Eckhardt and Shane, 2003; Stevenson and Jarillo, 1990). This definition highlights how,where and when entrepreneurs can look for opportunities to start their entrepreneurial activities. In addition, the establishment of new businesses provides employment and new markets can be added to the economic growth and improvement in the quality of life (Elam, 2014). Moreover, the gender entrepreneurship, the contribution of women in entrepreneurial activities, has become a trending subject for policymakers and researchers over the last decade (e.g., Bruni, Gherardi, and Poggio, 2004; Hanson and Blake, 2007; Langevang, Gough, Yankson, Owusu, and Osei, 2015). However, the reasons for these interests were changing during the time. Although women are about half as likely as men to create and start new businesses, the policies aimed at women entrepreneurship development were based on efforts to support equal status and social inclusion of women (Kelley, Singer, and Herrington, 2012; Lotti, 2006; Wilson, Kickul, and Marlino, 2007).

Economic issues like inflation and more importantly unemployment are the key problems faced by governments in the majority of nations. This kind of challenge puts the entrepreneurship in the position of jobs creation not only regarding self-employment, but also in the context of creating new employment opportunities for others (Holienka, Jančovičová, and Kovačičová, 2016). With this perspective, the participation of women alongside men in entrepreneurial activities can lead to economic growth of nations. For this purpose, gender entrepreneurship and exploring the differences between men and women in terms ofcreating new business has become one of the major researches in this field.

This study contributes to the literature that explores the variations between men and women in entrepreneurship and prospects their motivational intentions by performing an analysis for the United States of America, Italy and France.

To present a more detailed description of the variations between gender type in entrepreneurship, we outstrip the current studies and examine the influencing factors in entrepreneurship. We used Global Entrepreneurship Monitor statistics, which presents information about entrepreneurs involved in the total early-stage entrepreneurship (TEA), including all new, young and nascent entrepreneurial activities.

This paper aimsto contribute to the literature by the following objective: we examine the role motivation has over both male and female entrepreneurs. GEM (2017) classified motivational intentions of entrepreneurs in two categories: necessity and opportunity. Necessity entrepreneurs create a new business because of economic condition, unemployment or lack of appropriate job opportunities while opportunity entrepreneurs have a novel idea and look forward to starting a new venture because they have identified good business opportunities (Fuentelsaz, González, Maícas, and Montero, 2015). This study intends to investigate the motivational tendencies of men and women to create new ventures. In addition, we explore the impact of different age groups, education and income level on gender entrepreneurship through empirical analysis.

The rest of the paper is organised as follows. Initially, we bring forward the literature and theory overview, the differences between men and women in entrepreneurial activity and the impact of motivation on entrepreneurs. Then, we present the data and methodology. The subsequent section deals with the presentation of the empirical results of data analysis. Eventually, in the last section, we discuss the empirical findings and extract conclusions.

2. Theory overview

Entrepreneurship can be, shortly, defined as being self-employed and owner – managers (Sköld and Tillmar, 2015). However, some scholars conceptualise entrepreneurship regarding an outcome, such as the self-employment rate or the incidence of startups (Warnecke, 2013). Others consider that as a way of thinking or acting- being creative, innovative, risk-taking, or resilient (Dana and Wright, 2009; Foss and Klein, 2012).

Researchers have been interested the motivation to become an entrepreneur, differentiating between two different types of entrepreneurship, namely opportunity and necessity entrepreneurship (Reynolds, Bygrave, Autio, Cox, and Hay, 2002). On the one hand, opportunity motive entrepreneurs are ones who create a business in order to pursue an opportunity, not being a forced choice. They usually start the business because they want to either earn more money or be more independent. On the other hand, in an entrepreneurship by necessity motive, individuals feel obliged to start their own businesses because of involuntary job loss and the scarcity of vacancies. Consequently, the decision to become involved in an entrepreneurial activity is a forced choice, given that all other employment options are either absent or unsatisfactory (Angulo-Guerrero, Pérez-Moreno, and Abad-Guerrero, 2017).

Fossen and Büttner (2013) assessed the relevance of formal education on the productivity of the self-employed, distinguishing between opportunity entrepreneurs versus necessity entrepreneurs. Based on the original theory (Douhan and van Praag, 2009), entrepreneurs should benefit higher returns to education than paid employees because they have better control over the employment of and the accruals from their own human capital. Fossen & Büttner found lower returns to education for necessity entrepreneurs than for opportunity entrepreneurs.

Motivational-based entrepreneurship is also important for nations in terms of economic growth and social development. Using a conceptual framework of institutional economics, Aparicio, Urbano, and Audretsch (2016) analysed the influence of informal (control of corruption and confidence in one's skills) and formal institutions (the number of procedures involved in starting a business and private coverage to obtain credit) on opportunity entrepreneurship, which at the same time allow the achievement of economic growth. They found a positive relationship between opportunity TEA and economic growth.

In this paper, we are going to explore the motivation of entrepreneurs to receive opportunities; in other words,opportunity-driven entrepreneurs. For this reason, it is more intelligible to explore the opportunities for entrepreneurs. Entrepreneurial opportunities are defined as situations in which new goods, services, raw materials, markets and organising methods can be introduced through the formation of new means, ends or means-ends relationships. These situations do not need to change the terms of economic exchange tobe entrepreneurial opportunities, but only need to have the potential to alter the terms of economic exchange. In addition, unlike optimising or satisficing decisions, in which the ends that the decision maker is trying to achieve and the means that the decision maker will employ are given, entrepreneurial decisions are creative decisions. That is, the entrepreneur constructs the means, the ends or both (Casson, 1982; Eckhardt and Shane, 2003; Shane and Venkataraman, 2000).

Empirical consideration on the drivers of opportunities has concentrated mainly on the entrepreneurs who identify opportunities. In general, research has focused on both aspects of knowledge stocks and the behaviours of entrepreneurs (Short, Ketchen, Shook, and Ireland, 2010). In fact, the prior distribution of knowledge not only specifies who is more likely to find opportunities (Shane, 2001), but also affects the quality and quantity of discovered opportunities (Shepherd and DeTienne, 2005). DeTienne and Chandler (2007) figured out that although both gender types use unique stocks of human capital and show various processes of opportunity recognition, the innovativeness of opportunities did not differ. However, it is proved that past failures keep opportunity formation processes flexible while commitment emerges (Mitchell, Mitchell, and Smith, 2008; Short et al., 2010). Researchers have also found that opportunities can be discovered through more search activities and different analysis of data against non-entrepreneurs and highlighted the role of experience by detecting that the cognitive representations of opportunities of experienced entrepreneurs differ from those of novice entrepreneurs (Baron and Ensley, 2006; Kaish and Gilad, 1991; Short et al., 2010).

Women and men have, basically, the same crucial needs including innovative ideas, entrepreneurial personality characteristics, business plans and long-term strategies to start an entrepreneurial business. While the motivations of some female entrepreneurs may be similar to their male counterparts (e.g. desire for independence and financial gain), there is an argument that large numbers of women, unlike men, choose to start a business to balance work responsibilities and earning potential with domestic and familial responsibilities (Mattis, 2004; McGowan, Redeker, Cooper, and Greenan, 2012). However, the fact that an entrepreneurial career is gendered can also shape the interaction between entrepreneurs and various service providers and, as a result, limit women's ability to access the necessary resources or receive the necessary support to become successful entrepreneurs. This may cause women to perceive the environment to be challenging and unsuitable for entrepreneurial activity with insurmountable barriers (Shinnar, Giacomin, and Janssen, 2012; Zhao, Seibert, and Hills, 2005).

Entrepreneurs may also suffer from the lack of confidence. This barrier is unavoidable because societal gender roles, stereotypes and occupational gender typing can shape the perceptions individuals have of themselves (Shinnar et al., 2012). In her analysis of GEM data, Thebaud (2010) figured out that, in general, male entrepreneurs are more likely to believe that they have the necessary knowledge, skills and experience to be an entrepreneur. The importance of perceived skills was also examined by Krueger (2007) who adds that when certain occupations are typed as masculine, women's intentions to pursue these occupations will be weaker because they perceive themselves as less able or less skilled. As a result, literature confirms that the barrier of lack of confidence in female entrepreneurs is harsher than male entrepreneurs.

The nature of entrepreneurship is incorporated with the risk of failure, addressing the fear of failure as one of the barriers to the creation of new ventures. Wagner (2007), on the study of German individuals, found gender-specific differences in risk aversion to be an important reason not to become self-employed with only 44 percent of all men, but 56 percent of all women in his sample considered fear of failure as a reason to avoid entrepreneurship. In another research, Carter and Robb (2002) discovered female founders to be more risk averse and less likely to expect debt financing, investing a higher level of their assets relative to wealth. However, the idea that women have lower risk tolerance has been used to explain low growth rates in female-owned firms. In comparison with male entrepreneurs, women may experience more fear of failure when starting a venture because doing so would constitute the pursuit of a career that is socially discouraged for women. Furthermore, some research evidence indicates that women aremore risk averse than men and that this has a negative influence on their propensity to step into self-employment (Shinnar et al., 2012).

Global entrepreneurship monitor

The Global Entrepreneurship Monitor is the world's foremost study of entrepreneurship, providing custom datasets, special reports and expert opinion. To create a comprehensive database, GEM conducted numerous interviews of professors, researchers, specialists and entrepreneurs from more than a hundred countries. Using tried-and-tested methodology and a network of local experts, GEM promotes evidence-based policies towards entrepreneurship around the world (GEM, 2017).

GEM has a special interest in ascertaining what makes a country entrepreneurial. Researchers especially focus on studying the role of adult populations' attitudes and social values toward entrepreneurship. The GEM research community indicates, in general, the importance of values and attitudes of entrepreneurship, such as capability to identify opportunities, having skills, knowledge and experience starting up businesses, knowing recent entrepreneurs, not having fear of failure, thinking that entrepreneurship is a good career choice, and successful entrepreneurs getting high social status and recognition (Coduras, Clemente, and Ruiz, 2016). Figure 8.1 reports the contribution of our targeted economies (United States, Italy and France) in TEA. As it is shown, the United States, with a considerable distance, stands in the highest level of job creation.

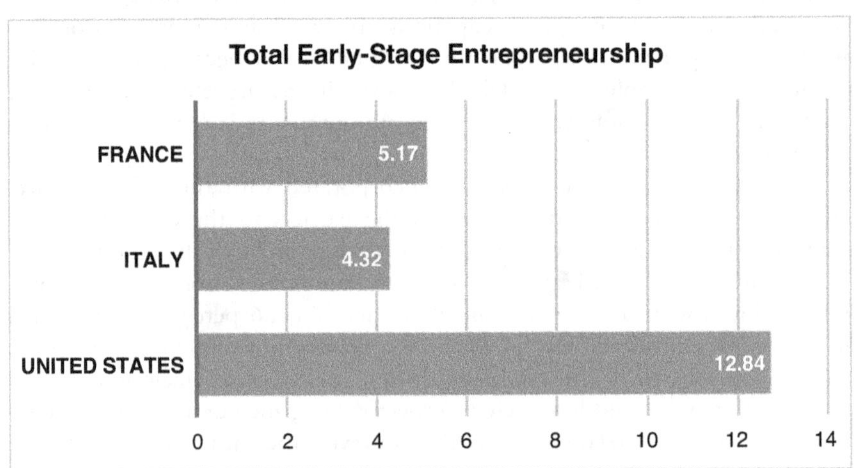

Figure 8.1 TEA involvement by country in 2012 (percentage)

Source: GEM database

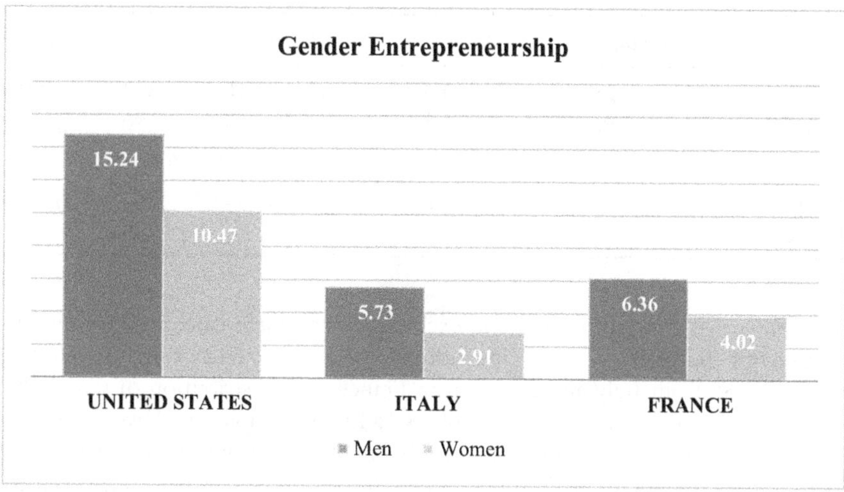

Figure 8.2 The gender gap in TEA by country in 2012 (percentage)

Source: GEM database

Moreover, Figure 8.2 represents the percentage of the gender gap in entrepreneurial activities among these countries. While the United States presents the most engagement of female entrepreneurship, we can see a better situation of gender equality in Italy and France.

3. The empirical study

Sample

This study for the analysis uses the data derived fromGlobal Entrepreneurship Monitor (GEM) as the biggest scholar study in entrepreneurial activities. GEM captures attributes of entrepreneurship in two different data collection methods – National Expert Survey (NES) and Adult Population Survey (APS) – representing specific perceptions on the trends in all kind of entrepreneurship (Singer, Amoros, and Arreola, 2015). The APS collects individual-level data through a standardised survey instrument administered to representative samples of a minimum of 2,000 individuals from adult populations (18 to 64 years old) in each participating country (Holienka et al., 2016).

For our study, we created a pooled sample using GEM APS individual level data for the United States, Italy and France in 2012, resulting in a sample of 11,545 individuals (5,542 from the United States, 2,000 from Italy and 4,003

Table 8.1 Distribution of entrepreneurship by gender and country

	United States		*Italy*		*France*		*Total Size*	
Male	277	3.80%	37	0.51%	80	1.10%	394	5.41%
Female	206	2.83%	19	0.26%	45	0.62%	270	3.71%
N/A	2,922	40.13%	1,110	15.24%	2,586	35.51%	6,618	90.88%
Total by Gender	3,405	46.76%	1,166	16.01%	2,711	37.23%	7,282	100%

from France). After purification and excluding incomplete data, the final sample formed the number of 7,283 individuals, including 5,542 from the United States, 1,166 from Italy and 2,711 from France. The distribution of sample by country and gender is shown in Table 8.1. In the sample, we have identified 664 early-stage entrepreneurs, out of which 394 are owned and managed by men, while women created 270 businesses (6,618 individuals have not specified their gender).

Measure

Dependent variable

GEM explains total early stage entrepreneurial activities as the percentage of the 18 to 64 population who are either nascent entrepreneurs or owner-manager of a new business. We considered the involvement of men and women in TEA as our dependent variables: a) Men (yes = 1, no = 0); b) Women (yes = 1, no = 0).

Explanatory variable

A) motivation – the most important motive for pursuing the opportunity to become an entrepreneur (greater independence, increase personal income, maintain income, other motivation); b) household income – total annual household income classified for country into one of three ranges (lowest/middle/upper 33rd percentile); c) age category (18–24, 25–34, 35–44, 45–54 or 55–64 years); d) education – highest educational attainment (up to some secondary, secondary degree, graduate experience, no education); d) Confidence – perception of having knowledge, skill and experience required to start a new business (yes = 1, no = 0); e) fear of failure – having a fear of failure would prevent one from starting a new business (yes = 1, no = 0).

Control variables

We control for the country of the survey as dummy variables (USA, Italy, France).

Model specification

To explore the motivational drivers in gender entrepreneurship we employed a binomial logistic regression modelling. This model estimates the probability of an event happening. In our case, this event was running an early-stage business activity based on men or women contribution. Thus, we applied two regression model analyses with two different dependent variables – male or female entrepreneurship. The maximum likelihood estimations were used to calculate the logit coefficients denoting changes in the log odds of the dependent variable. Correlations between independent variables were tested and proved not to be problematic (Table 8.2). The selections of final models were conducted through a stepwise regression function using Akaike Information Criterion and then were compared to the real observation using Hosmer and Leme show goodness of fit (GOF) test, which indicated that the models are well fitted.

4. Results

The results of binomial logistic regression applied in order to identify the drivers of men involvement in total early-stage entrepreneurship suggest that ten out of sixteen analysed variables are significant (Table 8.3). The coefficients represent the effect of a variable on the odds of men involvement in entrepreneurship against not being involved in early-stage business at all. The positive coefficient confirms that an increase in a variable raises the likelihood of engagement in ventures through men, keeping all other variables equal.

According to our result, the odds of creating a new business by men are positively affected by motivational perspectives of entrepreneurship. Among all motives, monetary issues, including keeping current income (with the highest coefficients value in the model) and the increase of personal income, stimulate intensively the odds of men entrepreneurship. The sense of having greater independence and other motivations are factors that positively motivate men to start a new business.

Our results also represent that belonging to age categories 25–34 years, 45–54 years and 35–44 years, in order of their coefficients, significantly increase the odds of men's engagement in entrepreneurial activities. Moreover, men holding a secondary degree of education significantly decreases the odds of involvement in early stage business through men. Finally, our results suggest that while confidence of having required knowledge and skill positively lead men into entrepreneurship, the fear of failure significantly decreases the likelihood of involvement in early stage business out of men. Regarding the income category, our results showed no significant behaviour in men entrepreneurship.

The results of binomial logistic regression applied in order to identify the drivers of women's engagement to total early-stage entrepreneurship suggest that eight out of sixteen analysed variables are significant (Table 8.4).

Table 8.2 Correlation matrix

	1	*2*	*3*	*4*	*5*	*6*	*7*	*8*	*9*	*10*	*11*
1. Men											
2. Women	–.047**										
3. Independence	.376**	.283**									
4. Increase	.409**	.222**	-0.023								
5. Maintain Income	.235**	.123**	-0.013	-0.012							
6. Other Motivation	.064**	.156**	-0.007	-0.007	-0.004						
7. Lowest 33% Tile	–.024*	–.023*	–.025*	–.054**	-0.015	-0.021					
8. Middle 33% Tile	–.045**	-0.003	-0.014	–.034**	-0.006	-0.001	–.519**				
9. Upper 33% Tile	.070**	.026*	.040**	.089**	0.021	0.022	–.464**	–.517**			
10. 18–24 Years	–.023*	-0.005	-0.005	-0.005	-0.017	-0.016	.080**	–.027*	–.052**		
11. 25–34 Years	0.022	.026*	0.018	0.002	0.013	0.003	0.004	.037**	–.042**	–.173**	
12. 35–44 Years	.035**	0.009	.043**	.024*	-0.003	0.014	–.047**	-0.003	.050**	–.184**	–.285**
13. 45–54 Years	0.001	-0.017	-0.017	-0.017	0.010	0.006	–.034**	–.032**	.067**	–.189**	–.293**
14. 55–64 Years	–.042**	-0.014	–.041**	-0.005	-0.008	-0.011	0.021	0.020	–.042**	–.174**	–.270**
15. Some Secondary	-0.015	–.055**	–.026*	–.038**	0.004	–.025*	.146**	.036**	–.183**	0.007	-0.001
16. Secondary Degree	–.057**	-0.014	–.034**	–.039**	-0.022	-0.004	.083**	.040**	–.124**	.098**	-0.022
17. Post–Secondary	.037**	.049**	.041**	.045**	0.016	.037**	–.197**	-0.008	.205**	–.025*	.061**
18. Graduate	.060**	.045**	.034**	.060**	0.004	-0.007	–.139**	–.058**	.199**	–.091**	-0.013
19. No Education	-0.016	–.033**	-0.016	–.026*	-0.001	-0.012	.159**	–.046**	–.112**	–.029*	–.061**
20. Confidence	.221**	.153**	.139**	.130**	.061**	.037**	–.113**	–.066**	.181**	–.102**	0.011
21. Fear of Failure	–.089**	–.048**	–.069**	–.059**	–.025*	–.028*	-0.006	.040**	–.035**	-0.022	.052**
22. USA	.113**	.116**	.066**	.103**	.034**	.040**	–.074**	–.116**	.194**	.057**	–.030*
23. Italy	–.043**	–.048**	–.054**	–.059**	–.028*	-0.021	.100**	0.022	–.123**	–.047**	0.000
24. France	–.084**	–.083**	–.028*	–.061**	-0.014	–.025*	0.000	.103**	–.107**	-0.023	.031**

i.*: Correlation is significant at the 0.05 level (2–tailed).
ii. **: Correlation is significant at the 0.01 level (2–tailed).

12	*13*	*14*	*15*	*16*	*17*	*18*	*19*	*20*	*21*	*22*	*23*
–.311**											
–.287**	–.294**										
–.044**	.055**	–0.017									
–0.004	–.033**	–0.012	–.324**								
.042**	–.030*	–.054**	–.379**	–.447**							
.041**	0.000	.038**	–.176**	–.208**	–.244**						
–.050**	.026*	.108**	–.135**	–.159**	–.187**	–.087**					
.056**	0.014	–0.008	–.125**	–.043**	.143**	.095**	–.108**				
.034**	0.008	–.080**	.039**	.023*	–.044**	–0.009	–0.013	–.143**			
–.046**	0.004	.031**	–.251**	–.037**	.188**	.194**	–.116**	.262**	–.130**		
.039**	0.007	–0.013	.140**	.175**	–.316**	.077**	–.038**	–.114**	.113**	–.409**	
0.018	–0.010	–0.022	.153**	–.095**	.046**	–.259**	.149**	–.184**	.048**	–.722**	–.336**

Table 8.3 The analysis of men involvement in entrepreneurial activities, results of logistic regression

Variable	*Odds ratio*	*Coefficient*	*Std. error*	*Z-value*	*P-value*
(Constant)	0.005	–5.324	0.412	–12.933	0.000
Motivation: Greater Independence	44.992	3.806	0.197	19.369	0.000
Motivation: Increase Personal Income	67.880	4.218	0.210	20.118	0.000
Motivation: Maintain Income	80.583	4.389	0.344	12.753	0.000
Motivation: Other	16.951	2.830	0.544	5.204	0.000
Income: Lowest 33%	1.321	0.279	0.179	1.557	0.119
Income: Middle 33%	0.908	-0.096	0.171	-0.562	0.574
Income: Upper 33%	(omitted)				
Age Category: 18–24 Years	1.500	0.405	0.300	1.352	0.176
Age Category: 25–34 Years	1.723	0.544	0.224	2.434	0.015
Age Category: 35–44 Years	1.574	0.454	0.218	2.078	0.038
Age Category: 45–54 Years	1.706	0.534	0.220	2.431	0.015
Age Category: 55–64 Years	(omitted)				
Education: Up To Some Secondary	0.925	–0.078	0.348	–0.225	0.822
Education: Secondary Degree	0.439	–0.824	0.353	–2.333	0.020
Education: Post-Secondary	0.590	–0.527	0.340	–1.552	0.121
Education: Graduate Experience	0.756	–0.280	0.374	–0.749	0.454
Education: No Education	(omitted)				
Confidence	6.577	1.884	0.193	9.782	0.000
Fear of Failure	0.703	–0.353	0.148	-2.381	0.017
Country: USA	1.617	0.481	0.177	2.715	0.007
Country: Italy	2.233	0.803	0.247	3.257	0.001
Country: France	(omitted)				
No. of Observation	7,282				
Residual df	7,263				
Deviance	1732.746				
Log likelihood	–866.373				
GOF test of Hosmer – Lemeshow	0.441				
Akaike Information Criterion (AIC)	1770.746				

Table 8.4 The analysis of women involvement in entrepreneurial activities, results of logistic regression

Variable	*Odds ratio*	*Coefficient*	*Std. error*	*Z-value*	*P-value*
(Constant)	0.002	–6.141	0.522	–11.754	0.000
Motivation: Greater Independence	22.563	3.116	0.199	15.631	0.000
Motivation: Increase Personal Income	15.844	2.763	0.209	13.219	0.000
Motivation: Maintain Income	18.935	2.941	0.330	8.908	0.000
Motivation: Other	65.173	4.177	0.542	7.703	0.000
Income: Lowest 33%	1.601	0.471	0.192	2.445	0.014
Income: Middle 33%	1.655	0.504	0.172	2.929	0.003
Income: Upper 33%	(omitted)				
Age Category: 18–24 Years	1.276	0.244	0.281	0.868	0.385
Age Category: 25–34 Years	1.288	0.253	0.211	1.198	0.231
Age Category: 35–44 Years	0.865	–0.145	0.216	–0.674	0.500
Age Category: 45–54 Years	0.893	–0.114	0.221	–0.514	0.607
Age Category: 55–64 Years	(omitted)				
Education: Up To Some Secondary	1.151	0.141	0.489	0.288	0.773
Education: Secondary Degree	1.968	0.677	0.465	1.455	0.146
Education: Post-Secondary	2.120	0.751	0.458	1.640	0.101
Education: Graduate Experience	2.347	0.853	0.486	1.755	0.079
Education: No Education	(omitted)				
Confidence	3.027	1.108	0.183	6.056	0.000
Fear of Failure	1.079	0.076	0.150	0.505	0.614
Country: USA	2.281	0.824	0.191	4.319	0.000
Country: Italy	1.505	0.409	0.303	1.351	0.177
Country: France	(omitted)				
No. of Observation	7,282				
Residual df	7,263				
Deviance	1678.941				
Log likelihood	–839.470				
GOF test of Hosmer – Lemeshow	0.065				
Akaike Information Criterion (AIC)	1716.941				

Pursuant to the result of Table 8.4, the odds of women entrepreneurship are positively influenced by motivational agents of entrepreneurship. Although the other motivation and having greater independence have a severe impact on female entrepreneurship, the maintenance of current income and the increase of personal income motivate women to start their activities in entrepreneurship.

Our findings also represent the positive relationship between household income (belonging to the lowest and especially middle 33rd percentile) and the odds of being an early-stage female entrepreneur. Finally, as can be seen from the results, females not only were significantly influenced by graduate educational attainment, but also their confidence of having required knowledge and skills stimulates them to be involved in the process of job creation. As for the remaining hypothesized variables, we found no significant relationships in terms of age categories and fear of failure with female entrepreneurship.

5. Discussion

There is a general consensus that the contribution of men in entrepreneurial activities is more than women. The evidence derived from GEM (See Figure 8.1 and Figure 8.2) reveals that in our targeted countries there is a significant gap in gender entrepreneurship. In accordance with the literature and using logistic regression analysis, we found significant effects on gender entrepreneurship, focusing on the motivational drivers and their differences between male and female entrepreneurs. As it is mentioned in prior literature, motivation influences entrepreneurship in three ways: effects on the choice of the individual, influences the intensity of the action and impacts the persistence of action (Braga, Proença, and Ferreira, 2014; Locke, 2000). For this study, we focused on the different motivational aspects of entrepreneurship assessed by GEM – greater independence, increase personal income, maintain income and other motivation.

Our findings on drivers of motivational perspectives of gender entrepreneurship in the United States, Italy and France identify certain common factors as well as some distinctive features. Our analysis reveals that monetary and financial motives have less influence on the intention of women, in comparison with men, to become an entrepreneur. Based on our results, men tend to start a new business with the priority to keep the current income and to increase their income. Their next preferences are to be more independent and other motives (like family business, etc.), while on the opposite side, the sense of being more independent is a significant enthusiasm for female entrepreneurs. Women try to keep their current income, and they look to entrepreneurship as an opportunity to increase their income as their last option.

Regarding household income, our results represent the significant positive relationship between household income and involvement of women in entrepreneurial activities, with the middle-income category showing a stronger relationship than the lowest category, but no significant connection to the men entrepreneurship. It supports the findings of Holienka et al. (2016) who state that this relationship does not mean causality from income to entrepreneurial activity, but rather in the opposite way. To be more precise, women probably do not start businesses because of high income of their household, but, vice versa, they perhaps achieve higher income thanks to being involved in entrepreneurship. It supports our previous claim that confirms the increase of income is one of the significant drivers of female entrepreneurship.

Concerning age, our results indicate that although there is no significant relationship between age categories and female entrepreneurship, men at the age of between 25 to 54 years have positively enhanced entrepreneurship. In terms of education, our evidence suggests that individuals with a graduate degree influence female entrepreneurship while men require a secondary educational attainment to start a new business and enhance entrepreneurship.

Confidence about having the skills, knowledge and experience required to start a business was found as the most important driver leading men and women towards engagement in entrepreneurial efforts, irrespective of their motivation (Holienka et al., 2016; Krueger, Reilly, and Carsrud, 2000). Moreover, our findings illustrate that having confidence stimulates men toward entrepreneurship in comparison with women. Moreover, the impact of fear of failure on the tendency of starting new ventures has been studied frequently and introduced as the main barrier entrepreneurs face (e.g., Cacciotti, Hayton, Mitchell, and Giazitzoglu, 2016; Morgan and Sisak, 2016). Thus, our results are in line with previous literature, indicating that fear of failure stops entrepreneurs, here female entrepreneurs, in their business venturing.

6. Conclusion

Employing the GEM Adult Population Survey 2012 individual-level data for the United States, Italy and France, we analysed the gender entrepreneurship drivers, with the distinction between male and female. This paper aims at adding substantiality to the previous literature addressing the variations between men and women in their motivation of becoming an entrepreneur. Therefore, focusing on keeping current income, increasing personal income, being independent and other motives, we used the motive category provided by GEM to explain the differences between genders in their tendency of starting a new business. In order to acquire a comprehensive perspective, we also investigated the impact of household income, age, education, confidence and fear of failure in the two opposite genders of entrepreneurs and explained their variations.

Our findings suggest there are several similarities, together with certain differences, in men and women entrepreneurship drivers. Based on our findings, different types of motivation, age category, education level, confidence and fear of failure are significantly related to male entrepreneurship, while different types of motivation, household income, education level and confidence have been identified as significant drivers of entrepreneurial activity arising out of women. Although types of motivation were in both cases the most important and, similarly, strong drivers, men were stimulated more by financial motives, like keeping and/or increasing their income, while women were influenced by being more independent and other motives to create a new venture.

As for the implication of our finding, we can create a lot of jobs and increase the number of employment in each economy by recognising the crucial drivers of gender types, specifically women, in entrepreneurship and, eventually, by enhancing their competencies. Another implication of this research warns the government to support entrepreneurs and provide an opportunity for men and women to start new businesses that help to decrease the rate of unemployment. From the micro perspective, we help to identify the importance of particular factors about the support of entrepreneurship focusing on the motivations people choose to become entrepreneurs. If policy makers desire to develop entrepreneurial activities among men and women, emphasis should be put on measures supporting opportunity recognition, entrepreneurial skills and knowledge, enhancing the personal motivation and reducing fear of failure.

As limitations of our analysis, we used the motivational category of entrepreneurship provided by GEM, which has limitations in the capturing of not only different motives but other drivers of gender entrepreneurship. Thus, further directions could expand inquiry on gender entrepreneurship from an individual to also a social and institutional level, applying multi-level analytical techniques and using a customised survey and/or questionnaire. Future research also can be developed in developing countries, as compared to advanced countries. With this classification, we can monitor the different types of motivation for entrepreneurship in the wide spectrum of economies.

References

Angulo-Guerrero, M. J., Pérez-Moreno, S., and Abad-Guerrero, I. M. (2017). How economic freedom affects opportunity and necessity entrepreneurship in the OECD countries. *Journal of Business Research*, 73, 30–37. http://doi.org/10.1016/j.jbusres.2016.11.017

Aparicio, S., Urbano, D., and Audretsch, D. (2016). Institutional factors, opportunity entrepreneurship and economic growth: Panel data evidence. *Technological Forecasting and Social Change*, 102, 45–61. http://doi.org/10.1016/j.techfore.2015.04.006

Baron, R. A., and Ensley, M. D. (2006). Opportunity recognition as the detection of meaningful patterns: Evidence from comparisons of novice and experienced entrepreneurs. *Management Science*, 52(9), 1331–1344.

Braga, J. C., Proença, T., and Ferreira, M. R. (2014). Motivations for social entrepreneurship – Evidences from Portugal. *Tékhne – Review of Applied Management Studies*, 12, 11–21. http://doi.org/10.1016/j.tekhne.2015.01.002

Bruni, A., Gherardi, S., and Poggio, B. (2004). Doing gender, doing entrepreneurship: An ethnographic account of intertwined practices. *Gender, Work and Organization*, 11(4), 406–429. http://doi.org/10.1111/j.1468-0432.2004.00240.x

Cacciotti, G., Hayton, J. C., Mitchell, J. R., and Giazitzoglu, A. (2016). A reconceptualization of fear of failure in entrepreneurship. *Journal of Business Venturing*, 31(3), 302–325. http://doi.org/10.1016/j.jbusvent.2016.02.002

Carter, N. M., and Robb, A. (2002). The role of risk orientation on financing expectations in new venture creation: Does sex matter. *Frontiers of Entrepreneurship Research*, 2002, 170–181.

Casson, M. (1982). *The Entrepreneur: An Economic Theory*. Rowman & Littlefield.

Coduras, A., Clemente, J. A., and Ruiz, J. (2016). A novel application of fuzzy-set qualitative comparative analysis to GEM data. *Journal of Business Research*, 69(4), 1265–1270. http://doi.org/10.1016/j.jbusres.2015.10.090

Dana, L. P., and Wright, R. W. (2009). International entrepreneurship: Research priorities for the future. *International Journal of Globalisation and Small Business*, 3(1), 90–134. http://doi.org/10.1504/IJGSB.2009.021572

DeTienne, D. R., and Chandler, G. N. (2007). The role of gender in opportunity identification. *Entrepreneurship Theory and Practice*, 31(3), 365–386.

Douhan, R., and van Praag, M. (2009). Entrepreneurship, wage employment and control in an occupational choice framework. Working Paper, Copenhagen Business School, Copenhagen, Denmark.

Eckhardt, J. T., and Shane, S. A. (2003). Opportunities and entrepreneurship. *Journal of Management*, 29(3), 333–349. http://doi.org/10.1016/S0149-2063(02)00225-8

Elam, A. B. (2014). *Gender and Entrepreneurship*. Cheltenham, UK: Edward Elgar Publishing.

Foss, N. J., and Klein, P. G. (2012). *Organizing Entrepreneurial Judgment: A New Approach to the Firm*. Cambridge: Cambridge University Press.

Fossen, F. M., and Büttner, T.J.M. (2013). The returns to education for opportunity entrepreneurs, necessity entrepreneurs, and paid employees. *Economics of Education Review*, 37, 66–84. http://doi.org/10.1016/j.econedurev.2013.08.005

Fuentelsaz, L., González, C., Maícas, J. P., and Montero, J. (2015). How different formal institutions affect opportunity and necessity entrepreneurship. *BRQ Business Research Quarterly*, 18(4), 246–258. http://doi.org/10.1016/j.brq.2015.02.001

GEM. (2017). *GEM Global Entrepreneurship Monitor*. Retrieved January 26, 2017, from www.gemconsortium.org/

Hanson, S., and Blake, M. (2007). Changing the gender of entrepreneurship. In *A Companion to Feminist Geography* (pp. 179–193). Nelson, L. and Seager, J. (Eds) Blackwell Publishing Ltd, Oxford, United Kingdom. http://doi.org/10.1002/9780470996898.ch13

Holienka, M., Jančovičová, Z., and Kovačičová, Z. (March 2016). Drivers of women entrepreneurship in Visegrad countries: GEM evidence. *Procedia – Social and Behavioral Sciences*, 220, 124–133. http://doi.org/10.1016/j.sbspro.2016.05.476

Kaish, S., and Gilad, B. (1991). Characteristics of opportunities search of entrepreneurs versus executives: Sources, interests, general alertness. *Journal of Business Venturing*, 6(1), 45–61.

Kelley, D. J., Singer, S., and Herrington, M. (2012). The global entrepreneurship monitor. *2011 Global Report, GEM 2011*, 7.

Krueger, N. F. (2007). What lies beneath? The experiential essence of entrepreneurial thinking. *Entrepreneurship Theory and Practice*, 31(1), 123–138.

Krueger, N. F., Reilly, M. D., and Carsrud, A. L. (2000). Competing models of entrepreneurial intentions. *Journal of Business Venturing*, 15(5), 411–432.

Langevang, T., Gough, K. V, Yankson, P.W.K., Owusu, G., and Osei, R. (2015). Bounded entrepreneurial vitality: The mixed embeddedness of female entrepreneurship. *Economic Geography*, 91(4), 449–473. http://doi.org/10.1111/ecge.12092

Locke, E. (2000). Motivation, cognition, and action: An analysis of studies of task goals and knowledge. *Applied Psychology*, 49(3), 408–429.

Lotti, F. (2006). *Entrepreneurship: Is there a Gender Gap*? LEM Working Paper Series, Pisa.

Mattis, M. C. (2004). Women entrepreneurs: Out from under the glass ceiling. *Women in Management Review*, 19(3), 154–163.

McGowan, P., Redeker, C. L., Cooper, S. Y., and Greenan, K. (2012). Female entrepreneurship and the management of business and domestic roles: Motivations, expectations and realities. *Entrepreneurship & Regional Development*, 24(1–2), 53–72. http://doi.org/10.1080/08985626.2012.637351

Mitchell, R. K., Mitchell, J. R., and Smith, J. B. (2008). Inside opportunity formation: Enterprise failure, cognition, and the creation of opportunities. *Strategic Entrepreneurship Journal*, 2(3), 225–242.

Morgan, J., and Sisak, D. (2016). Aspiring to succeed: A model of entrepreneurship and fear of failure. *Journal of Business Venturing*, 31(1), 1–21. http://doi.org/10.1016/j.jbusvent.2015.09.002

Reynolds, P. D., Bygrave, W. D., Autio, E., Cox, L. W., and Hay, M. (2002). *Global Entrepreneurship Monitor Executive Report 2002.* Kauffman Center for Entrepreneurial Leadership at the Ewing Marion Kauffman Foundation, Kansas City, MO.

Shane, S. (2001). Technological opportunities and new firm creation. *Management Science*, 47(2), 205–220.

Shane, S., and Venkataraman, S. (2000). The promise of entrepreneurship as a field of research. *Academy of Management Review*, 25(1), 217–226.

Shepherd, D. A., and DeTienne, D. R. (2005). Prior knowledge, potential financial reward, and opportunity identification. *Entrepreneurship Theory and Practice*, 29(1), 91–112.

Shinnar, R. S., Giacomin, O., and Janssen, F. (2012). Entrepreneurial perceptions and intentions: The role of gender and culture. *Entrepreneurship Theory and Practice*, 36(3), 465–493. http://doi.org/10.1111/j.1540-6520.2012.00509.x

Short, J. C., Ketchen, D. J., Shook, C. L., and Ireland, R. D. (2010). The concept of 'opportunity'in entrepreneurship research: Past accomplishments and future challenges. *Journal of Management*, 36(1), 40–65. http://doi.org/10.1177/0149206309342746

Singer, S., Amoros, J. E., and Arreola, D. M. (2015). Global entrepreneurship monitor 2014 global report. *Global Entrepreneurship Research Association* London Business School, London, 1: 1–116.

Sköld, B., and Tillmar, M. (2015). Resilient gender order in entrepreneurship: The case of Swedish welfare industries. *International Journal of Gender and Entrepreneurship*, 7(1), 2. http://doi.org/10.1108/IJGE-09-2013-0057

Stevenson, H. H., and Jarillo, J. C. (1990). A paradigm of entrepreneurship: Entrepreneurial management. *Entrepreneurship: Concepts, Theory and Perspective*, 11, 17–27. http://doi.org/10.1007/978-3-540-48543-8_7

Thebaud, S. (2010). *Institutions, Cultural Beliefs and the Maintenance of Gender Inequality in Entrepreneurship Across Industrialized Nations.* SSRN. Retrieved from: https://ssrn.com/abstract=1664554 or http://dx.doi.org/10.2139/ssrn.1664554

Wagner, J. (2007). What a difference a Y makes-female and male nascent entrepreneurs in Germany. *Small Business Economics*, 28(1), 1–21.

Warnecke, T. (September 2013). Entrepreneurship and gender: An institutional perspective. *Journal of Economic Issues*, 47, 455–464. http://doi.org/10.2753/JEI0021-3624470219

Wilson, F., Kickul, J., and Marlino, D. (2007). Gender, entrepreneurial self-efficacy, and entrepreneurial career intentions: Implications for entrepreneurship education1. *Entrepreneurship Theory and Practice*, 31(3), 387–406. http://doi.org/10.1111/j.1540-6520.2007.00179.x

Zhao, H., Seibert, S. E., and Hills, G. E. (2005). The mediating role of self-efficacy in the development of entrepreneurial intentions. *Journal of Applied Psychology*, 90(6), 1265.

9 The impact of family structure, marital status and the parental model on the business creation process among young Tunisian entrepreneurs

Emna Baccari-Jamoussi, Adnane Maâlaoui and Severine Leloarne-Lemaire

1. Introduction

Family is a social system that is governed by laws and habits, which enable it to take care of its members and meet their needs. Family offers cohesion among its "members" over time and through hardships. It works to protect the interpersonal relationships, emotion and affection within the family and cultivates a sense of responsibility and loyalty to the family system. It also provides economic security to its members. Thus, family satisfies deep needs for emotional and social belonging, affection and intimacy and provides a sense of identity (Kepner, 1983: 60).

Families are the most important providers of start-up capital to new ventures around the world (Astrachan, Zahra, and Sharma, 2003; Astrachan, 2010); yet their roles remain relatively little understood. We are interested to contributing toward filling that gap. Aldrich and Cliff (2003), Heck and Mishra (2008), Rogoff and Heck (2003) and others have worked at the intersection of family and entrepreneurship. Stewart (2003) focused on kinship and family business, and his research may be useful. However, as Dyer and Handler (1994) and Basco (2013) have indicated, there is a lack of explanatory theories that can help us to understand the complex relationship between entrepreneurs and their families through the time variable.

A review of the literature on entrepreneurship, and particularly the work of Saporta (2002), shows that the family as a variable is largely underestimated, if not occluded, in most of this research. Nevertheless, some authors have begun to consider the family's impact, noting, for example, that successful entrepreneurs could be distinguished from others by the richness of their "vision." This difference is not *a priori* the result of a spontaneous generalization, but in many cases had its origin in the paternal family environment and even in a "great father" figure who served as a sort of "incubator" (Filion, 1991).

Whether seen as an institution or as a system of relationships, the family is the first social space in which the resources of the organization are identified and put into practice by individuals. Indeed, Dagenais (2000) argues, "the family is neither more nor less than the rooting mode of beings in existence, acting directly as an assignment and reappropriation vector by individuals, under their action and organization possibilities." Thus, it is fair to say that we organize ourselves through our family experience.

Our research goal is to scrutinize family involvement in the entrepreneurial process among young entrepreneurs in the context of Tunisia. The seminal work by Pierre Bourdieu – a pioneer in developing our current understanding of cultural, social and symbolic capital, who studied North African countries – is useful in framing these ideas in a context, and Zahra (2007) highlights the unique context of our study for entrepreneurship research. Considering the typology of the business forms in Tunisia, family firms take on the traditional and dominant form; parental is the historical structure, but the marital structure is running its course according to the socio-cultural evolution of the country.

Some years ago, unemployment had tensed the situation in Tunisia, making it awkward; then decision-makers believed private initiative was the cure. Entrepreneurial activities in Tunisia, especially after the 14/1/2011 events, are being boosted by exogenous (e.g. foreign NGOs) and endogen (e.g., official incentives) factors. In recent years, Tunisia has witnessed a considerable increase in business start-ups by young people as more and more young Tunisians dash into the business world with an interest in an entrepreneurial career. In 2005, the Centre for Young Leaders (CJD) had an opinion poll with 80 young company directors, each younger than 40. The majority responded, "Yes" to "I am a potential investor" and agreed that investment is the mainspring of the economy, as well as the mainspring of their activity. Such a situation is leading to an "entrepreneurial explosion", according to project launching statistics, but entrepreneurship is not only the launching act; it is a continuous process, and we are seeking to explore some success factors of such processes.

First, we propose a review of the entrepreneurial process based on family as an institution. Then, we discuss that process from an anthropological perspective. Therefore, we do not consider the family as a venture resource, but it focalizes on the family structure as a factor explaining the entrepreneurial process modelling. Next, we present the propositions of this research. Finally, we interpret the results obtained using this exploratory qualitative approach and the characteristics of the different entrepreneurship models that are relevant to young Tunisian entrepreneurs.

2. Literature review

According to Danes, Lee, Stafford, and Heck (2008):

> members of family and business may interact with the community. The impetus for the manner and degree to which that interaction with community occurs is rooted in meanings family members give to that interaction. For the ethnic families, interaction with their communities is imbued with multiple meanings. As an intermediary between the community and the firm, the owning family provides a fertile environment of community values,

attitudes, and beliefs that serve as inputs to the firm and may add further meaning to the firm's direct interaction with the community.

However, for the Tunisian context, ethnic families' and communities' interaction are insignificant to be validated by a specific study. Therefore, this work is looking to explain the interaction of some key variables, along the entrepreneurial process, without examining eventual underlying business success factors (family business, etc.).

2.1 Entrepreneurial process of young entrepreneurs

Fayolle (2004) argued that the process of starting a business is a subject of modelling that has generated many approaches. This process has become the focus of many studies of entrepreneurship, and the dominant concepts in this field are at the heart of many research agendas. Gartner (1985) identified six behaviours that are components of entrepreneurial activity: "the entrepreneur locates a business opportunity," "the entrepreneur accumulates resources," "the entrepreneur market products and services," "the entrepreneur produces products," "the entrepreneur builds an organization" and "the entrepreneur meets the requirements of government and society." Other researchers have also adopted this idea of the entrepreneurship process.

Bygraveet al.'s (1991: 14) definition of the entrepreneurial process involves "all the functions, activities and actions associated with the perception of opportunity and creation of an organization." In sum, according to Gasse (2002), the creation of a business involves several steps, which can be divided into three stages: namely, the design or pre-incubation, starting-up and operationalization phases. We are interested primarily in the start-up phase. However, the literature is full of entrepreneurial models of the process of starting a business without reaching a consensus. Research now suggests that the latter is marked by various stages. According to Bruyat (1993), there are three phases that characterize the creative process: initiation, commitment and survival/development.

2.1 The conceptual approach to the institution and family anthropology

An institution is a system of rules that prescribes behaviour and limits the free will of individuals (Huault, 2002). Complying with social norms generates many advantages for businesses, ranging from legitimacy and increased prestige to social support through the recognition of the profession and its activity. Everyone agrees that institutions can take many forms and can include family, school, government, church, businesses, collective agreements and ministerial decrees. Indeed, institutions can be defined very broadly as habits of thought and behaviour, values, rules, representations, beliefs, and cultures. In addition to this very general vision of the institution, three main types of institutions have been identified: cognitive institutions, coercive institutions and normative institutions.

It is to Di Maggio and Powell (1983) that we owe this distinction. A cognitive institution can be defined as a pattern of thought that arises from patterns of behaviour.

Routinely, according to Berger and Luckman (1989), habits of thought and reason become institutions in a relatively conscious and rapid manner. Deeply rooted habits that become cognitive institutions transition from a state of social construction into a state of social reality. The cognitive institution is the habitus of Bourdieu (1972) that shapes the representations of groups and individuals who "streamline" their behaviour and legitimizes decisions based on concern regarding identity and identification. Therefore, for Bourdieu, the rationality can be determined to the emotional level by the unconscious or the sociocultural determiners

In this framework, the company is considered a cognitive institution with the habits, history, culture, values and skills associated with that concept. Bouchikhi and Kimberly (1996) include all of these components in the "corporate identity" of the company. This institutional line of thinking is "a set of practices and symbolic constructions constituting the structural principles of a field and are available to organizations and individuals to build this field" (Friedland and Alford, 1991: 248). It includes all of the belief systems of actors in the field, which orient their activities and give them meaning (Scott, Ruef, Mendel, and Caronna, 2000: 20).

2.1.1 *Family as an institution*

The family as a socio-cultural reality manifests through daily discourse and practices. The socio-cultural process through which we build this institution called the family is revealed as we participate in the business of life. However, the concept of the family is not fixed; instead, it derives from the meaning attributed to that concept in light of experiences and understanding developed in daily life (Gubrium and Holstein, 1990). In this sense, family is a language that we all use every day and that we use to describe our relationships.

Family is a universe of representations and sensations that, through language, can persuade, suggest and inform. Thus, family is as much a way of thinking about and developing relationships as it is a set of concrete emotional, cognitive and political ties. When we speak of the character of the family, its structures and its functions, we refer to a concrete and obvious purpose (either tangible or intangible) and to experiences marked by substance and borders.

2.1.2 *Family anthropology*

Anthropology illustrates the extreme variability of family arrangements based on specific contexts and rules. It is obvious that the concept of family is not universal and does not always feature the same structures and the same dynamics. Instead, family anthropology and sociology enable us to isolate the particular character of family in the multiple contexts (economic, political and symbolic) in which it operates. From this perspective, it may be the social form of family that is most multifaceted and least unique. Goode (1970) and Todd (1983,1984) are expert authors who have examined the various existing family types in the world in different eras. They note that comparing field studies suggest that the family institutions have existed in every society but have taken various forms. The examples of Western, Islamic, African, Indian, Chinese and Japanese families (Goode, 1970) are excellent ones. The work of Todd (1983) indicates that the family structure is a system that influences the behaviour of all family members and their perception of reality (Parker, 2016).

One author develops a typology of family structures, including one that is centred on an authoritarian patriarch and others that are very liberal and give more autonomy to children. The same author supports the hypothesis that family relationships (between parents and children or between husband and wife) are used as a model for political relationships and define the relationship of the individual to governmental authority. The author examines freedom and equality in several societies in both Western and Eastern cultures. Based on these basic criteria, four typical family structures emerge: the absolute nuclear family, the egalitarian nuclear family, the authoritarian family and the community family. Todd (1985) presents those family structures as follows:

- The absolute nuclear family is liberal and egalitarian. Family members are independent and oriented towards personal accomplishment. There is no specific norm regarding inheritance.
- The egalitarian nuclear family emphasizes the concepts of freedom and fairness. Property is divided equally among the heirs. Children are also independent and are oriented towards personal achievement.
- The authoritarian family emphasizes inequality and authority. Ultimate authority is granted to the father, and a sole heir is appointed. The relationship between father and son is pre-determined. The other children have to leave the family circle.
- The community family values fairness and authority. The children live with their parents in an extended family, and all are treated equally in terms of their rights to inheritance. Still, the patriarch retains the ultimate authority in such families.

In testing these assumptions, we seek to identify a link between young entrepreneurs and the family structure that dominates the Tunisian context. We suggest that family structure influences young entrepreneurs in creating businesses and conducting the entrepreneurial process. However, the diversity of family structures identified by Todd implies that the behaviour of young entrepreneurs will differ according to their particular family structures. More specifically, does belonging to an absolute nuclear family or to an egalitarian, authoritarian or community-based family really influence young Tunisian entrepreneurs in the creation of their businesses?

Goode and Todd are author specialists who examined the various existing family typologies all over the world at various periods.

The use of Todd's work was motivated by his studies of the Arabic/Oriental family context and was limited to determine the family structure type.

2.2 Marital status and family support

In his work, Todd (1983) specified that family structure in the Arab world is characterized by community-sharing among family members, respect for the values of fairness and authority and a minimum of independence. This finding has been verified for Tunisia. A young entrepreneur who lives in a community family will be dominated by a strong family coalition. In the Tunisian environment, singles live with their parents and are strongly supported by them. However, when a child marries, he leaves his family and his childhood home, and he begins to create a new community family structure of his own. The structure that is created is largely independent of the parents. A husband who has founded a company will be less able to seek support from his parents. This leads us to propose the following:

Proposition 1: The origin of family support depends on the marital status of the entrepreneur.

Proposition 1.1: In the Tunisian context, a single entrepreneur is primarily supported by his/her parents.

Proposition 1.2: In the Tunisian context, a married entrepreneur is primarily supported by his/her spouse.

2.3 Influence of the parental model

Most of the literature argues that a high percentage of entrepreneurs have fathers who were themselves entrepreneurs (Hisrich and Brush, 1987). Many researchers have shown that history, traditions and family involvement in business promote the development of future entrepreneurs. The role of family (parents, uncles, aunts, cousins) provides an environment that encourages young entrepreneurs to learn from the experiences of others and to develop a positive attitude towards business (Mann, 1990).

The family environment is an incentive for a young person, and the child may mimic a family member (usually the father) and decide to create his/her own business. Most entrepreneurs have parents who own or have started their own business (Sweeney, 1988). It is therefore assumed that this filial link explains the desire to form a business (Collins and Moore, 1964). Other authors argue that having parents who are entrepreneurs or craftsmen gives children a taste for entrepreneurship. Studies by Jacobowitz and Vilder showed that 72 percent of entrepreneurs have one or more parents who are entrepreneurs. Litvak and Maule, Kierulff and Scanlan reported an average figure of 50 percent (as cited by Lacasse (1990). The family environment and the sociocultural context exert an influence on potential entrepreneurs but does not solely generate the intention to start a business. However, for graduates, as for the rest of the population, having a father who is a business owner doubles or triples the probability of becoming an entrepreneur.

An extensive survey conducted with more than 50,000 people in 28 countries found that the perception of business opportunities in one's context and the presence of model entrepreneurs are significantly associated with being an entrepreneur. Knowing an entrepreneur reduces the uncertainty inherent in the process of entrepreneurship, thus encouraging aspiring entrepreneurs to execute their projects. For Rocher (1964), the parental relationship is the backbone of traditional social organization. This relationship is the hub of the entire collective life, which unfolds around it and is shaped by it.

Bandura (1977) argues that the actions of others influence the behaviour of individuals. He stresses the action of those who really matter to us, especially our parents. Self-efficacy is achieved through personal experience, learning through sharing experiences with others and verbal persuasion. For example, Bandura argues that if a son sees his mother, a female entrepreneur, as a positive and successful model, he will tend to try to imitate her in the future. According to Scherer, Adams, Carley, and Wiebe (1989), individuals who perceive their parents' entrepreneurial experience as successful tend to follow the parental model (Bee and Neubaum, 2014) more than those who do not have a parental model to follow. Admittedly, however, many children who do have this type of model refuse to be confined by it and reject the entrepreneurial path as a career choice (Brockhous and Horwitz, 1986).

Similarly, Dunn and Holtz-Eakins (1996) indicate that the presence of a mother entrepreneur will not necessarily inspire her children to choose to become entrepreneurs. In addition, in yet another scenario, some young people will choose the entrepreneurial path and create a company despite not having a parental model for this type of work.

Other researchers, such as Ronstadt (1984) and Dyer (1992), support the idea that entrepreneurs are born in a home in which the father and/or mother work independently. For these children, this parenting model encourages and promotes entrepreneurial behaviour. According to Gasse and D'Amours (2000), entrepreneurs are usually from families in which parents or relatives are themselves in business or work on their own. Still more research indicates that this applies to 50 percent of entrepreneurs. Presumably, a child who grows up in this kind of family considers his/her parents or relatives to be his/her role models.

Children of entrepreneurs generally prefer to set up their own business rather than working for others (Dyer, 1992. They are destined to be future entrepreneurs themselves (Hout, 1984; Lentz and Laband, 1990;Holt, Madison, and Kellermanns, 2016). This trend originates in family support for the entrepreneurial path.

In investigating the role of family size and family structure in the probability of choosing self-employment, Hout and Rosen (2000) suggest that the nature of family relationships depends on the ancestral origins of each family. For example, there are parents who are involved in the lives of their children beginning at a young age and others who are not. The success of a young person who seeks to set up his/her own business is dependent on human capital, which varies from one group to another.

The sociological and economics literature suggests that it is obvious that family structure affects the education and orientation of a child, helping to ensure that s/he chooses a career that suits him/her (Butcher and Case, 1994). These assumptions converge with what we have advanced in the family anthropology section above. However, in Arab-Muslim societies, which are characterized by a high level of commitment of individuals to their families, relationships and links between parents and sons persist even after they become autonomous and independent. Thus, "The most favourable environment for a creative candidate seems to be a family environment that combines a positive image of private business" (Bragard, 1987: 10). Moreover, Saporta (2002) reached a conclusion that is both ambiguous and complex. Family can play a powerful, encouraging role in families with a business model, but unfortunately, a more nebulous family influence can discourage young graduate school students from choosing entrepreneurship as a career.

The extended family can be an obstacle to individual motivation for work and entrepreneurship. This negative evaluation is challenged by researchers like Wong (1985), Lau (1988) and Redding (1990), who show that the "family business" is directly responsible for the extraordinary success of the Chinese in Hong Kong.

This example refutes the argument that traditional family culture is an obstacle to economic development. Dyer (1992) noted that entrepreneurs are discouraged from creating their own businesses because they are not backed or supported by their families. A family usually wants its children to earn a stable income in a traditional occupation. The uncertain nature of an entrepreneurial career is perceived by the family as a burden to be avoided. However, the family can play an important role for an entrepreneur, providing him/her with liquidity, contacts, and access to markets. It can also provide support and relief for an entrepreneur who is starting a business. Thus, the family is seen as a success factor in business creation.

Dyer and Handler (1994) argue that the role of the family is a more important determinant than any other traditional success factor. As a result, they insisted on conducting more systematic research on the subject. However, the family can also play another role by discouraging the entrepreneur and can therefore act as an obstacle to business creation by withholding funding and support and by decreasing the potential entrepreneur's confidence.

In our research we consider "the parental model" is a person having a significant effect (inspirational, mentoring, etc.) over the entrepreneur and having necessarily a parental relation with him.

Based on this overview of the parental model, we present the following proposition and underlying sub-propositions:

Proposition 2: The types of family capital enjoyed by the young entrepreneur depend on the following:

- **The parental model.**
- **The marital status (single or married) of the young entrepreneur.**

According to socio-cultural perception, married young people must fend for themselves; on the other hand, families with no entrepreneurs have an aversion to enterprising, preferring for their children a salary employment to entrepreneurial adventure; young entrepreneurs who belong to such families receive family inhibition instead of capital, and regarding the marital state, this negative leverage is accentuated for married ones. Based on proposition 2, three sub-propositions emerge:

Proposition 2.1: Young single entrepreneurs who belong to a family with an entrepreneur benefit from a wider range of capital than those who belong to a family with no entrepreneurs.

Proposition 2.2: Young single entrepreneurs who belong to a family with no entrepreneurs benefit only from financial capital.

Proposition 2.3: Married young entrepreneurs who belong to a family with no entrepreneurs receive minimal family capital.

These path proposals and sub-propositions allow us to present proposition 3, as we are interested in the allocation of family capital.

Proposition 3: The allocation of family capital throughout the creation process depends on

- **The parental family model**
- **The marital status (single or married) of the young entrepreneur.**

Proposition 3.1: Young single entrepreneurs who belong to a family with an entrepreneur benefit from family capital throughout the process.

Proposition 3.2: Married young entrepreneurs who belong to a family with an entrepreneur benefit from family capital only at the beginning of the creation process.

Proposition 3.3: Young single entrepreneurs who belong to a family with no entrepreneurs receive family capital only at the beginning of the creation process.

Proposition 3.4: Young single entrepreneurs who belong to a family with no entrepreneurs receive no family capital.

Interestingly, family capital also generates disadvantages. These disadvantages are mainly dependent on the parental model (whether or not the person belongs to an entrepreneurial family). We can assume that a young entrepreneur will benefit from his/her parent's experience as an entrepreneur.

Proposition 4: The disadvantages associated with family capital depend on the parental model of the young entrepreneur. Young entrepreneurs who belong to families with no entrepreneurs will experience more disadvantages than those who belong to families with entrepreneurs.

3. Research methodology

According to Baumard and Ibert (2003), "one of the main choices that the researcher must make is that of an approach and data adequate to the research question." This finding incorporates two aspects of methodological thinking. On the one hand, there is the pursued aim of exploring, building, testing and improving what is known and discovering what is not. On the other hand, there is what is already available, accessible and feasible: what has already been done. In this sense, the qualitative approach is doubly justified in our case because we are examining a less studied population and a less explored phenomenon. Influenced by Dana and Dana (2005), this qualitative approach will enable us to identify the impact of family structure, marital status and the parental model on the business creation process among young Tunisian entrepreneurs. Indeed, these methods seek to explore and analyse social phenomena and therefore are intended to help researchers understand them in context. Thus, we collected data through semi-structured interviews.

Our sample consists of 20 young Tunisian entrepreneurs. This choice is consistent with what is proposed by Glaser and Strauss (1967: 62), concerning theoretical saturation: "In trying to reach saturation, he maximizes differences in his groups in order to maximize the varieties of data bearing on the category, and thereby develops as many diverse properties of the category as possible" (Glaser and Strauss, 1967).

The interviewees were contacted by email to present our purpose and research objectives; then, we used telephone calls to make appointments. We experienced substantial difficulty identifying young entrepreneurs and making appointments during this step. This difficulty was no doubt due to their very busy schedules.

The individuals were identified partly through the updated directory of entrepreneurs that is generally available at the Agency for Promotion of Industry (API). The group of young entrepreneurs (Table 9.1) was selected through rational choice based on predefined criteria.

Table 9.1 Profile of the respondents

	Age when firm was created/ Current age	*Gender*	*Marital status*	*Formal education*	*Sector/industry*	*Number of employees*	*Duration of the interviews*
Interview 1	24 /35	M	M	Master's degree in tax law, Tunisia	Services (advice and multidisciplinary assistance	6	1H27
Interview 2	27 / 31	F	S	Master's degree in international trade, Tunisia	Catering services	7	1H18
Interview 3	24 / 35	M	S	Engineering school, Algeria	Rental services	40	2H06
Interview 4	27 /31	M	S	Master's degree, researcher in entrepreneurship and project management, Tunisia	Real estate services	5	1H11
Interview 5	25 / 35	M	M	Engineering degree in food processing, Tunisia	Food-processing industry	8	1H27
Interview 6	26 /31	M	M	Doctor in science of management, France	IT service	9	1H13
Interview 7	28 /35	M	S	Master's degree in finance and international trade, USA	Industry building materials	14	1H26
Interview 8	26 /31	M	S	Master's degree in entrepreneurship and project management, Tunisia	Food-processing industry	40	1H08
Interview 9	28/ 34	M	S	Engineering school, Tunisia	IT service	7	1H42
Interview 10	26/31	F		Master's degree in management at HEC, Tunisia	Services (training)	11	1H06

	Age when firm was created/ Current age	*Gender*	*Marital status*	*Formal education*	*Sector/industry*	*Number of employees*	*Duration of the interviews*
Interview 11	24 /34	M	S	Engineering school, France	IT service	22	1H22
Interview 12	25 /31	F	M	Master's degree in Management at ISG, Tunisia	Services (training)	12	1H18
Interview 13	27 / 32	M	S	Master's degree in public communication, Canada	Trade	11	1H33
Interview 14	28 /33	M	M	Master's degree in finance, Tunisia	Cleaning services	10	1H18
Interview 15	28 /33	M	S	Advanced technician diploma, Tunisia	Parapharmaceutical industry	7	1H21
Interview 16	25 /31	F	M	Master's degree in firm management, Belgium	Painting services	25	1H37
Interview 17	25 /35	M	S	Master's degree in international trade, Tunisia	Materials rental services	6	2H03
Interview 18	25 /33	M	S	Master's degree in Management, France	Industry	25	1H03
Interview 19	26 / 33	M	S	Master's degree in management, Tunisia	Industry/services	7	1H23
Interview 20	28 /33	M	M	Engineering school, Tunisia	Industry	6	1H29

The sample selection criteria were:

- Under 30 entrepreneur age
- Ex-nihilo enterprise type
- Entrepreneur supported by their family independently of the family opinion (favourable, unfavourable, neutral)
- Rejection of entrepreneurial team creations; only individual creations are selected
- Non specific business line

The respondents had a mean age of 26.1 and a fairly high level of education (Baccalauréat + 2, Bac + 4, and Bac + 5). The young entrepreneurs whom we interviewed facilitated our access to other young people starting businesses. There was no random selection; all of the young entrepreneurs were interviewed using the same approach. Our sample is non-probability-based and was not chosen randomly; rather, it is rational and includes cases with the same characteristics.

All creations are *ex nihilo* creations. The data were subjected to a thematic content analysis. According to Creswell (1998), the richness of a qualitative research process is generated by the attempt to create a profile of complex phenomena, analyse words, provide a detailed account of the vision of the informants and conduct a study within the framework of a set of lived experiences. We also attempted to connect the conceptual framework of this research with the field overall to ensure theoretical sensitivity. This approach allowed us to analyse the various interviews in depth while remaining open to the emergence of new explanations for the studied phenomenon.

As we are in a relatively young age as a field and according to Gioia et al. (2013), it is imperative that we remain open to new concept development and new theory development as well. It is clear, though, that we should have approaches or methods that can generate new concepts and grounded theories not only via impressionistic studies, but also via qualitatively rigorous inductive studies. So we suggest for future studies adopting such approach.

The use of case study approach for research purposes was motivated by the nature of young entrepreneurs researches that should be, as a first interim step, exploratory, due to scarcity of similar studies. Paturel (2004) had the same position specifically for francophone entrepreneurship studies.

In the sense of Robichaud (2001), collection of information relative, in the conditions of starting up, to the approach pursued by the young Tunisian entrepreneurs and the main difficulties which they face are imbued with a "hard to do" nature. To address this difficulty, the most obvious solution was to use qualitative tools through case studies.

However, it does not mean the rejection of the quantitative methodologies option, which seems to be appropriate for the validation of the empirical.

The case study is chosen as a data gathering method. This choice is driven by two reasons: the first one is that the research does not seek for checking an actual comportment of an event, but it's an exploration of the real context of the enterprise creation by young Tunisian entrepreneurs. The second reason motivating our choice is that we are concentrated upon contemporary events (those more recent) rather than historical ones.

The computer software used in our analysis is Nvivo, which seems suitable for the thematic analysis adopted in our case. This software allows the researcher to treat important masses of data in a more iterative, less linear way. It is the format that helps him to study dynamically measure the complexity of the data. The Nvivo process starts with the categorization of gathering data

The coding represents operations consisting in cutting the data (speeches, texts, etc.) in analysis units and in defining the categories, then it places the units in those categories. It is a crucial and important stage of the data analysis.

The coding consists in dividing our corpus in so many segments relative to each of the codes that suggests to us its reading. The procedure is simple; it is enough to read the text and to attribute a specific coding to each sentence, or the sentences set, being the same theme.

Once the whole corpus was codified, it is a question of refining these multiple codes to transform them into free categories. We leave codes generated in the reading of the text, and we compare the portions of texts codified with terms semantically close, so as to eliminate doubloons, by merging under the same code the portions of texts codified by synonyms, but also so as to raise the ambiguities by creating new codes within textual sets codified in a too vague way.

This progressive refining of the coding leads to transform the codes into categories. This primary categorization of our whole corpus led us to isolate 111 free categories (free nodes), each of them sending back in a set of comments moved forward on themes identical but held by diverse interviewees. They are said free categories because they are not connected. So, in the term of this first stage of the analysis, we divided our corpus into 111 thematic segments, which were suggested to us by the reading of all the re-transcribed interviews.

The second stage of the analysis consists in giving coherence to this juxtaposition of themes by operating a hierarchical organization of the free categories by creating thematic arborescence. It is a question of moving closer to the categories cross-referenced with the same theme. This process of sequencing came along with a new work of refining the categories not according to the immanent sense of the text, but compared with the variables of our model. From 111 free categories, we passed to 93 categories, which are arranged in thematic arborescence (hierarchic levels of a main subject topics and sub topics) carrying the personal motivations in the creation by young entrepreneurs, the stages of the process of new business start-up, the received family capital and the performance of the created companies.

The validity of this codification depends on the quality of the reserved categories. That's why the constitution of the corpus has to obey, according to Bardin (2001), to four main rules:

- the rule of the exhaustiveness;
- the rule of the representativeness;
- the rule of homogeneity;
- the rule of relevance to the research target.

3. Research findings and discussion

Here some interviews excerpts, with our discussion and some propositions cross-referenced.

Entrepreneur LZ

The entrepreneur LZ is married. For the origin of the family support, she makes reference partially to her husband (quoted 6 times at the level of the interview [maintenance]). She evokes, ironically that her parents (relatives) supported her in a very negative way (quoted 4 times at the level of the interview).

> *The only source (spring) of help (assistant) which I had it was the support of my husband who was not at the top. My parents doesn't helped me at all; they were very reluctant to the idea. For them as a woman, I have to stay at home to occupy me of my children.*

Her comments confirm that for LZ, the origin of the family support emanates essentially from her husband. This is in adequacy with our under proposition P1 and under proposition P1.2.

The types of invested capitals

LZ was the first one in her own family but also in her family by law to become an entrepreneur. Nobody of either parts (parties) appreciated her initiative. LZ announced that she was autonomous at the beginning until the end of the elaboration of her project. Indeed, she moved forward and she (it) had no intervention of family capital seen in her (its) circumstances. She showed patience and a strong will for the necessary capital.

"I rowed alone, I had no family capital, nobody helped me."

- For the financial capital: LZ resorted, at the same time, to a bank credit (Tunisian Bank of Solidarity). She said that it was the only solution, that it was a credit granted without any guarantee. But also, she was able to rely on her own savings. When she had the financing, she had decided to go up to the end of her project.
- The social capital: LZ announced that she relied on her friends' network a lot. As she studied at HEC TUNIS, she had a portfolio of qualified persons. She tried the contacts with them and she was very surprised by the support that she was able to have. She relied on her personal skills of management to seize emergent opportunities, but also she (it) had her competent people to intervene at the level of the training (formation) that she was going to propose.

As she (it) worked as sales agent in hotels, this had too much helped him (it) because she (it) maintained very good reports (relationships) with the general managers. She managed to develop loyalty of them to become her service providers (trainers).

"*By putting me in touch with the general managers, I managed to have their agreements to become my service providers (trainers). This had very encouraged me seen that there was already a good agreement between us thanks to my former job.*"

- The moral support: LZ moves forward that she was at the beginning very encouraged by her husband but, as she moved forward in her realisation, he became very jealous of her. On the other hand, her friends encouraged her because they appreciated the idea of her business creation.

Entrepreneur BD

BD asserts that he benefited from allowances of the capital throughout the process. By way of its culture shock, which he felt by returning from the United States, his family was involved since his decision to launch his own business. BD announced that the availability of its family allowances increased more and more when he made a commitment definitively in this way. Once his well-founded decision was made, he was very confident in the realization of his target.

> "*It is very comforting to know that I was supported throughout the approach (initiative) of creation of my company. We become more and more confident, and in case of stagnation of this approach (initiative), I did not complicate things seen that I had my own soldiers in the good timing.*"

BD asserts that by being young, it is really difficult to begin its approach without support at the level of the phases of creation of the project. The intervention of his family was necessary at every level of the process. For example, his mother was an interface between him and the bank. Thanks to her, he admits that he very well lived the experience of progress of his entrepreneurial process because he had no experience (experiment) with the bankers and because he did not even know how it was necessary to manage things.

> *The family was an asset which worked in my favour. My mother was an interface of communication with the bankers, she had too much facilitated me many things. Already, to be confident at this level, it is a load at least. She collected the positive feedbacks and the negatives of my debts and in the same time, she made sure that I have a better situation and in the releases of appropriations as soon as possible. To know it already allowed me to feel at ease for the continuation of my progress at the level of my process. It was a concern less.*

On the basis of the presentation of the twenty cases of the study, they were grouped under two categories according to the parental model and marital status. This drawing of four groups was useful for the propositions testing. The four groups are:

- Group S+PM: single with the presence of a parental model (8 cases)
- Group S-PM: single without the presence of a parental model (4 cases)
- Group M+PM: married with the presence of a parental model (5 cases)
- Group M-PM: married without the presence of a parental model (3 cases)

Based on this table, we prepared a chart that combines the civil status of our entrepreneurs and their parental models. This chart indicates how the two variables interact.

Introducing marital status into the analysis of the factors that affect family support shows the importance of this neglected variable. Marital status reflects the influence of anthropology and family structure in a community-based context. Tunisian culture prioritizes family very strongly.

In this environment, the relationships between family members are strong and are based on relationships of trust and social solidarity. However, the departure of children influences the support that they will grant in starting a business. When an entrepreneur is single, his/her parents' involvement will be greater than when s/he is married. The marital status of the young married entrepreneur requires that s/he assume the responsibility to create a new family unit, disengage from his/her parents and rely more on himself/herself. However, some authors (Cramton (1993)) suggest that research should be conducted on married couples who have started businesses. These authors have shown that married couples help each other to mobilize resources for the creation phase. However, they also show that despite their marital status, these individuals can count on parental support. The resources provided depend on the nature of the children's relationships with their family members (Aldrich (1999) and Aldrich and Zimmer (1986)). Additionally, having an entrepreneurial parent affects the propensity for entrepreneurship (Cooper and Dunkleburg, 1987;

Table 9.2 Summary of the validation of the study propositions

Propositions	*Validation*
P1	P1.1 is validated; P1.2 is not validated for both cases for single children. **P1** is partially validated.
P2	P2.1 is validated, P2.2 is validated, P2.3 is validated. **P2** is validated.
P3	P3.1 is validated, P3.2 is not validated, P3.3 is validated, P3.4 is validated. ***P3*** is partially validated
P4	**P4** is validated

Table 9.3 The intersection of marital status and the parental model

Marital status *Parental model*	*Single*	*Married*
Family member = entrepreneur	✓ Origin of family support: parents ✓ All types of family capital ✓ Allocation throughout the process ✓ Few disadvantages.	✓ Origin of family support: parents and spouses ✓ All types of family capital ✓ Allocation early in the process ✓ Few disadvantages
No family member who is an entrepreneur	✓ Origin of family support: parents ✓ Only financial capital ✓ Allocation at the beginning of the process. ✓ Many disadvantages associated with family capital	✓ Origin of family support: spouses ✓ No capital

Duchesneau and Gartner, 1988; Scherer, Brodzinsky, and Wiebe, 1991; Davidsson, 1995; Delmar and Gunnarsson, 2000). This factor generates easier choices and more capacity for action in the process of starting a business.

There are many studies that indicate that the family is one of the most important influences on major life decisions, such as the selection of a career path. Individuals from families with entrepreneurs are much more likely to start a business. In the same vein, Gray, Foster and Howard (2006) argue that exposure to a business climate within the family at a young age seems to develop an entrepreneurial spirit in children and facilitate the implementation process. A parental role model provides support in the creation process for potential young entrepreneurs who choose the same career. The family history provides an example, and the family member acts as a mentor for the young entrepreneur who wants to embrace this adventure. Nevertheless, our research shows that it is very important to highlight the intersection of marital status and the parental model. Indeed, the intersection of the two variables is significant because we obtain differing results when both are considered.

In practical terms, the Tunisian organizations that seek to support the business creation process should consider marital status and whether an entrepreneur has a parental role model. Considering these two variables may help organizations to distribute support more efficiently and effectively and may assist them in creating equal opportunities for young entrepreneurs. However, some of our assumptions are only partially validated. These findings cause us to consider a third variable that may influence family support: is the young entrepreneur the only child?

Table 9.4 Refined propositions taking into account whether the new entrepreneur is an only child

Propositions
P1': The origin of family support depends on the marital status of the entrepreneur as well as whether the new entrepreneur is an only child.
P1.1': A single entrepreneur, whether or not s/he is an only child, is primarily supported by his/her parents.
P1.2': A married entrepreneur who is not an only child is primarily supported by his/her spouse.
P1.3': A married entrepreneur who is an only child is primarily supported by his/her parents.
P3': The allocation of family capital throughout the creation process depends on **– The parental model.** **– The marital status (single or married) of the young entrepreneur.** **– Whether the young married entrepreneur is an only child or not.**
P3.1': Young single entrepreneurs who belong to a family with an entrepreneur receive family capital throughout the process.
P 3.2': Young married entrepreneurs who are only children and belong to a family with an entrepreneur receive family capital throughout the process.
P 3.3': Young married entrepreneurs who are not only children but belong to a family with an entrepreneur receive family capital only at the beginning of the business creation process.
P 3.4': Young single entrepreneurs who belong to a family with no entrepreneurs receive family capital only at the beginning of the business creation process.
P 3.5': Young married entrepreneurs in a family without an entrepreneur, whether they are only children or not, receive no family capital.

According to our interviewees, having only one child will cause a Tunisian family not to decrease support for the child despite his or her marital status. In such a case, the young entrepreneur will benefit from the support of his/her family even after leaving the family to create one of his/her own. This long-term family support is characterized by continuity and commitment. Indeed, the cases in our study that included a married only child (case 1, case 14) are similar to the cases of single individuals with entrepreneurial parents. Thus, in future research, whether a new entrepreneur is an only child should be considered because doing so generates different results for married individuals. On this basis, we refine our propositions (Table 9.4) as follows:

In our sample, the average age of the Tunisian entrepreneurs interviewed at the time of business creation is 26.1 years. We note that going into business is easier for individuals of a certain age. Creating a company at younger than 20 years of age is challenging. In contrast, it appears that an age between 24- and 28-years-old is ideal for business creation for young Tunisians.

The entrepreneurial process involves several steps. First, the entrepreneurial awakening occurs. This awakening primarily involves an awareness of the possibilities inherent in starting a business as well as the legitimacy of entrepreneurship as a professional career. This awakening is also powered by other factors: the potential entrepreneur's personal traits and ability to undertake this type of challenge, the individual's resources and skills and the business opportunities that exist in the market. The beginning and the evolution of this consciousness depend on age. In persons younger than 22 years of age, such consciousness is rare.

Prior to that age, young people tend to be overwhelmed by their studies and by financial difficulties. In contrast, the initial awakening and the growth of this consciousness are consolidated by young people's first jobs and their active entry into professional life. This is the route to entrepreneurship. Young people are more interested in entrepreneurship when they can begin the search for resources, skills and knowledge through personal experience.

Although their resources and skills are underdeveloped during this period, these young people view the world more clearly, have more confidence and become more responsible. As a result, they start to create. Desire and motivation to become an entrepreneur are likely to be at high levels during this period. The new entrepreneur's decision to start a business may be supported by his/her family and friends as well as by government aid. During the creation process, the Tunisian family appears to be a very important and decisive factor, especially for young Tunisian entrepreneurs. Family support facilitates the creative process. However, this influence depends both on the presence of a fellow entrepreneur in the family and on the marital status of the young Tunisian entrepreneur. The role of the family in this context is as follows:

- To provide physical and financial aid as well as the benefits of personal knowledge, all of which can be understood as family resources.
- To facilitate access to loans through involvement with creditors and thus support the entrepreneurial child in the process of launching a business. This involvement increases the probability of the new entrepreneur's receiving a loan.
- To support the decision and the proposed business of the young entrepreneur (there will be much more support of this type if one of the parents is also an entrepreneur).

Thus, according to our results regarding marital status and parental role models, we cannot offer a single model of entrepreneurship for young Tunisian entrepreneurs. Instead, we propose four specific models for single entrepreneurs with parental role models (S + PM), single entrepreneurs without parental role models (S-PM), married entrepreneurs with parental role models (M + PM) and married entrepreneurs without parental role models (M-PM).

During the process of starting a business, the family plays an important role in mobilizing financial resources (e.g., Waldinger, Aldrich and Ward, 1990; Steier

Parental support
Financial capital,
Financial capital, Social capital
Financial capital, Social capital, Moral support
Financial capital, Social capital, Moral support capital
Financial capital, Social capital, Moral support capital
Time
Entrepreneurial survey
Awareness
Commitment
Decision-making
Creation

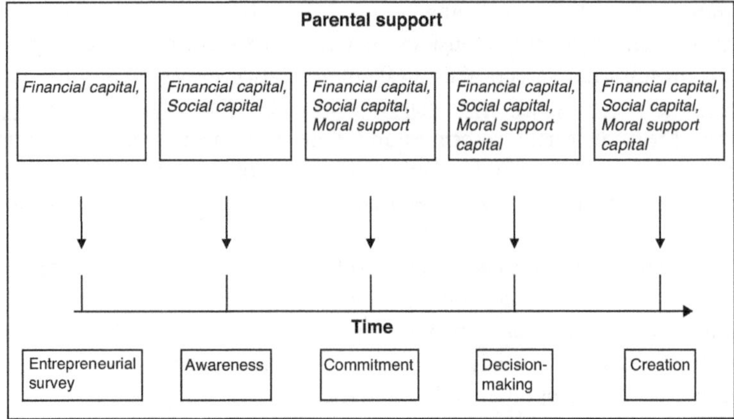

Figure 9.1 Model 1: single entrepreneurs with parental role models

Parental support
Financial capital, Social capital
Possible involvement of the spouse
Time
Entrepreneurial survey
Awareness
Commitment
Decision-making
Creation

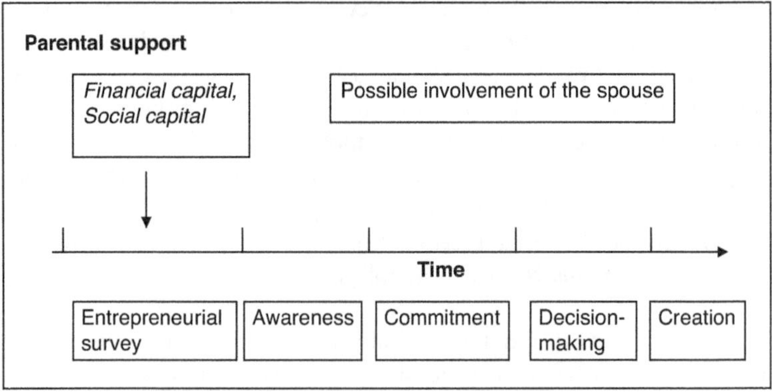

Figure 9.2 Model 2: married entrepreneurs with parental role models

Business creation process for young entrepreneurs
NB: We removed the two mixed cases that were similar to the PM + S cases.

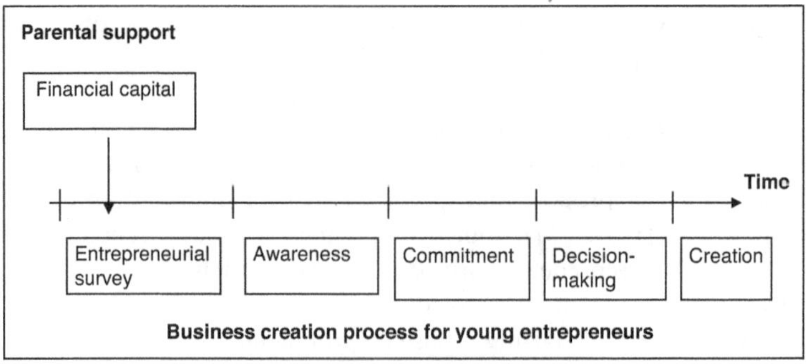

Parental support
Financial capital
Time
Entrepreneurial survey
Awareness
Commitment
Decision-making
Creation
Business creation process for young entrepreneurs

Figure 9.3 Model 3: single entrepreneurs without parental role models

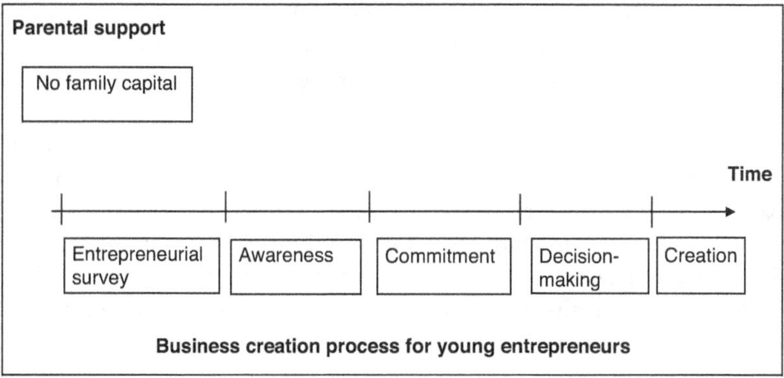

Figure 9.4 Model 4: married entrepreneurs without parental role models

and Greenwood, 2000), human resources and physical resources (Aldrich and Langton, 1998). For young singles, family intervention is inevitably a source of success during the business creation process. In the Tunisian context, young people often live with their parents before marriage and therefore depend heavily on them. They therefore frequently benefit from support from their parents at all levels. We note also that there is a spirit of support, brotherhood and solidarity among family members besides parents and children (e.g., brothers, sisters, uncles, cousins). This support is especially visible among those in business and those who have developed successful projects.

In families with a parental entrepreneur, children are frequently encouraged to start their own business and to invest all of their available resources in that business. In contrast, families that do not include an entrepreneur are reluctant to provide such assistance, and the assistance provided is not very effective. Parents are more likely to desire stable employment for their children. Marriage in most cases is associated with independence and the departure of the children from the family. At this level, the role of the family decreases, and the relationship is irrevocably changed. The parents expect that the husband or wife of the married child will provide the support that they once provided, and as a result, they let their child live in his/her own way. At this time, the parents begin to pay much more attention to the future of their other children.

4. Conclusions

The concept of the family is a fruitful one. The interaction between young entrepreneurs and their families can be used to explore the role of the family in the process of creating a business. Because of the diversity of elements of the family universe (e.g., affection, physical and psychological conflicts, money, work, feelings, name, moral principles, education, culture, memories, tangible and intangible goods), it is important to study this concept to decipher how family influences the entrepreneurial process among young entrepreneurs.

The data showed the importance of two variables that are often neglected: the presence of entrepreneurship within the family and the marital status of the young entrepreneur. Indeed, we find that the allocation of household resources depends on these two variables for the young entrepreneur. The presence of a business role model stimulates and facilitates the phases of the creation process: awareness, commitment and creation. For entrepreneurs with no parental role model, entrepreneurship will be more difficult. The entrepreneur will partly rely on parental support (financial assistance only) but will also rely on friends and personal acquaintances to fill the resource gap. Entrepreneurs in these categories exhibit a moderately good level of performance. Additionally, in combination with the presence or absence of an entrepreneurial role model, marital status also plays a role. For young single entrepreneurs, parental involvement is inevitably a cause of success.

Throughout this research, we have attempted to connect the empirical data to the theory so that it reflects the outcome of this exploratory qualitative research. This approach has allowed us to expand our investigation of the studied phenomenon. Our theoretical sensitivity has allowed us to propose four theoretical models of business creation that are specific to young Tunisian entrepreneurs.

Particularly in the Tunisian context, which features a community family structure, young people often live with their parents before marriage and therefore depend heavily on them. They can therefore benefit from the frequent support of their parents at all levels. In most cases, marriage is associated with independence and the departure of children. At that time, the role of the family in a child's life decreases, and the relationship is irrevocably changed. Parents expect the husband or wife to assume the responsibilities that they once had and let the child live in his/her own way. At this time, parents pay much more attention to the future of any other children who are still living under their roof. However, young entrepreneurs who are only children are exceptional cases. Parental support is the same for these entrepreneurs whether they are single or married. If this research *a priori* presents all possible intersections of marital status and parental role models, one might wonder about the potential to generalize these results to the national level (to the entire population of young Tunisian entrepreneurs) and the regional or international level (to entrepreneurs in countries similar to Tunisia). At the first level, simple generalization would be inappropriate because even if all intersections of marital status/parental model are presented in this research, it is unclear whether their proportions in the sample used for this research (which included only 20 cases) are similar to those of the entire population of young Tunisian entrepreneurs.

Methodological contributions

The case study allowed us the crossing of the speeches of the various young entrepreneurs, which limited itself to 20 semi-directive conversations. In the methodological frame, our qualitative work allowed us to generate an arborescence of codes integrating elements on the personal objectives of the young entrepreneurs, the family and the process of creation. This arborescence, obtained after coding of our conversations with the software of data processing qualitative Nvivo, is reusable by other researchers wishing to study elements on variables quoted above. Our work will guide and clear the way for future researchers.

Given the importance of the coding in the process of analysis and construction of sense, this stage was very time consuming. So, the use of the software Nvivo for the coding of the conversations facilitated this stage. The interest of the software lies essentially in the possibility of quickly reaching the extracts of conversations, which refer to the same code. This feature allowed us to refine as we went along our coding, while assuring us of the coherence of the verbatim, which relates to the same code.

Managerial contributions

Our work is, in itself, a first managerial contribution. Indeed, this study joins within the framework of the main objective of the Tunisian government, which is to create a new generation of young entrepreneurs. We give a perspective on the approach of creation seen that the constraints remain numerous and the entrepreneurial process remains a route difficult to borrow for the young Tunisian creator. In the practice, the results of this research can be useful at the same time for the persons in charge of government policies and for the experts who fuss on the ground of the development.

The second managerial contribution of our work lies in the revealing of the state of the social status as well as the entrepreneurial model, which we proposed. Indeed, in a perspective of accompaniment, these two variables, as well as four models of the process of new business start-up, allow the guides to realize that a very young entrepreneur does not have the same chance of success in his process of new business start-up as an older person does.

It is rather a question of granting the adequate assistance to the people who really deserve to be supported. The implied participants have to put in contact, for example, those who have no entrepreneurial model within the family (who cannot take advantage of family resources) with more experimented entrepreneurs who are going to adopt them and to act voluntarily as guide. Consequently the young people will more be stimulated to use the network of contact of the latter as well as the services of external support. In the same sense, we suggest to deploy a system of accompaniment during all the stages of the process of new business start-up and not to limit itself at the beginning of this approach. Certain categories borrow a longer and more difficult process of creation (single without entrepreneurial model, married without entrepreneurial model).

Limitations

Our first limitation, considering the research timeline, was to define the objective criteria set of business success, especially mixed with the scarcity of trusted companies' information. That is why our sample was thus a sample of suitability with all the well-known negative aspects. Our research is exposed to some biases:

1 It is about the collection of historic data (memory effect), the collected (harvested) information may be contaminated by the passing of time and even by the effect of the real-life experience.
2 The complexity of data illumination and protectionism (aversion of the persons interviewed to reveal the stages of the entrepreneurial genesis).
3 A way of social evaluation. The young Tunisians exaggerate their business route, which could be explained by the need of self-respect.

But the main limitation for us is the to verify the truthfulness of the interviewee's answers. They may consider themselves as visionary persons, and they don't want to share their business success, a kind of copyright complex.

Future research

Due to the exploratory nature of the research, it will be necessary in future research to conduct a quantitative study that incorporates the previously identified variables for a representative sample of the population. Likewise, future research should extend the study of this population of young Tunisian entrepreneurs by considering similar populations in comparable countries.

The clear results, as well as the observed limits, open new ways of research. Indeed, we suggest spreading the exploratory study through a quantitative study on a more representative sample. That would allow us to generalize the results. On the other hand, such an approach would allow us a better understanding of the degree of influence of every variable. Then other investigations could lead a comparison of two populations with different intrinsic and extrinsic characteristics, in particular characterizing different family structures. This type of approach would allow researchers to confirm or to counter the results we managed, especially to deepen aspects bound to the granted family resources, the entrepreneurial model and the civil status of the young entrepreneur in the context of different family structures.

It would also be interesting to lead a symmetric study on the cases of young entrepreneurs who failed their initiatives of new business launches. These researches would allow the identification and the understanding of the most relevant determiners to retain in terms of efficiency the resources in this approach. On the practical plan, we suggest to lead an evaluation of the various Tunisian bodies of promotion of the entrepreneurial activity. This action is going to allow a better understanding about who needs help and under which form would benefit them best.

References

Aldrich, H. E. (1999). *Organizations Evolving*. London: Sage.

Aldrich, H. E., and Cliff, J. E. (2003). The pervasive effects of family on entrepreneurship: Toward a family embeddedness perspective. *Journal of Business Venturing*, 18(5), 573–596.

Aldrich, H.E., and Langton, N. (1998). Human resource management and organizational life cycles. In P. D. Reynolds, W. Bygrave, N. M. Carter, P. Davidsson, W. B. Gartner, C. M. Mason and P. P. McDougall (Eds.), *Frontiers of Entrepreneurship Research 1997* (pp. 349–357). Babson Park, MA: Babson College, Center for Entrepreneurial Studies.

Aldrich, H. E., and Zimmer, C. (1986). Entrepreneurship through social networks. In D. Sexton and R. Smilor (Eds.), *The Art and Science of Entrepreneurship* (pp. 3–23). New York: Ballinger.

Astrachan, J. H. (2010). Strategy in family business: Toward a multidimensional research agenda. *Journal of Family Business Strategy*, 1(1), 6–14.

Astrachan, J. H., Zahra, S. A., and Sharma, P. (2003). *Family-Sponsored Ventures: The Entrepreneurial Advantage of Nations.* Report presented at The First Annual Global Entrepreneurship Symposium, April 29, 2003, United Nations, New York.

Bandura, A. (1977). *Self-Efficacy: The Exercise of Control.* New York: W.H. Freeman.

Basco, R. (2013). The family's effect on family firm performance: A model testing the demographic and essence approaches. *Journal of Family Business Strategy*, 4(1), 42–66.

Baumard, P., and Ibert, J. (2003). Quelles approches avec quelles données? In Thiétart Raymond Alain et coll (Eds.), *Méthodes de recherche en management* (2ème ed., pp. 82–103). Dunod.

Bee, C., and Neubaum, D. O. (2014). The role of cognitive appraisal and emotions of family members in the family business system. *Journal of Family Business Strategy*, 5(3), 323–333.

Berger, P., and Luckman, T. (1989). La construction sociale de la réalité. *Paris Méridiens Klincksieek*, 1, 296.

Bragard,L. (1987). *La formation Chef d'entreprise.* Centre de Recherche et de Documentation PME, Etude réalisée à la demande de l'Institut Francophone de Formation Permanente des Classes Moyennes, Bruxelles.

Brockhaus, R. H. Sr., and Horwitz, P. S. (1986). The psychology of entrepreneurship. In D. L. Sexton and R. W. Smilor (Eds.), *The Art and Science of Entrepreneurship.* Cambridge, MA: Ballinger.

Bruyat, C. (1993). *Création d'entreprise: contributions épistémologiques et modélisation.* Thèse de doctorat en Sciences de Gestion, UPMF, Grenoble 2, France.

Butcher, K. F., and Case, A. (1994). The effect of sibling sex composition on women's education and earnings. *The Quarterly Journal of Economics*, 109, 531–563.

Collins, O., and Moore, D. (1964). *The Enterprising Man.* East Lansing: Michigan State University Press.

Cooper, A. C., and Dunkleburg, W. C. (1987). Entrepreneurial research: Old questions, new answers, and methodological issues. *American Journal of Small Business*, 11(3), 11–23.

Creswell, J. W. (1998). *Qualitative Inquiry and Research Design: Choosing Among Five Traditions.* Thousand Oaks, CA: Sage.

Dagenais, D. (2000). *La fin de la famille moderne: signification des transformations contemporaines de la famille.* Saint-Nicolas: Les Presses de l'Université Laval.

Dana, L., and Dana, T. (2005). Expanding the scope of methodologies used in entrepreneurship research. *International Journal of Entrepreneurship and Small Business*, 2(1), 79–88.

Danes, S. M., Lee, J., Stafford, K., and Heck, R.K.Z. (2008). The effects of ethnicity, families and culture on entrepreneurial experience: An extension of sustainable family business theory. *Journal of Developmental Entrepreneurship*, Special Issue titled Empirical Research on Ethnicity and Entrepreneurship in the U.S., 13(3), 229–268.

Davidsson, P. (1995). *Determinants of Entrepreneurial Intentions.* Paper presented at the RENT IX Workshop, November 23–24, Piacenza, Italy.

Delmar, F., and Gunnarsson, J. (2000). How do self-employed parents of nascent entrepreneurs contribute? In P. D. Reynolds et al. (Eds.), *Frontiers of Entrepreneurship Research 2000.* Wellesley, MA: Babson College.

Di Maggio, P. J., and Powell, W. W. (1991). *The New Institutionalism in Organizational Analysis.* Chicago: University of Chicago Press.

Diochon, M., Gasse, Y., and Menzies, T. (2002). *Attitudes and Entrepreneurial Action: Exploring the Link.* Paper presented to the ASAC Conference, Winnipeg, Manitoba.

Duchesneau, D. A., and Gartner, W. B. (1990). A profile of new venture success and failure in an emerging industry. *Journal of Business Venturing*, 5, 297–312.

Dunn, T., and Holtz-Eakin, D. (1996). *Financial Capital, Human Capital, and the Transition to Self-Employment: Evidence From Intergenerational Links.* Metropolitan Studies Occasional Paper No. 181, Center for Policy Research, Syracuse University.

Dyer, W. G. (1992). *The Entrepreneurial Experience: Confronting Career Dilemmas of the Start-Up Executive.* San Francisco: Jossey-Bass.

Dyer, W. G., and Handler, W. (1994). Entrepreneurship and family business: Exploring the connections. In *Entrepreneurship Theory and Practice* (pp. 71–83). Baylor University, USA.

Fayolle, A. (2004). *Entrepreneuriat et processus: faire du processus un objet de recherche et mieux prendre en compte la dimension processus dans les recherches.* 7ème Congrès International Francophone en Entrepreneuriat et PME 27, 28 et 29 Octobre, Montpellier, France.

Filion, L. J. (1991). *Visions et relations: clefs de succès de l'entrepreneur.* Montréal: les éditions de L'Entrepreneur.

Gartner, W. B. (1985). A conceptual framework for describing the phenomenon of new venture creation. *Academy of Management Review*, 10(4), 696–706.

Gasse, Y. (2002). Functional diversity in university entrepreneurship development: The Laval University Model. In Teresa V. Menzies (Ed.), *Entrepreneurship and the Canadian Universities* (Chapter 11, pp. 71–76). St. Catharines, Ont.: Brock University.

Gasse, Y., and D'Amours, A. (2000). *Profession: Entrepreneur: Avez-vous le profil de l'emploi?* Montréal: Les Éditions Transcontinental and Fondation de l'Entrepreneurship.

Gioia, D. A., Corley, K. G. et al. (2013). Seeking qualitative rigor in inductive research: Notes on the Gioia Methodology. *Organizational Research Methods*, 16(1), 15–31.

Goode, W. J. (1970). *World Revolution and Family Patterns.* New York: The Free Press.

Gray, K. R., Foster, H., and Howard, M. (2006). Motivations of Moroccans to be entrepreneurs. *Journal of Developmental Entrepreneurship*, 11(4), 297–318.

Gubrium, J. F., and Holstein, J. A. (1990). *What Is Family?* Mayfield: Mountains View Publishing.

Heck, R.K.Z., and Mishra, C. S. (2008). Family entrepreneurship. *Journal of Small Business Management*, 46(3), 313–316.

Hisrich, R. D., and Brush, C. G. (1987). Women entrepreneurs: A longitudinal study. In N. C. Churchill, J. A. Hornaday, B. A. Kirchhoff, O. J. Krasner and K. H. Vesper (Eds.), *Frontiers of Entrepreneurial Research* (pp. 187–199). Boston, MA: Babson College.

Holt, D. T., Madison, K., and Kellermanns, F. W. (2016). Variance in family members' assessments the importance of dispersion modeling in family firm research. *Family Business Review*, 30(1): 61-83.

Hout, M. (1984). Status, autonomy, and training in occupational mobility. *American Journal of Sociology*, 89, 1379–1409.

Hout, M. (1989). *Following in Father's Footsteps: Social Mobility in Ireland*. Cambridge, MA: Harvard University Press.

Hout, M., and Rosen, H. (2000). Self-employment, family background, and race. *The Journal of Human Resources*, 35, 670–924.

Huault, I. (2002). Paul DiMaggio et Walter W. Powell – Des organisations en quête delégitimité. In S. Charreire and I. Huault (Eds.), *Les grands auteurs en management* (chapitre VII, pp. 99–112). Grands Auteurs, Editions EMS.

Kepner, E. (1983). The family and the firm: A coevolutionary perspective. *Organizational Dynamics*, 12(1), 57–70.

Lacasse, R. M. (1990). *La petite entreprise au Canada: le cas particulier de l'entrepreneuriat féminin dans le secteur manufacturier*. Thèse de doctorat en Sciences de Gestion, Université de Nice Sophia Antipolis.

Lau, S.K. (1988). *The Ethos of the Hong Kong Chinese*. Hong Kong: The Chinese University Press.

Lentz, B. S., and Laband, D. N. (1990). Entrepreneurial success and occupational inheritance among proprietors. *Canadian Journal of Economics*, 23(3), 563–579.

Mann, P. H. (1990). Nontraditional business education for black entrepreneurs: Observations from a successful program. *Journal of Small Business Management*, 28(2), 28–41.

Parker, S. C. (2016). Family firms and the 'willing successor' problem. *Entrepreneurship Theory and Practice*, 40(6), 1241–1259.

Paturel, R. (2004). Les choix méthodologiques de la recherche doctorale française en entrepreneuriat: remise en cause partielle d'idées préconçues. *Revue de l'Entrepreneuriat*, 3(1), 47–65, http://asso.nordnet.fr/r-e/RE0301rp.pdf.

Redding, S.G. (1990). *The Spirit of Chinese Capitalism*. New York: Walter de Gruyter.

Robichaud, D. (2001). *La création d'entreprises par les immigrants: le cas des Québécois d'origine portugaise de la région métropolitaine de recensement de Montréal*. PhD thesis, HEC Montréal.

Rocher, G. (1964). *Rapport de la Commission royale d'enquête sur l'enseignement dans la province de Québec*. Deuxième partie ou tome II: Les structures pédagogiques du système scolaire. Les structures et les niveaux de l'enseignement.

Rogoff, E. G., and Heck, R.K.Z. (2003). Evolving research in entrepreneurship and family business: Recognizing family as the oxygen that feeds the fire of entrepreneurship. *Journal of Business Venturing*, 18, 559–566.

Ronstadt, R. C. (1984). *Entrepreneurship*. Dover: Lord Publishing.

Ruef, M. A., Rogge, M., Velten, U., and Gieseke, W. (2002). *Hacking Intern – Attacks, Strategies, Defense*. Düsseldorf: Data Becker.

Saporta, B. (2002). 'Famille, création d'entreprises et entrepreneuriat', dans la gestion des entreprises familiales. *Economica*, 107–125.

Schein, H. (1994). Commentary: What is an entrepreneur? *Entrepreneurship Theory and Practice*, 19(2), 87–88.

Scherer, R. F., Adams, J. S., Carley, S. S., and Wiebe, F. A. (Spring 1989). Role model performance effects on development of entrepreneurial career preference. *Entrepreneurship Theory & Practice*, 13(3): 53–71.

Scherer, R. F., Brodzinsky, J. D., and Wiebe, F. A. (1991). Examining the relationship between personality and entrepreneurial career preference. *Entrepreneurship & Regional Development*, 3, 195–206.

Steier, L. P., and Greenwood, R. (2000). Entrepreneurship and the evolution of angel financial networks. *Organization Studies*, 21(1), 163–192.

Stewart, A. (2003). Help one another, use one another: Toward an anthropology of family business. *Entrepreneurship Theory and Practice*, 27(4), 383–396.

Sweeney, G. (1988). *Entrepreneurs and Regional Development, European Foundation for Management Development.* 18ème séminaire sur les PME, Gand.

Todd, E. (1983). *Latroisième planète: structures familiales et systèmes idéologiques.* Paris: Éditions du Seuil.

Todd, E. (1984). *L'enfance du monde: structures familiales et développement.* Paris: Éditions du Seuil.

Waldinger, R., Aldrich, H., and Ward, R. (1990). *Ethnic Entrepreneurs: Immigrant Business in Industrial Societies.* New York: Sage Publications.

Wong, S. L. (1985). The Chinese family firm: A model. *British Journal of Sociology*, 36(1), 58–72.

Zahra, S. A. (2007). Contextualizing theory building in entrepreneurship research. *Journal of Business Venturing*, 22(3), 443–452.

10 Heteronormativity and the family firm

Will we ever see a queer family business?

Börje Boers

Introduction

Gender aspects are a small niche in family business research. Extant research is limited and focuses on illuminating the role of women in family businesses, which has been described as a gap in the literature (Sharma, 2004). Recent research has looked at the role of women having an important but subtle role (Martinez Jimenez, 2009; Sonfield and Lussier, 2009). Other research has looked at daughters in the succession process (Vera andDean, 2005). Research in this tradition is important but it needs to be complemented with a perspective that goes beyond the male-female dichotomy. In other words, the nuclear family, which is perceived as the standard for and of family businesses, is not the only possible type of family within family business. Folgerø (2008) introduces the term of "queer nuclear family" as also gay or lesbian couples can have children.

Therefore, we should discuss the concept of family within the family firm context as it is represented in family business research. I argue that the social construction of family is based on heteronormative expectations, i.e. the family consists of a married couple with children. Although this assumption is rarely made explicit, it dominates the view when talking about family business. Support for this claim can also be found in how women are treated in family businesses. This can be seen as a consequence of roles that women are associated with in family businesses as being associated with the mother role (Bjursell and Bäckvall, 2011). Research on women's role in family business is important, but it needs to be extended to include further gender aspects. Karataş-Özkan, Nicolopoulou, İnal, and Özbilgin (2011: 7) argue, "With respect to control, power relations and resistance, family business context may be rather hierarchical, repressive and paternalistic, representing contradictions and negative implications for equality and diversity." So the meaning of family and family business is traditional and emphasizing the male norm of family businesses (Bjursell and Bäckvall, 2011; Karataş-Özkan et al., 2011). I argue that it is necessary to go further and extend the meaning of family, including non-traditional families, i.e. queer families.

There is an emerging stream of research in the entrepreneurship literature that deals with minorities. The entrepreneurship literature often refers to female entrepreneurship or immigrant entrepreneurship as minorities in that they deviate from the male norm of the entrepreneur (Ahl, 2006; Galloway, 2012). Ahl argues that the female entrepreneur is often celebrated in publications, but it also recreates women's secondary position in society (Ahl, 2002), which corresponds the depiction of women in family businesses (Bjurselland Bäckvall, 2011). Morgan (1996) argues that organizations are depicted by following patriarchic patterns predominantly describing male and Western values.

As a consequence of the appearance of non-traditional, or queer, families (Andersson, Noack, Seierstad, and Weedon-Fekjær, 2006; Folgerø, 2008), it is about time to also look into their economic activities, i.e. as business owners and managers. Galloway reports of gay male entrepreneurs and the problems they encounter in relation to being a business owner (Galloway, 2012). Galloway concludes that these face similar problems as other minority groups who deviate from the male norm.

A discussion on what is meant by family will be followed by a part where the concept of queer is discussed. Further, I discuss how this relates to family business research and why researchers should care about non-traditional or 'queer' family firms. Before concluding the paper, I discuss inequality regimes as an alternative perspective of studying family businesses.

What is family?

Family is a social construction, which is seen by Gabb (1999) as a representation of 'blood kinship'(p. 11). Stewart (2003) argued that the term 'family' is not useful as the meaning attached to it varies over time and culture. The claim of many gay or lesbian activists to have the right to start a family or get married is eventually nothing more but a reinforcement of the legitimacy of the institution 'family'. Still, the existence of gay or lesbian couples and their claim to be a family is a deviation from the norm that a family has to consist of a man and a woman. However, there are trends indicating changing cultural norms and values, i.e. allowing same sex marriages and partnerships (Andersson et al., 2006). For instance, Andersson et al. (2006) found in their study of demographics of same-sex marriages in Norway and Sweden that there are similarities and differences with opposite-sex marriages. A big different was a higher risk for divorce, particularly for lesbian couples. Andersson et al. (2006) explain that the difference can be due to the lower normative pressure from society to maintain lifelong unions as it exists for opposite-sex marriages. This means that the concept of family is not as simple as it is often taken in family business research. Weston already argued in 1991 that the concept of family contains richness and diversity in terms of family models and structures (Watson, 1991, cited in: Folgerø, 2008). Folgerø illustrates that homosexual family constellations with children challenge conventional norms and understandings of the concept 'family' (Folgerø, 2008). Further, Folgerø found in his study that homosexual couples with children reproduce heteronormative assumptions of family and kinship (Folgerø, 2008). Davies and Robinson argue that queer families often, seen from a consumer

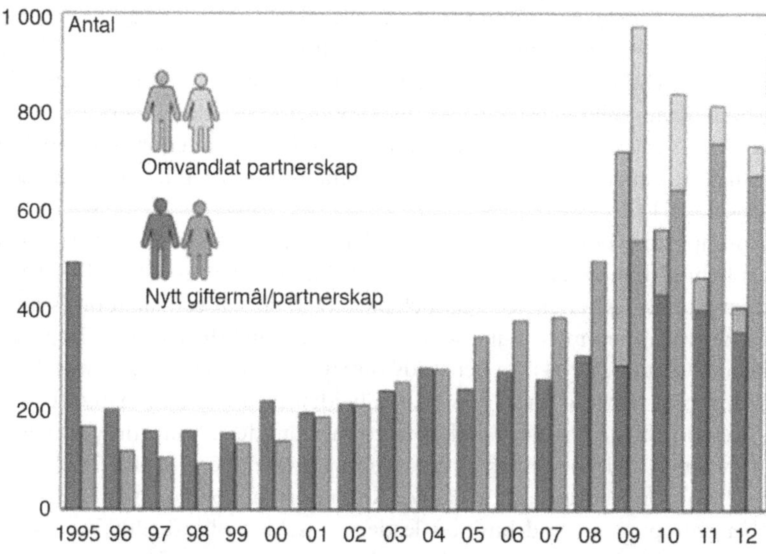

Figure 10.1 Registered partnerships from 1995 to April 2009. Marriages from May 2009 (scb.se)

perspective, are still in harsh contradiction to the normative family as being heterosexual (Davies and Robinson, 2013). They further emphasize the heterogeneity of queer families. However, Silin (2013), acknowledging the importance of queer families, also cautions further research with regards to children involved.

Sweden is often described as a forerunner in terms equal rights for same-sex relationships. Recently, the Swedish Statistical Bureau (SCB) reported on the population of same sex marriages in Sweden.

Ultimately, the population of Swedish queer families consists of several thousand and the phenomenon is not going to disappear as many other European countries have introduced forms of marriage and partnership for same-sex partners. The Nordic countries of Sweden and Norway can be seen as forerunners with already some years of experience, which allows a further investigation.

Research in the literature

There are very few studies that have dealt with the phenomenon of queer families in the entrepreneurship or family business literature. Schindehutte, Morris, and Allen (2005) found that a 'gay' identity has an impact on the venture-creation process.

Butler (1999) argues that an identity is constructed or constituted through performativity. The family business as such can be reproduced as 'male' through this kind of performativity. This means that the family business is performing/

constituting the identity it pretends to be. What does this mean? Going back to Sharma (2004), who pointed to a role behind the scenes, or Mulholland (2003), who found women to be invisible although they contributed financially and ideally to the success of the business, it can be assumed that women's role in family firms will continue to be undervalued (Martinez Jimenez, 2009; Vera and Dean, 2005). That women are presented in an inferior position towards the male norm has been shown in different research (Ahl, 2002; Bjursell and Bäckvall, 2011).

An important point to make here is that women not always take the invisible roles behind the scenes. For instance, Javefors Grauers concluded that women running a business often see it as a chance for their self-actualisation (sometimes together with their men) but also as a means to fulfill their societal responsibility (Javefors Grauers, 2004). In her study on Swedish (ICA) stores, it was, however, also apparent that the founder was usually identified with the man, even though the woman or the couple together were the founders. Still, through performativity women will be seen as a resource in the periphery of the family business whose real contribution is not valued. An important consequence in this context is that entrepreneurs and business leaders – as Mulholland (2003) calls them – are perceived to have certain attributes that are in close association to masculinity. Mulholland criticizes that this view of the 'self-made man' and the entrepreneur implies the reliance on personal 'male' traits as success factors, which ignores the resources needed and used to be successful. Specifically, she refers to family, i.e. women labor (2003: 15). An illustration could be the stereotypical representation of women as wives who stay in the background and support their husbands in the business press.

Another sign for the heteronormative character of the family firm is the role daughters play when it comes to succession. Although Chrisman, Chua, and Sharma (1998) argue that birth order and gender are of minor importance when choosing a successor, there is also evidence that it matters whether the successor is a son or a daughter (Gilding, 2000; Mulholland, 2003). Moreover, there are findings that implicate that daughters become successor when there are no sons available or their respective husbands take a leading role in the family business. Not surprisingly, Vera and Dean (2005) report in line with Cole (1997) problems of daughters as successors in a problematic position. Their parents expect them to take over the business but also to 'produce' children, which constitutes an awkward situation for daughters. There is some evidence that daughters take over the family business later than sons do because they wait until they have given birth to children (Vera and Dean, 2005). This is clearly an inequality regime based on gender because even if sons are forced by their parents to produce heirs, it is easier for them to follow both demands when the 'wife' takes care of the children, as she has to give birth.

Moreover, men refer to their wives in a personal way, thereby ignoring their contribution to the success and their management position but also claiming the business as their merit (Mulholland, 2003). A notable dimension in a family business is formed by the different roles that men and woman occupy in that setting, which are due to inequality based on gender. First, there is the business role where the man often becomes the entrepreneurial man who determines the direction of the business and his other role as a husband or father is subordinated. Second, the woman is often, especially in the beginning of the business, the one who supplies her labor for free and sometimes also capital or other assets, which is taken for granted, as well as her role as wife who takes care of the household and children. The importance of producing heirs is especially important when the business should be passed on to the next generation, i.e. in order to stay in the family. Here, the marriage as institutional foundation for the family and, therefore, the family business also comes into play. Another important finding refers to the gendered character of resources, i.e. men have better access to them in comparison to women. This leads to a more limited access for women to certain industries. In her study, Mulholland revealed that women played an important role specifically in the start-up phase; however, their contribution was hidden. For instance, they did not have formal positions in the business and, if they had these positions, were hardly in the top-management (directorship).

The business is seen as a way to gain recognition for male entrepreneurs. Thereby it also functions as a way for promotion in social and class terms because it grants access to a sphere only accessible for 'men' of class and wealth. Wives give up their job for helping out in the business start-up phase. Moreover, male entrepreneurs also benefit from so called 'emotional labor' and refers to the work mostly done by wives in the domestic sphere at home. Men deny their emotional commitment in their domestic role and instead focus on their role as breadwinner, neglecting their role as fathers and husbands. In addition, they also separate strictly between the domestic world at home and the work they perform outside the home. Then, being a workaholic is just a means to fulfill this role. Consequently, women are left in charge for the domestic labor and, almost ironically, are responsible for raising their children and successors. Hence, the emotional labor is a deeply gendered task whereby women compensate the absence of men at home. Part of this emotional labor is also the nurturing of men, enabling men to work with the business. Interestingly, this behavior seems to be independent of class, age, ethnicity or education (Mulholland, 2003). Looking at female entrepreneurs, it seems that they do not differ much in their behavior from male entrepreneurs. They also negotiate their role with their partners and follow a similar pattern, like giving their wealth to sons. It has to be mentioned that women come into position from an instance when men as heirs are lacking. Mulholland raises the question whether these women can be categorized as 'honorary men' because they follow the male pattern.

Family firms are the most dominant form of organising business activities, and researchers agree that family firms are different from non-family firms (Chrisman, Chua, and Sharma, 2005; Faccio and Lang, 2002; La Porta, Lopez-De-Silanes, and Shleifer, 1999). Still, researchers have not agreed upon a universally valid and generally accepted definition (Chrisman et al., 2005; Litz, 1995; Sharma, 2004; Westhead and Cowling, 1998). Although some scholars have argued for the superiority of one particular definition, they tend to agree that the most important issue is that each researcher is clear upon the definition in use in each study. Following Sharma (2004), most definitions regard the family as a decisive source for unique resources and capabilities as well as important for the vision and control mechanisms of the firm. Besides the relative and absolute importance of family firms, it is also important to mention that there are different types of family firms. Different efforts have been undertaken to capture the variety in family firms (Astrachan, Klein, and Smyrnios, 2002; Sharma, 2004). Scholars have made similar arguments with regards to the heterogeneity of family firms as well as with the boundaries of the field (e.g. Zahra and Sharma, 2004). Looking at the family as the unit of analysis, it becomes obvious that the family is regarded as an institution that represents the heterosexual norm of (western) society. Women in family businesses seem to be the exception that proves the male norm. In a recent review of the family business field, Sharma (2004) indicated that women in family firms seem to stay in the background taking care of the household. Women are seen as wives whose real contribution is not valued or seen (Rowe and Hong, 2000; Mulholland, 2003). Recently, researchers began to acknowledge the diverse and dual roles of women in family firms as unpaid and invisible resources or stewards of the business (Poza and Messer, 2001; Mulholland, 2003). For the US, Carrington and Troske (1995) found that small firms were highly segregated by sex. Moreover, the sex of the business owner influences the composition of the firm's workforce in terms of sex. That means that men usually work in firms where primarily men work and women work in firms where primarily women work. Carrington and Troske also found that firms where primarily women work pay less than firms where primarily men work. However, the men-dominated firms also have higher revenues, which could explain the wage differences according to Carrington and Troske. In the next section of the paper heteronormativity will be discussed.

Heteronormativity

People hold, often implicitly, assumptions about sexual orientations of people. The most commonly held assumption refers to heterosexuality. It was Rich (1980) who questioned this assumption even within feminist theory. A similar term is heterosexism, which refers to a certain kind of heterosexual lifestyle that is promoted within the public discourse (Pilcher and Whelehan, 2006). Heterosexuality is sometimes even seen as compulsory. This normative character of heterosexuality has consequences for the way we view the world, and it leads people to assume that a family consists of man and woman. The dominance of heterosexual expectations also have been illustrated in the context of entrepreneurship (Bruni, 2006; Bruni, Gherardi, and Poggio, 2004). Even more importantly, Butler (1999) argues convincingly that gender is culturally constructed. It was Ahl (2002) who showed in her dissertation that female entrepreneurs are perceived to be the exception from the male norm, thereby reproducing the inferiority of women. Often, people see heterosexuality as the norm. When some people violate the norm, for instance men polishing their nails or women wearing moustaches, they question the heteronormative expectations (Nielsen, Walden, and Kunkel, 2000). Further, men behaving woman-like were attributed to be homosexual whereas women behaving man-like were attributed to be 'hyper-heterosexually' active and promiscuous.

Similar experiences of daughters taking over the parents' business are to be found (Vera and Dean, 2005). Daughters reported that they faced problems with non-family members within the firm because they doubted the daughters' ability to run the firm. The implications for family businesses are obviously that the owning family should consist of a heterosexual couple (and kids) and a man heads the business. This is a visible sign of inequality regimes working against daughters. Moreover, it also illustrates the heteronormative expectations people hold when it comes to leading a family business. In a study by Rowe and Hong (2000) it was revealed that the role of women in the family business is often undervalued. Especially in husband and wife businesses, the ignorance to the woman's role became striking. The man is seen as the entrepreneur and the business is his business (Dumas, 1998). Lee, Hong, and Rowe (2006) came to characterise married women working in their families' business being confronted with a three shift situation, that is they "work in the family business, in the marketplace, and at home" (p. 73). These performative mechanisms constitute the heteronormative family business. In a recent publication, Van Auken and Werbel (2006) underlined the importance of spousal commitment for the success of a family firm. This is a similar argument to what Mulholland (2003) has found. Van Auken and Werbel argue in line with Poza and Messer (2001) and emphasise the economic bonds between spouses due to marriage. This is a sign of the heteronormatively-gendered understanding of the field of family business research. Of course, not every women engaged in a family business is in a three shift situation. However, Rowe and Hong (2000) point out that wives, irrespective of their double or three times occupation, contribute an important amount of financial income to the family household, which again illustrates the functioning of inequality regimes in the context of family and business.

Why care about queer family firms?

Queer, lesbian or gay families do exist, but why care about it in the field of family business research? The question can be turned around as well: why not? It is not certain that the population of queer family businesses is of large size. However, this is also true for listed family-controlled firms on the stock exchange. In terms of the share of the total population of family firms, they very likely account for less than 1 percent of all family firms. My argument is that there is a need to also highlight the diversity within the population of family firms and the impact it has on certain issues, like succession.

When studying family firms, one reason to do so is because of its high empirical relevance. Depending on the context and definitions used, it can be assumed that the majority of all firms can be categorized as family firms (Astrachan and Shanker, 2003; Klein, 2000). Just by chance it is very likely that considerable differences between those firms do exist. Probably these firms differ in many ways, i.e. they are very heterogeneous in terms of size or industry, besides the common label 'family firm'. Thus, at the core of this question is the definition of what constitutes a family firm. As indicated already, the definition-problem is still unsolved. There are different approaches and a common criticism is related to the operational nature of definition (Chrisman et al., 2005; Chua, Chrisman, and Sharma, 1999). According to Chrisman et al. (2005) there are two principally different ways of defining the family firm: the 'components-of-involvement' approach and the 'essence' approach (p. 556). The former approach views family involvement as a sufficient condition to define a firm as a family firm whereas the latter additionally requires a behavior that leads to distinctiveness to make a firm a family firm (Chrisman et al., 2005). In line with the essence approach is also the suggestion that family firms have distinctive attributes due to the family involvement that lead to potential competitive advantages over non-family firms (Habbershon and Williams, 1999). However, we argue that based on this dichotomous view on family versus non-family firms the differences between family firms, and thus its heterogeneity, has been understudied. Westhead et al. (2002) also criticize the ignorance towards heterogeneity. Specifically, they mention the study of family firms in isolation or on an aggregate level. Thus, studies fail to compare different types of family firms and non-family firms (p. 263).

One distinct and typical feature of research within family business is succession (Zahra and Sharma, 2004). The intention to pass on the ownership to the next generation is often used to determine if a business is a family business. This option might lack when having a gay or lesbian family that runs a business. Well, maybe not the intention but the potential. However, it should be considered that gay or lesbian families could have children, and why couldn't they continue the business? In some countries it is even legal for homosexual couples to adopt children. Gender theory is a broad field and from my point of view there is potential to enrich the discussion by taking those families in. Besides, it might also posit an opportunity to give something back to the more mainstream literature. In a recent article in *Family Business Review* the issue of homosexuality was touched (Hubler, 2005). In an article about forgiveness, Hubler was giving an illustration from a case he experienced where a son admitted to be gay. As a consultant, Hubler could report things that might be undisclosed to the academic discourse otherwise. Hence, this 'problem' has to be recognized and addressed.

Inequality regimes

Nonetheless, it can be argued that the heterosexually-gendered family business is a means of oppression. For instance, Acker argues that in every organization 'inequality regimes' are at work that maintain, amongst others, gender inequalities (Acker, 2006) Inequality regimes can be part of practices, processes or actions that together lead systematic differences between people in the business, hierarchy being the obvious example. Inequality regimes lead to and maintain inequalities within an organization in terms of class, gender and race (Acker, 2006). Inequalities are based on systematic imbalances between people in terms of power and control over "goals, resources, and outcomes" (p. 443). Hence, decisions on how to organize work, who gets promoted, social and financial benefits of work and others are concerned. Equality can exist in certain areas whereas not in others. Acker (2006) underlines that inequality regimes are various, fluid and changing, and they are related to inequalities within the respective societal context. Moreover, inequalities can even vary within subunits of one organization. Still, hierarchy is a very appropriate illustration of inequality regimes, as in the majority of cases white men occupy the highest positions within Europe and the US. An important aspect is also the legitimacy and visibility of inequalities. It can be assumed that those who benefit from inequalities may be more reluctant to change anything, whereas when inequalities have a low legitimacy and are highly visible, change might be easier. Apparently, it is necessary to look at these inequality regimes in family businesses and how they are dealt with.

Conclusion

As suggested in the previous paragraph, it seems worthwhile investigating inequality regimes at family firms. Moreover, family business researchers claim that family firms are different from non-family firms. This can almost be perceived as a 'dogma'. Applying Butler (1999), family firms are different as long as we constitute them to be different! Of course, there is evidence that the 'population' of family firms is not homogeneous. Nevertheless, it seems that the majority of empirical research has been conducted within the Western world. But have we investigated enough how family firms are? I think not. Where are the queer family firms? Do they exist? And do they make a difference? I would think they do.

Why is it necessary to take a feminist perspective on family businesses? The easiest answer is, of course, to say that it matters. But how, in what respect and why? From an organization studies point of view, Calás and Smircich (1996) argue that feminist theory helps to uncover problems in theory and practice that would have stayed undetected otherwise. One area that concerns practioners, such as owners and consultants, refers to succession. What options do queer family businesses have for succession? Are they at all interested to keep the business in the family, and if so, how? Do they have children? Are there siblings or other relatives who can and want to take over the business? Another area of interest is growth. What is their attitude towards growth? Are queer businesses lifestyle businesses or are they interested in sustainable growth? What exit options exist?

Although female participation in family business and coverage in the literature is increasing, women are often victims of inequality regimes that favor men. This is obvious when it comes to succession where sons still dominate. But it is also obvious when it comes to the support wives give their husbands in different phases where they stay invisible. Family business researchers have acknowledged this. However, what is, in my point of view, lacking is the acknowledgement of different forms of family firms. Scholars are arguing for different, queer families (Gabb, 1999) as well as gay and lesbian interest groups are fighting for equal legal rights for same sex partnerships. Family business researchers should also hear this call. In order to grasp the diversity and richness, I think it is necessary to include 'alternative' families and their firms in the discussion. It will be interesting to see whether queer family firms can gain recognition within the field as within the society. It is certain, based on a simple probability calculation, that there are queer family controlled firms. They just need to be brought to the surface.

References

Acker, J. (2006). Inequality regimes: Gender, class, and race in organizations. *Gender Society*, 20(4), 441–464.

Ahl, H. J. (2002). *The Making of the Female Entrepreneur: A Discoursive Analysis of Research Texts on Women's Entrepreneurship*. Jönköping: JIBS.

Astrachan, J. H., Klein, S. B., and Smyrnios, K. X. (2002). The F-PEC scale of family influence: A proposal for solving the family business definition problem. *Family Business Review*, XV(1), 45–58.

Astrachan, J. H., and Shanker, M. C. (September 2003). Family businesses' contribution to the U.S. economy: A closer look. *Family Business Review*, XVI(3), 211–219.

Bruni, A. (2006). 'Have you got a boyfriend or are you single?': On the importance of being 'straight' in organizational research. *Gender, Work & Organization*, 13(3), 299–316.

Bruni, A., Gherardi, S., and Poggio, B. (2004). Doing gender, doing entrepreneurship: An ethnographic account of intertwined practices. *Gender, Work & Organization*, 11(4), 406–429.

Butler, J. (1999). *Gender Trouble: Feminism and the Subversion of Identity* (Tenth Anniversary Edition ed.). London, UK: Routledge.

Calás, M. B., and Smircich, L. (1996). From 'The woman's' point of view: Feminist approaches to organization studies. In S. R. Clegg, C. Hardy and W. R. Nord (Eds.), *Handbook of Organization Studies* (pp. 218–257). London: Sage Publishing.

Carrington, W. J., and Troske, K. R. (1995). Gender segregation in small firms. *The Journal of Human Resources*, 30(3), 503–533.

Chrisman, J. J., Chua, J. H., and Sharma, P. (1998). Important attributes of successors in family businesses: An exploratory study. *Family Business Review*, 11(1), 19–34.

Chrisman, J. J., Chua, J. H., and Sharma, P. (September 2005). Trends and directions in the development of a strategic management theory of the family firm. *Entrepreneurship Theory and Practice*, 11(1), 555–575.

Chua, J. H., Chrisman, J. J., and Sharma, P. (Summer 1999). Defining the family business by behavior. *Entrepreneurship Theory and Practice*, 23(4), 19–39.

Cole, P. M. (1997). Women in family business. *Family Business Review*, 10(4), 353–371.

Dumas, C. (1998). Women's pathways to participation and leadership in the family-owned firm. *Family Business Review*, 11(3), 219–228.

Faccio, M., and Lang, L.H.P. (2002). The ultimate ownership of Western European corporations. *Journal of Financial Economics*, 65(3).

Gabb, J. (1999). Imag(in)ing the queer lesbian family. *Journal of the Association for Research on Mothering*, 1(2), 9–20.

Gilding, M. (2000). Family business and family change: Individual autonomy, democratization, and the new family business institutions. *Family Business Review*, 13(3), 239–250.

Habbershon, T. G., and Williams, M. L. (1999). A resource-based framework for assessing the strategic advantages of family firms. *Family Business Review*, 12(1), 1–25.

Hubler, T. M. (2005). Forgiveness as an intervention in family-owned business: A new beginning. *Family Business Review*, 18(2), 95–103.

Javefors Grauers, E. (2004). *Kvinnors företagande, en avspegling av samhälletKvinnor som företagare in Gnosjö och Jönköping*. Edited by C. Holmquist and E. Sundin. Stockholm: Verket för näringslivsutveckling (NUTEK).

Klein, S. B. (2000). Family businesses in Germany: Significance and structure. *Family Business Review*, 13(3),157–182.

La Porta, R., Lopez-De-Silanes, F., andShleifer, A. (April 1999). Corporate ownership around the world. *The Journal of Finance*, LIV(2), 471–517.

Lee, Y. G., Hong, G. S., and Rowe, B. R. (2006). Third shift women in business-owning families. *Journal of Family and Economic Issues*, 27(1), 72–91.

Litz, R. A. (1995). The family business: Toward definitional clarity. *Family Business Review*, 8(2), 71–81.

Morgan, G. (1996). *Images of Organization* (2nd ed.). Thousand Oaks: Sage Publications.

Mulholland, K. (2003). *Class, Gender and the Family Business*. New York: Palgrave MacMillan.

Nielsen, J. M., Walden, G., and Kunkel, C. A. (2000). Gendered heteronormativity: Emprical illustrations in everyday life. *The Sociological Quarterly*, 41(2), 283–296.

Pilcher, J., and Whelehan. (2006). *50 Key Concepts in Gender Studies*. London: SAGE Publications.

Poza, E. J., and Messer, T. (2001). Spousal leadership and continuity in the family firm. *Family Business Review*, 14(1), 25–36.

Rich, A. (1980). Compulsory heterosexuality and lesbian existence. *Signs*, 5(4), 631–660.

Rowe, B. R., and Hong, G. S. (2000). The role of wives in family businesses: The paid and unpaid work of women. *Family Business Review*, 13(1), 1–13.

Sharma, P. (2004). An overview of the field of family business studies: Current status and directions for the future. *Family Business Review*, 17(1), 1–36.

Stewart, A. (2003). Help one another, Use one another: Toward an anthropology of family business. *Entrepreneurship Theory and Practice*, 27(4), 383–396.

Van Auken, H., and Werbel, J. (2006). Family dynamic and family business financial performance: Spousal commitment. *Family Business Review*, 19(1), 49–63.

Vera, C. F., and Dean, M. A. (2005). An examination of the challenges daughters face in family business succession. *Family Business Review*, 18(4), 321–345.
Westhead, P., and Cowling, M. (Fall 1998). Family firm research: The need for a methodological rethink. *Entrepreneurship Theory and Practice*, 23(1), 31–55.
Zahra, S. A., and Sharma, P. (2004). Family business research: A strategic reflection. *Family Business Review*, 17(4), 331–346.

11 Family business management challenges

Understanding generational differences

Veland Ramadani, Angelka Ilioska, Gadaf Rexhepi and Hyrije Abazi-Alili

1. Introduction

Few topics in the popular business press over the past few decades have captured as much attention as the role of different generations in the workplace and their effects on businesses, families and individuals. Today, family businesses are dominating the global business, but in order to ensure their longevity, they must face their many challenges through understanding and managing their differences.

How different generations perceive their work is critical in this swiftly moving economy. Each generation involved in the business has its own preference in the working environment and expectations from their work. Family businesses not only need to understand the importance of family members' motivations, but they should also comprehend the variances in preferences of motivation factors between various generations (Nasser, 2014). Furthermore, the fast pace of change in the business world only accelerates the tension between different generations, which is why family members need to establish strong and well-structured business relationships, especially since being a family may not be enough at times. Failure in satisfying these aspects could result in bad management, overall decline of organizations and can even lead to closing a business.

This chapter brings together two different streams of research: generational differences and how they affect the family business. It identifies effective strategies in decreasing the gap and resolving the differences between family members. Family members need to understand the source of the clash between them so they can put conflict resolution mechanisms in place, avoid conflicts or deal with conflicts before they escalate. The starting point in resolving the problem is enhancing organizations' awareness on their business practices and taking steps to understand generations' differences. To do that it is crucial to identify key generational differences that exist across key employees, within family businesses in particular.

For years now the literature discusses various generational stereotypes and ways to address them, but almost all are theoretical. To date no empirical research in the context of family businesses in Macedonia has been performed. The intent is not to side with a certain viewpoint in the debate of generational differences, but it is to reveal insights to generational differences and their implications on family businesses. Family businesses must understand generational differences, which will help them to create a sustainable, competitive business.

2. Literature review

2.1 Defining generation

A traditional definition of generation is "the average interval of time between the birth of parents and the birth of their offspring" (Collins English Dictionary, n.d.). In term of years, this definition has placed a generation roughly at around 20–30 years in span. However, because the dynamic of today's life is changing rapidly, mainly in response to new technologies and shifting societal values, two decades is too broad for a generational span. In today's fast-paced world, it is perhaps better to define generations sociologically rather than biologically (Ng, Schweitzer, and Lyons, 2010).

Generations are shaped by its history, and according to McCrindle (2007), there are three aspects that define a generation and those are:

- age,
- conditions and
- experiences.

Age is a defining factor because it differentiates one generation from another while conditions (economic, political, social conditions, etc.) and experiences define the characteristics of a generation (Schweitzer and Lyons, 2010).

Kupperschmidt (as cited in Zemke, Raines, and Filipczak, 2000) defines a generation or cohort as "an identifiable group that share birth years, age, location, and significant life event at critical developmental stages, divided by five-seven years into the first wave, core group, and last wave" (p. 148). Ultimately generations are defined by key life events that capture the attention and emotions of thousands of individuals (Zemke et al., 2000). These shared experiences influence the course of an individual's life and distinguish one generation from another; generational differences are ultimately the result of different life experiences (Zemke et al., 2000; Strauss and Howe, 1991). Due to these key life experiences, each generation develops a set of unique characteristics, personalities, aspirations and expectations that influence a person's feelings toward organizations, what they expect from work and how they interpret subsequent life experiences (Zemke et al., 2000.

Shaped by its place and role in history, each generation brings something new and distinctive, yet crucially important, to the workforce. This is why it is so important to understand and regularly address generational differences in the workplace.

If generational differences regarding work are not understood correctly by organizations, this can lead to conflicts, issues in communication and negatively influence productivity. All generations equally desire a workplace that not only allows but also encourages him or her to be a productive and influential contributor. This is the challenge that family businesses face today. Therefore, they need to find a way to create an environment that meets the needs and expectations of all employees, regardless of the generation to which they belong.

2.2 Theories about generations

The two most prevalent generational theories are the well-established Strauss-Howe generational theory and Mannheim generations' theory.

2.2.1 Strauss-Howe generational theory

William Strauss and Neil Howe analyzed history cyclically rather than in a linear fashion. The study they released, even if it was irrespective of its heavy American characteristics, has been widely used by other scholars, and their findings could greatly help us understand recurring characteristics and traits of generations.

Strauss and Howe discovered a pattern in the historical generations they examined that revolved around generational events, which they called turnings. In generations, and in greater detail in *The Fourth Turning*, they identify the four-stage cycle of social or mood eras, i.e. turnings (Strauss and Howe, 1997).

Strauss-Howe theory aims to give a clear picture of the future by studying "recurring dynamics of generational behavior and how and when it results in social change" (Howe and Strauss, 1996). Their theory can be reduced to the idea that each new generation responds to the previous generation.

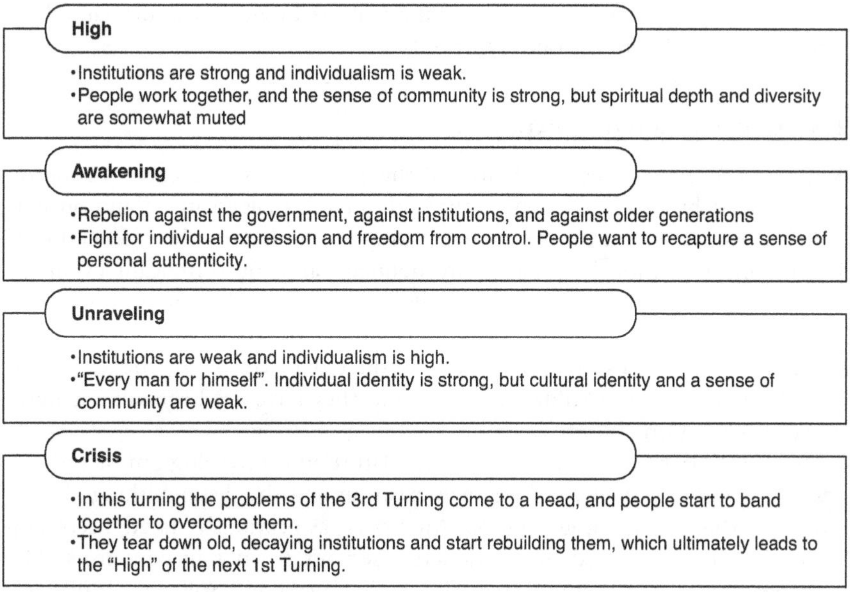

High

- Institutions are strong and individualism is weak.
- People work together, and the sense of community is strong, but spiritual depth and diversity are somewhat muted

Awakening

- Rebelion against the government, against institutions, and against older generations
- Fight for individual expression and freedom from control. People want to recapture a sense of personal authenticity.

Unraveling

- Institutions are weak and individualism is high.
- "Every man for himself". Individual identity is strong, but cultural identity and a sense of community are weak.

Crisis

- In this turning the problems of the 3rd Turning come to a head, and people start to band together to overcome them.
- They tear down old, decaying institutions and start rebuilding them, which ultimately leads to the "High" of the next 1st Turning.

Figure 11.1 Four-stage cycle of social or mood eras

Source: Strauss and Howe (1997)

2.2.2 Mainannheim's theory of generations

Dr. Karl Mannheim explains his Theory of Generations from a sociological point of view. He proposes a less-structured theory that compliments the Strauss-Howe Generational Theory, emphasizing social location and class factors as dominant variables affecting generational traits while believing that social change occurs at a slower pace. Mannheim's theory can be summarized by the idea that people resemble their times more than they resemble their parents (Corsten, 1999).

Mannheim theorizes that major historical events change society quickly in a much more direct, linear way. Mannheim also emphasizes social location and class factors as dominant variables affecting generational traits that explain different behaviors and approaches attributed to different generations. According to Mannheim, it is necessary to look at social and cultural factors that may justify the commonness of certain characteristics among specific generations (Pilcher, 1993).

Mannheim indicates that generations can be primarily characterized by special behavior and collectively shared knowledge (Corsten, 1999). He argues that the development of the distinct generational consciousness and altered approaches depends on social changes (Pilcher, 1993). Therefore, it is important to consider social, political, economic and historical factors that can help shape and change common generational characteristics and features. These factors will eventually lead in the development of certain traits and qualities in each generation that might distinctively distinguish it from others. Although these differences might not be as distinctive as some of the existing similarities among different generations, it is necessary to be aware of them so as to identify the values system and behavioral pattern of each generation as to eventually understand how generations are different from each other.

2.3 Classification of generations

As previously mentioned, generational theory suggests that each generation is influenced by their experiences throughout life that creates common personality, value, and attitude distinguishing them from other generations. Therefore, generation boundaries are defined based on significant events in the society. Since each generation is defined based on its age and location, generations are usually characterized based on the boundaries of each country. Most generational research has been conducted in the U.S., the U.K. and Canada (Lancaster and Stillman, 2002), and they have used the same generational classification.

Despite the lack of consistency in nomenclature and chronology, most authorities agree that a great deal of variance exists among the distinguishing characteristics within any given generation. Moreover, as previously stated, according to the literature reviewed, the parameters set out are not in consensus. The most prominent classifications are based on Lancaster and Stillman (2002) and Strauss and Howe (2000).

Table 11.1 Generation's birth years

Generation	*Born Between (Lancaster and Stillman, 2002)*	*Born BetweenStrauss and Howe (2000)*
Silent Generation	1925–1946	1925–1942
Baby Boomers	1946–1964	1943–1960
Generation X	1965–1981	1961–1981
Generation Y	1982–2000	1982–2002

Source: Lancaster and Stillman (2002) and Strauss and Howe (2000)

Table 11.2 Personal and lifestyle characteristics by generation

	Silent Generation	*Baby Boomers*	*Generation X*	*Generation Y*
Core values	Respect for authority Conformers Discipline	Optimism Involvement	Skepticism Fun Informality	Realism Confidence Extreme fun Social
Family	Traditional Nuclear	Disintegrating	Latch–key kids	Merged families
Education	A dream	A birthright	A way to get there	An incredible expense
Dealing with money	Put it away Pay cash	Buy now, pay later	Cautious Conservative Save, save, save	Earn to spend

Source: Based on Hammill (2005)

To understand how individuals in different generations act and react we must consider the individual underlying values, or personal and lifestyle characteristics, that seem to correspond with each generation, as shown in the following table (Hammill, 2005).

The characteristics listed in the table are in general; it does not necessarily means that every person in a generation will share all of the characteristics with others in the same generation. However, these characteristics are indicative of general patterns in the relationships between and among family members, friends and people in the workplace.

Understanding individual characteristics makes it easier to look at workplace characteristics and how they manifest themselves in business. The workplace characteristics are shown in Table 11.3.

Table 11.3 Workplace characteristics

	Silent generation	*Baby Boomers*	*Generation X*	*Generation Y*
Work ethics and values	Hard work Respect authority Sacrifice Duty before fun Adhere to rules	Workaholics Work efficiently Crusading causes Personal fulfillment Desire quality An exciting adventure	Eliminate the task Self-reliance Want structure and direction Skeptical	What's next Multitasking Tenacity Entrepreneurial Tolerant Goal orientated
Work is . . .	An obligation	An exciting adventure	A difficult challenge A contract	A means to an end Fulfillment
Leadership style	Directive Command-and-control	Consensual Collegial	Everyone is the same Challenge others Ask why	*TBD
Interactive style	Individual	Team player Loves to have meetings	Entrepreneurial	Participative
Communication style	Formal Memo	In person	Direct Immediate	E-mail Voicemail
Feedback and rewards	No news is good news Satisfaction in a job well done	Don't appreciate it Money Title recognition	Sorry to interrupt, but how am I doing? Freedom is the best reward	Whatever I want at a push of a button Meaningful work
Messages that motivate	Your experience is respected	You are valued You are needed	Do it your way Forget the rules	You will work with other bright, creative people
Work and family life	Ne'er the twain shall meet	No balance Work to live	Balance	Balance

*As this group has not spent much time in the workplace, this characteristic has yet to be determined.
Source: FDU Magazine (2005) http://ww/fdu.edu/newspubs/magazine Winter/Spring 2005

Today, as a result to the dramatic changes in the world, the differences between generations are more pronounced than ever before. Being aware of these differences can help individuals understand each other better; after all, good business is based on understanding others. For business to work effectively and efficiently and to increase productivity and quality one needs to understand generational characteristics and learn how to use them effectively in dealing with each individual (Hammill, 2005).

4. Family-owned businesses

Globally, family-owned businesses are the cornerstones of economic growth and more than two thirds of all businesses in the world are estimated to be family owned businesses Furthermore, family owned businesses have proven to contribute significantly towards employment creation, poverty reduction and wealth creation (Baron, 2016).

As a type of company, family businesses have many distinguishable forms: sole proprietorships, partnerships, limited liability companies, regular corporations, holding companies and even publicly traded, albeit family-controlled companies. .

However, even today there is no single, comprehensive definition that encompasses all divergent views about family business (Chua, Chrisman, and Sharma, 1999). Researchers define the elements of the family business, yet have difficulty finding a common frame to establish a consensus as to what constitutes a family business (Litz, Pearson, and Litchfield, 2012).

Through the years many scholars have attempted to define family-owned businesses and have focused primarily on distinguishing family-owned businesses from other businesses (Sharma, 2004). Even so, none of these definitions have yet gained widespread recognition or approval (Astrachan, 2003). The majority of definitions seem to focus on the vital role of family in terms of determining the management and control methods used in the business, but the main confusion is separating small businesses from family businesses (Sharma, 2004). Many large corporations are considered to be family-owned businesses, but the clear majority of family businesses are considered to be small businesses with less than 20 employees.

As stated previously, there are various definitions of family business looking at the different aspects of the business itself. All definitions have been broadly classified into two categories based on the structure and the process involved in family business. There are structured and process definitions of family business. Structured definitions are given based on ownership and/or management of family business while process definitions are based on how the family is involved in the business.

Shankar and Astrachan (Ward, 1991) note that the criteria used to define a family business can include:

- Percentage of ownership;
- Voting control;
- Power over strategic decisions;
- Involvement of multiple generations and
- Active management of family members.

In order to resolve the ambiguity surrounding family business research, a business can be defined as a family business when its ownership and management are concentrated within a family unit where the business' members must strive to achieve, maintain and/or increase intra-organizational family-based relatedness (Litz et al., 2012).

Regardless of how broadly or narrowly family businesses are defined, it is critical to recognize their significance and contributions to the local economy. Family businesses are considered to be a separate and emerging sector and a field of academic study because there are certain intentional variables due to a different combination of resources, needs and goals compared with intentions of non-family organizations (Chrisman, Chua, and Sharma, 1998).

4.1 Participants in the family business

In general, participants in a family business can be divided into two groups: family members and non-family members. According to Sharma (2001), these groups are divided into internal and external family business members. Internal members are those who are involved with the business (employees, owners and/ or family members). External members are those who are not linked to the family business (through employment, ownership or family membership).

Venter, van der Merwe, and Farrington (2012) categorize participants in family business into four groups:

1 Non-family members (non-family employees, outside professionals, experts, consultants, advisors),
2 Inactive family members (members who are not directly involved in the family business in terms of interfering in the business decision-making or disagreements),
3 Senior generation (parents who share important information related to the business and should resign control),
4 Incumbent generation (children as active family members that are willing to satisfy their career needs in the context of the family business).

Each participant has personal approaches and abilities to put pressure on the business and the family itself (Sharma, 2004).

4.2 Key elements of family-owned business

Family-owned business organizations have very distinct characteristics; they have its own set of rules, values and methods of communication (Bork, Jaffe, Lane, Dashew, and Heisler, 1996). These characteristics have either a positive or negative impact on the business. The family-owned business system is impacted by two different worlds: one is the family and the other one is the business. These two systems are demonstrated in Figure 11.2.

The needs and objectives of the family can easily conflict with the business system (Bork et al., 1996). The family relies on caring for each other while the business depends on generating profit through working efficiently in a competitive environment. Family needs can supersede the business needs in certain situations when family members expect the business system to operate on the same rules as within the family. The opposite situation can occur also. The intersection

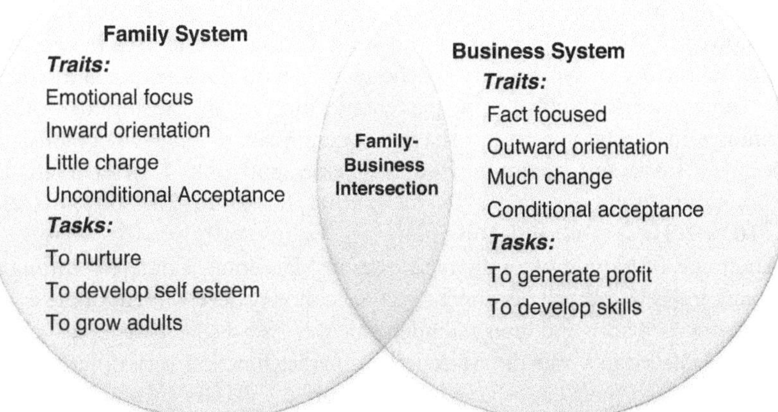

Figure 11.2 Intersecting family business system

Source: Bork et al., (1996)

area in the circle includes those decisions that have implications on both the family and the business.

Jaffe (1990) also described certain characteristics of the family and business systems. He identifies the family as an "emotional support system" while business has to "produce tangible results". The two systems (family and business) can impact or influence each other in any family business. Adding the qualities of one system to the other can have positive as well as negative impacts (Jaffe, 1990). For example, family system characteristics like caring for each other while developing effective and controlled informal relationships and adopting a long-term time frame can help to develop effective work environments in the family business. On the other hand, if the family business involves too much paternalistic authority, informal relationships and family loyalty, the business can become an oppressive and inefficient place to work. Therefore, in order to have an effective family business, a family should try to capitalize on bringing the positive qualities of the family into the business while controlling or limiting the negative qualities of the family system.

5. Family businesses in Macedonia

Most small businesses in Macedonia are family owned, and they have always had an important place in the economy. Family business importance refers to the ability to accumulate a great deal of the workforce, provide employment opportunities, provide greater competitiveness and achieve accelerated economic growth and development. Macedonian economy is in the form of microeconomics; 92 percent of the companies in Macedonia have between 0–10 employees, representing a figure of 80 percent of the total number of employees who generate more than 60 percent of the gross domestic product of Macedonia.

The trend of steady increase in the share of small businesses in the overall economic picture of the country is synonymous with the size, position and role that family businesses play. The percentage increase in the number of small businesses in Macedonia shows that, in recent years, 99 percent of businesses belong to small and medium sized businesses and only 1 percent are large corporations ("Official Gazette" No. 28/2004, 84/2005, 25/2007, 87/2008, 42/10, 48/10, 24/11 and 166/12).

The trend of growth of family businesses in Macedonia is different throughout the years and is very much dependent on the economic development of the country in the periods before and after its independence. As a Federal Republic in Yugoslavia, the Macedonia and the Macedonian market function very differently.

As part of former Yugoslavia, Macedonian companies produced for many major markets, and the requirements of the economy then were quite different from the trends and expectations now. During that time, there were a number of "Giants", large companies with full internal structural formulation and a very small number of small family businesses that could not penetrate the market easily. After independence and over the years, new horizons were opened, policies were put in place that started implementing measures to provide faster and better development of the business sector and it was easier for family businesses to thrive in the market (Suklev, 2006).

Although steps were taken to improve the business climate in the Macedonian market, there are reasons that limit the formation and threaten the success of family business in the territory of the Republic of Macedonia. Family businesses in Macedonia don't have to deal only with generational differences but have to adapt and learn to prevail in a, at times, hostile business environment.

Some of the difficulties that family owned businesses in Macedonia have to face are (Dana and Ramadani, 2016):

- *Ownership rights* – the protection of property rights are still a serious challenge for Macedonia. What makes things more difficult is the fact that the judicial system in Macedonia is relatively inefficient and remains a subject to political influence.
- *Corruption* – despite all efforts, the existence of corruption in Macedonia is evident. Corruption increases the rate of entry for family businesses and decreases the interest of potential investors to invest money, expertise and time in these companies.
- *Administrative and bureaucratic obstacles* – even though the time needed for registration of new enterprises is significantly cut, there are other, time consuming bureaucratic procedures that make daily business transactions more difficult.
- *State regulation* – Macedonia needs to strengthen the independence of regulatory bodies and ensure fair regulation of different domains of the market,

stop deregulation and remove administrative and bureaucratic obstacles that obstruct the growth of businesses.

- *Infrastructure* – poor infrastructure is the key obstacle to development of businesses in Macedonia.

These factors are directly related to the success of family businesses in Macedonia.

6. Methodology

The primal objective of the research was to identify whether generational differences existed and what was their role in family owned businesses, particularly in Macedonia. In the research, different types of family owned businesses were studied. Through an interviewing process of selected cases and a questionnaire, common themes were identified that indicated that generational differences do exist and they affect how the business is run, cause tensions and result in conflict in the management of the family business.

The following is an overview of the sequential steps that were undertaken in the research:

a Specific outcomes of the research were decided and identified.
b The structure and questions of the questionnaire were developed.
c Interview structure and questions were determined for both successor (second generation) and the founder (first generation).
d The sample consisting of family owned businesses was identified.
e A majority of the interviews and questionnaires were conducted over a four-week period, one-to-one with a semi-structured interview format. Some were conducted by telephone.
f Each interview followed a protocol utilizing the established questions with each interview lasting less than 20 minutes.

6.1 Subject selection and description

The following criteria were used to select the sample of family owned businesses:

a Family owned businesses that were part of the study were small/medium-sized family owned businesses.
b The total sample consisted of 50 companies.
c The sample included a mix of different kinds of business sectors.
d All businesses were Macedonia based.

6.2 Data collection methods

Two research methods were used for the research, exploratory interviews and questionnaires. The preliminary research of the exploratory interviews has a qualitative nature. It was chosen to add a qualitative research method in order to give an extra depth to the quantitative research discussed below and to get a better understanding of the subject of this research. The qualitative method offered an opportunity to go more into depth on the main topics of the research and strengthened the basis of the quantitative research.

Quantitative research was selected, since it can be used to measure opinions, values and preferences as well as behavior from a larger population. Questionnaires containing 36 statements were used in order to be able to measure differences in values, preferences and characteristics between different generations.

The exploratory interviews were held with first and second generations to get a better understanding of the generation's dynamics in the workplace and to distinguish the generational differences that cause tensions and conflicts in the workplace. The interviews were structured to make sure that the responses could be compared properly.

For this research the structured interview method was used. The questions asked by the interviewer are identical in all interviews held and questions are open-ended.

The questionnaire was used to get information in a clearer, more organized way, and it was based on the findings of the interviews and the literature review.

All questions surveyed the following scale:

Level	*Strongly agree*	*Agree*	*Neutral*	*Disagree*	*Strongly disagree*
Scale	5	4	3	2	1

6.3 Hypothesis

H1 – Key differences between generations exist and affect the dynamics of an organization.

H2 – Generational differences are likely to cause conflicts in a family business.

H3 – Generational differences affect working relationships and undermine business effectiveness.

6.4 Descriptive statistics

The representative sample of the study included companies across different industries in Macedonia. In order to fit the criterion of the study, only family owned and operated businesses were chosen.

Two representative bodies were selected for the research: the owners of the business or the entrepreneurs that started the business and their children or close family members that were supposed to inherit and take over the business.

The research shows that the representatives were mostly male, which only confirms that in practice, even today, men heavily outnumber women in the world of entrepreneurship. In Macedonia gender equality has a de jure rather than de facto presence, and discrimination against women persists and is manifested in both the public and private sectors. Macedonia is a young country with a lot of social and religious customs in which women endure patriarchal stereotypes and have been perceived more as mothers and wives. Women are noticeably under-represented in decision-making roles; in fact, a very small percentage of women hold senior decision-making positions. This inequality is the effect of cultural factors and preferences and is linked to the double burden women face, which is work within and outside the household.

The numbers also indicate that when it comes to transferring or running a business, age and gender bias are still evident, even though they are weaker than they have historically been. Macedonia is a traditional society, and it is considered as some kind of a norm for a father to groom his son to succeed him in running the family business or take on an executive role. Most of the respondents from the first generation still see their sons as the "natural leader" of the business.

	Successor	*Founder*
Male	78%	22%
Female	88%	22%

The respondents from the first focus group (founders) were aged between 40 years up to60 years and above, whereas the second focus group (successors) was aged between 18 up to the age limit of 40–49.

7. Analysis per hypothesis

Below, the analysis of the data is discussed per hypothesis. For the analysis both crosstabs and symmetric measures were used.

Hypothesis 1: Key differences between generations exist and affect the dynamics of an organization.

Based on the general hypothesis the expectation is for it to be true. The cross tabulation is performed across the 7 variables.

Variable 1: Ambition – This variable looks at how ambitious respondents are when it comes to their work. We examined ambition as the driving force behind individual and business achievement with the power to motivate individuals to be the best that they can be.

Variable 2: Optimism – this variable focuses on the respondent's tendency to optimism. We examined the mindset of the two groups that affect everything a person does. Optimism, or the lack thereof, can impact performance at work and even family relationships. Pessimists believe that unsuccessful circumstances will endure and will undermine everything they do. Whereas optimists perceive setbacks as temporary, specifically confined to one occurrence. Pessimists usually give up and the optimists keep trying.

Variable 3: Build my own way – this variable looks at the respondent's tendency to follow their own ideas of success instead of conforming and following a set path. This variable was examined because entrepreneurship and family businesses can often collide, especially when new generations bring their own ideas or tend to drift away from the companies their parents or grandparents founded.

Variable 4: Follow the example of others – This variable refers to the respondent's tendency to learn from others' experiences and follow their path. Successors can always learn from the founder's experience and knowledge.

Variable 5: Activities outside of work – This variable focuses on how other aspects, like friends and family, are considered more important than work.

Variable 6: Job as a priority – This variable focuses on the role that the job plays in the respondent's lives.

Variable 7: Social interaction – This variable focuses on the degree of social interaction the respondent's desire at work.

Variables/Answers	*Successor*					*Founder*				
	do not agree at all	*do not agree*	*neutral*	*agree*	*completely agree*	*do not agree at all*	*do not agree*	*Neutral*	*agree*	*completely agree*
Ambition	–	–	–	26%	74%	–	4%	14%	16%	66%
Optimism	–	4%	4%	36%	56%	2%	20%	12%	16%	50%
Build my own way	2%	12%	22%	36%	28%	–	2%	14%	34%	50%
Follow the example of others	–	8%	24%	42%	26%	6%	16%	12%	46%	20%
Activities outside of work	–	6%	8%	40%	46%	4%	36%	16%	34%	10%
Job as a priority	8%	10%	16%	44%	22%	–	8%	2%	20%	70%
Social interaction	2%	2%	12%	18%	66%	14%	10%	38%	22%	16%

Cross tabulation was performed across the 7 variables, and the findings show that there was a moderate, positive association between them.

Successors have stronger positive association with the following variables: ambition, activities outside of work and social interaction.

They consider themselves to be more ambitious, find activities outside of work to be more important for them and place a higher value on social interaction in the workplace. These results are no surprise, as younger generations, in terms of preparation, are highly educated and many of them seek high-level job positions. They want a challenging work, to continuously learn and do better. And when it comes to family and social life, they are looking for a strong work-life balance. They want more time for their spouse, children and friends. Furthermore, the findings from the research indicate that successors value social interactions with coworkers more and that work relationships play an important role in their professional life.

Founders, or the older generation, have a stronger positive correlation with the following variables: build my own way and viewing their job as a priority. This generation values their job more than successors do, and they see it as a priority in their life. They also want to build their own way and find following the example of others less important. The social interaction in the workplace, as well as activities outside of work, is less important for them.

Different associations and the obvious dissimilarity in the strength of correlation between the 7 variables and generations show that there is, in fact, a difference between members of different generations. With this we accept the first hypothesis.

Hypothesis 2: Generational differences are likely to cause conflicts in a family business.

Based on the general hypothesis, the expectation is for it to be true. The cross tabulation is performed across the 6 variables.

Variable 1: Who is in charge of the business? – Companies managed by a committee of relatives can trigger bitter disagreements and lead to execution paralysis. This variable looks at who has the final say in decision-making within the family business.

	Successor	*Founder*
1st Generation	42%	58%
2nd Generation	65%	35%

Variable 2: Making business decisions – The decisions facing business families can be gut wrenching, and the implications of these decisions can be huge both for the future of the family and on the business. This variable takes a closer look at how decisions are made in the selected businesses.

Variable 3: Business Ownership – When it comes to family businesses, conflict can arise from any direction, but succession often poses a serious challenge for the family business. This variable looks at how respondents feel about business ownership.

Variable 4: Organizational practices –Formalized contracts, job descriptions and operating procedures are important in family-run companies. Relying on handshake agreements, though tempting, leaves room for interpretation conflicts. This variable looks at how participants from different generations feel about organizational practices.

Variable 5: Leadership – Poorly designed leadership roles set up a family business for failure. This variable in particular looks at how much guidance or leadership respondents seek in their job.

Variable 6: Challenges – Family members are raised under the same roof, thus their outlooks are similar, and while this is a great strength, it guarantees blind spots in many situations. This variable focuses on what are the respondent's views on the challenges their business is facing.

The analysis demonstrates that for the 6variables, significant results in cross correlation were found.

When asked, "Who's in charge of the family business?" both generations had different answers. 58 percent of the respondents from the successors said that they were in charge of the business, whereas 88 percent of the founders said that they were in control of the family business.

Designating someone as the leader with the final say ensures that the company can avoid a potentially toxic and damaging predicament. Who is in charge of the family business should be an easy answer; unfortunately, the answer is different for each generation and it is very unclear. The notion of who is in charge in the family business is far more fluid than it should be. The issue of control is often overridden by a family member (usually the founder) no matter what title is held or, in some cases, not held. But, bottom line, is that not knowing who has the leading role in the business can be extremely harmful to the business and cause conflicts between the two generations.

The results also show that both generations make decisions differently; while the successors seek the advice from family members (usually the founders), founders make decisions solely. How decisions are made in the business can lead to potential conflicts. For example, 76 percent of respondents from the founders say they do not share a role of making decisions and that other family members generally don't have an input into decision-making. Key business decisions should be discussed between at least two people before a decision is made so that the decision-making process is effective and conflicts are avoided.

Furthermore, when it comes to organizational practices, successors feel that organizational practices are important and want to have a formal organizational structure within the business. However, their opinion is not shared with the older generation. Most founders feel that there is no need for organizational practices and prefer a more laid back approach to running a business. The older generation, or the founders, is relying on handshake agreements. Organizational practices take into account effective business controls, placing the right people in the right jobs, providing incentives that work and having sufficient resources to fulfill the obligations of the business. Nonexistent organizational practices do not only hurt the business ability to maximize opportunities, but can also create conflicts between generations and ultimately lead to serious financial consequences.

In successors' responses about leadership where stronger positive association was found, we could say that the leadership of their supervisor is more important for them. On the other hand, the founders seek less leadership or guidance.

Both generations seem to have different perceptions about the challenges that their business is facing. This can lead to conflicts because they cannot identify the issues that affect their business negatively.

The data analysis shows that there is no significant difference between the responses of both generations about business ownership. Both generations agree that family members or members who partake in the business should have ownership of the business.

The difference in the strength in correlation between the variables and different generations is significant, which leads to the conclusion that the hypothesis could be accepted.

***Hypothesis* 3:** Generational differences affect working relationships and undermine business effectiveness.

***Variable 1*:** Prefer working individually – This variable asks the question of whether respondents prefer working individually or in a team. Individualistic or a team approach affects the overall work dynamic.

***Variable 2*:** Flexibility –Flexibility in the workplace allows employers and employees to decide about working conditions that suit them. This can either help improve the productivity and efficiency of their business or the lack of it can cause tensions and dissatisfaction.

***Variable 3*:** Work after work – This variable looks at how respondents feel about working overtime.

***Variable 4*:** Interesting job – This variable looks at how important it is for responders to have an interesting job.

***Variable 5*:** Management – This variable focuses on the respondent's views about the management team in their businesses.

Variables/Answers	*Successor*					*Founder*				
	Do not agree at all	*Do not agree*	*Neutral*	*Agree*	*Completely agree*	*Do not agree at all*	*Do not agree*	*Neutral*	*Agree*	*Completely agree*
Prefer working individually	16%	26%	20%	26%	12%	8%	20%	14%	40%	18%
Flexibility	–	2%	14%	12%	72%	4%	8%	36%	24%	28%
Work after work	18%	16%	16%	24%	26%	–	6%	6%	24%	64%
Interesting job	6%	–	2%	18%	74%	22%	10%	8%	18%	42%

A Pearson's product-moment correlation was run to assess the relationship between the two general generations (founders and successors) and the level to which they prefer working individually. There was a strong positive correlation between generations and their individualistic approach when it comes to work (r =, 060, p < .0005). These results show that by a slight difference there is a difference of perspective on individuality when it comes to work between members of different generations as founders tend to prefer to work individually more than successors.

The correlation between generation and flexibility shows that successors are associated with a higher tendency to value flexibility in their work.

The correlation between generation and working outside normal working hours shows that founders have a higher tendency to stay and work longer, that it is required, whereas 18 percent of the successors are strongly against working overtime.

When analyzing the fourth variable, based on the results above, we could report that the results of this study indicate that successors find it more important for them to have an interesting job, whereas founders do not place such importance on this variable.

The Pearson's product-moment correlation assessed the relationship between generation and the management team as strongly positive. The results indicate that both generations have a similar view when it comes to their management team. Most of the companies that were researched had a management team that consisted of family members.

The significant results show that generational differences do affect working relationships and that, because of different preferences and ways of approaching work, business effectiveness can sometimes be undermined.

Regression analysis

The primary objective of regression analysis is to estimate the value of a random variable (the dependent variable) given that the value of an associated variable (the independent variable) is known. Below we provide some regression analysis using the questionnaire data where we set the variable *generation* as dependent variable, and variables *Business and lifestyle, Leadership, Job security, Activities outside work, Family and friends, Factors for success, Work after work, Responsibility* and *Age* as predictors or independent variables.

Model Summary

Model	*R*	*R Square*	*Adjusted R Square*	*Std. Error of the Estimate*
1	,924[a]	,855	,840	,201

a. Predictors: (Constant), Business and lifestyle, Leadership, Job security, Activities outside work, Family and friends, Factors for success, Work after work, Responsibility, Age

ANOVA[a]

Model		*Sum of Squares*	*df*	*Mean Square*	*F*	*Sig.*
1	Regression	21.363	9	2,374	58,736	,000[b]
Residual	3.637	90	,040			
Total	25.000	99				

a. Dependent Variable: Generation
b. Predictors: (Constant), Business and lifestyle, Leadership, Job security, Activities outside work, Family and friends, Factors for success, Work after work, Responsibility, Age

Coefficients[a]

Model		*Unstandardized Coefficients*		*Standardized Coefficients*	*t*	*Sig.*
		B	*Std. Error*	*Beta*		
1	(Constant)	(.869)	.341		(2,547)	,013
	Age	.314	.022	.784	14,200	,000
	Work after work	.028	.018	.076	1,534	,129
	Activities outside work	(.098)	.020	(.225)	(4,866)	,000
	Job security	(.043)	.033	(.056)	(1,318)	,191
	Responsibility	.049	.022	.113	2,190	,031
	Leadership	(.056)	.021	(.127)	(2,678)	,009
	Family and friends	.037	.025	.067	1,470	,145
	Factors for success	(.013)	.006	(.087)	(2,035)	,045
	Business and lifestyle	.551	.211	.110	2,610	,011

a. Dependent Variable: Generation

After performing linear regression using the software package SPSS we found the following results. In the model summary table, the R-square shows the "goodness of fit" of the model. We find that the adjusted R^2 of our model is, 840 with the $R^2 = .855$ that means that the linear regression explains 85.5 percent of the variance in the data. Given the analysis, we can also assume that there is a linear relationship between the variables in our model.

In this case the R-square for this model is 0,840, which means that the X variable (variables) can explain about 84 percent of the change in Y (generation variable).

The ANOVA tells us whether our regression model explains a statistically significant proportion of the variance. Specifically, it uses a ratio to compare how well our linear regression model predicts the outcome to how accurate simply using the mean of the outcome data as an estimate is. Given the strength of the correlation, it is not surprising that our model is statistically significant ($p < ,0005$).

After generating the model for generational differences, one can interpret the coefficients of the independent variables. The results show significant coefficients for age, activities outside of work, responsibility, leadership and factors for success, which can be interpreted as follows:

- The coefficient of the age level is positive and statistically significant. This indicates that a change from one scale to another, higher scale (1–5) increases the probability of being the founder by 9,5 percent. This indicates that there is a positive relationship between age and ownership. The older the respondent, the higher is the tendency for him/her to be the owner of the business.

- The relationship between generation and activities outside of work is found to be statistically significant, in particular the younger generation, or successors, are more likely to value activities outside of work than the older generation, or the founders.
- The coefficient of the responsibility is positive and statistically significant. This indicates that the older the respondent, the higher is the tendency for him/her to want to be given more responsibility.
- It looks as though leadership has strong positive correlation with generation. Findings show that successors need leadership from their supervisors more than the founders.

In short, the empirical analysis suggests that the successor's probability of finding activities outside of work and leadership increase in significance over time. Additionally, the probability of participants being founders increases with the age. After generating the model for generational differences, one can interpret the coefficients of the independent variables.

Findings from the interview

Findings from the interview confirm that in family businesses, with very diverse generations in charge, obstacles involving respect, communication and work styles are piling up and are hard to handle.

Shortly, some of the most pivotal conclusions from the interviewing process are:

- Conflicts between first and second generation usually involve differences in core life experiences.
- Criticism between relatives is taken more seriously than criticism by colleagues or outside supervisors. Acting on constructive criticism is mandatory for business improvement. Family members delivering and receiving criticism must take extra time to frame it in a professional context and must both maintain maturity. Clearly documented expectations and good reporting procedures can objectify discussion and make things easier.
- In the workplace different generations are not acknowledged for the contributions they bring to the workforce, and usually the values and experiences unique to each generation are not understood correctly.
- In the interviewing process most successors said that they still feel like they are under their parent's thumb and that they're not treated as adults. They are still being told what to do or are watched over by their parents. This is a problem for many family businesses in Macedonia. By not letting go, founders deprive their beloved businesses of the full range of knowledge and skills that the next generation may have to offer. After all, the younger generation is often more in touch with changing trends, developing markets, and shifts in technologies than the older generation is.
- A high percentage of workplace conflicts arise from differences in generational values. Key players don't discuss their differences and the conflict

continues to be "you against me", or "my generation's values against your generation's values".

The results from the research show that generational differences can either drive the family business and help them to achieve outstanding performance for many years to come or drive them to fail, which will ultimately leave long-lasting pains for the involved families.

Every successful multi-generational family business develops its own history of gains and pains, highs and lows, but it is essentially based on resilience and an unshakeable commitment to succeed over the long term and preserve the family business that remains as a legacy.

The second part of the research refers to the findings from the questionnaires and interviews, which led to several conclusions. Family business combines tensions of the family life with the strains of business life but at no moment do both types of stress combine so forcefully as when generational change occurs. As more family members enter the family business, have a key role in management and come from different generations, they carry more complexity to the business itself, since they bring a diversity of interests, skills and needs.

Furthermore, some family members do not share the same values and vision for the business, and, therefore, they tend to opt out of ownership.

Even though family members of different generations are not the same, both generations carry the same burden of weighing and managing potential conflicts of interest between the family and the business. The most prevailing conflicts that are unavoidable involve generational transition. This is currently the highest risk for continuity of the business, and the vast majority of families in business in Macedonia fail to effectively deal with it.

Parents, or the first generation, may pass on the burden of management to the next generation, long before they give up the privilege of control. The first generation, or the founders, in family businesses in Macedonia pursue a path of personal gratification, which often is expressed as a sense of entitlement in today's work force. Even after their official retirement they feel like they are truly in charge of the business that they have built. 12 percent said that they never want to retire simply because they like working and feel like they continue to play a pivotal role in the business's success.

The first generation is more disciplined. They are also more control-oriented and feel most competent, confident and comfortable when their expectations of control, stability and predictability are being met. They dwell on changes and resist it as much as possible. Since they feel like they know best, they don't feel like there is a need for improvement or change. Their ultimate motto is "Why change what's not broken?" or "If it's not broken, don't fix it".

Most founders of the business have created an "I" culture and have a strong feeling that the capital, or assets, of the business reflects their entrepreneurial personality. It reflects how the business was built in creative and "revolutionary" ways.

The second-generation who run the business may not be as united or as driven as the founder. And the extended family usually tends to have less faith in the new management than they did in the original founder. The second generation enjoys less authority with the rest of the family than the individual who originally created the business.

Family business in Macedonia must acknowledge and deal with generational differences in the workplace. They must understand that the success of the business lies in the explicit and formal commitment to a shared vision for the family business. This is a powerful foundation for a constructive business growth backed by a unified family. After all, family business is a story about people, entrepreneurs and their families whose personal values and visions leave an imprint on the businesses that they have created and that subsequent generations continue to manage.

Family businesses have the potential to outperform any other form of business organization through their synergies between capital and management. This is because these businesses are guided by the uniquely powerful value of wanting to build a healthy business that they want to pass on to their children.

Limitations

There are some limitations to the use of structured interviews as well as questionnaires. The use of structured interviews limits the ability to elaborate on subjects further. The questions are set, and the interviewer is not supposed to add questions. Another limitation of the use of interviews is that the attitude of the interviewer can influence the interview, which can have a negative effect on the outcomes.

A limitation of using a questionnaire is that the structuring of the relevant answers in closed-ended questions might overlook some possible responses. Some also say that observation is more accurate in capturing the behavior of those being studied. The use of Scales can also result in limitations, in which respondents try to avoid using the most extreme answers, also known as the central tendency bias, or feel the need to agree with statements because they believe this is what is expected.

The sample size is too small to be able to generalize conclusions. This research is exploratory, and further research is needed to be able to generalize conclusions to the sample groups, etc.

Since a lot of research has not been performed on the topic of differences within a generation, there are several options for future research. For instance, the research could be applied to multiple, specific generations to see if the same differences or other differences are present. Another research option is to not look at work values but to look at social or personal values.

This research was limited to one country; one could also choose to expand on that research area. One could compare if there are differences within generation members of different countries. Another option is to look at the influence of religion, education or upbringing and to see if this results in differences between members of a generation.

References

Astrachan, J. H. (2003). Commentary on the special issue: The emergence of a field. *Journal of Business Venturing*, 18, 567–572.

Baron, J. (March 28, 2016). *Why the 21st Century Will Belong to Family Businesses.* Retrieved from: https://hbr.org/2016/03/why-the-21st-century-will-belong-to-family-businesses

Bork, D., Jaffe, D. T., Lane, S. R., Dashew, L., and Heisler, Q. G. (1996). *Working With Family Businesses.* San Francisco, CA: Jossey-Bass Publishers.

Chrisman, J., Chua, J., and Sharma, P. (1998). Important attributes of successors in family businesses: An exploratory study. *Family Business Review*, 11(1), 19–34.

Chua, J., Chrisman, J., and Sharma, P.(1999). Defining family business by behaviour. *Entrepreneurship Theory and Practice*, 23(4), 19–37.

Corsten, M. (1999). The time of generations. *Time Society*, 8(2–3), 249–272.

Dana, L.-P., and Ramadani, V. (2016). *Family Businesses in Transition Economies Management, Succession and Internationalization.* Cham: Springer.

Generation. (n.d.). *Collins English Dictionary – Complete & Unabridged 10th Edition.* Retrieved July 8, 2016 from Dictionary.com website: www.dictionary.com/browse/generationhttp://mccrindle.com.au/resources/The-ABC-of-XYZ_Chapter-1.pdf

Handler, W.C. (1994). Succession in family business. *Family Business Review*, 7(2), 133–157.

Jaffe, D. T. (1990). *Working With the Ones You Love.* Berkley, CA: Conari Press.

Lancaster, L. C., and Stillman, D. (2002). *When Generations Collide: Who They Are. Why They Clash. How to Solve the Generational Puzzle at Work.* New York, NY: Harper Collins.

Litz, R. A., Pearson, A. W., and Litchfield, S. (2012). Charting the future of family business research perspectives from the field. *Family Business Review*, 25(1), 16–32.

McCrindle, M. (2007). *Understanding Generation Y.* North Parramatta: Australian Leadership Foundation.

Nasser, A. (2014). Retrieved from: www.pwc.com/m1/en/assets/document/family-business-docs/understanding-family-dynamics-and-family-conflicts.pdf

Ng, E.S.W., Schweitzer, L., and Lyons, S.T. (2010). New generation, great expectations: A field study of the millennial generation. *Journal of Business and Psychology.* Retrieved March 20, 2016 from: www.springerlink.com/content/a2163v415p26h523/fulltext.pdf

Oficial Gazette No. 28/2004, 84/2005, 25/2007, 87/2008, 42/10, 48/10, 24/11 and 166/12 Retrieved from: www.slvesnik.com.mk/besplatni-izdanija.nspx

Pilcher, J. (1993). Mannheim's sociology of generations: An undervalued legacy. *British Journal of Sociology*, September, 481–495.

Sharma, P. (2004). An overview of the field of family business studies: Current status and directions for the future. *Family Business Review*, 17(1), 1–36.

Strauss, W., and Howe, H. (1991). *Generations: The History of America's Future, 1584 to 2069.* New York: Harper Collins.

Strauss, W., and Howe, N. (1997). *The Fourth Turning: An American Prophecy – What the Cycles of History Tell Us About America's Next Rendezvous With Destiny.* Portland, Broadway Books.

Ward, J. (1991). *Creating Effective Boards for Private Enterprises.* New York: Family Enterprise Publishers.

Zemke, R., Raines, C., and Filipczak, B. (November 1999). Generation gaps in the classroom. *Training*, 48–54.

Zemke, R., Raines, C., and Filipczak, B. (2000). *Generations at Work Managing the Clash of Veterans, Boomers, Xers, and Nexters in Your Workplace.* New York: American Management Association.

12 Father-daughter succession in family businesses

Current state of knowledge and future research challenges

Aleš Kubíček and Ondřej Machek

1. Introduction

Succession is a crucial moment in a family firm's life that has an immense impact on its future ability to meet strategic goals and maintain family wealth. Most family firms are not able to survive even the first generation, often being either sold or liquidated after the death or retirement of the founder (Beckhard and Dyer, 1983). Every family firm is exposed to the risk of intergenerational transition failure (Brockhaus, 2004). Naturally, the challenge of leadership succession is not unique to family firms. Professionally managed, non-family companies with separated ownership and control also often reach the point when efficient management succession becomes critical for their further existence. However, there are significant differences that make succession in family firms unique and more challenging. In family firms, emotional issues, which affect not only the firm, but also the family itself, come into play (Zellweger and Astrachan, 2008). Family relationships need to be realigned, traditional patterns of influence are redistributed, and longstanding management and ownership structures must give way to new structures (Lansberg, 1988). As a result, succession has been one of the dominant areas of family business research.

In the past, women were often seen as "family members" rather than potential owners or managers in family firms (Frishkoff and Brown, 1996). The family business literature frequently mentions the term "invisible women" to highlight the important, yet traditionally underestimated roles of female family members (Gillis-Donovan and Moynihan-Bradt, 1990). Instead of being seen as potential successors, daughters often played the roles of assistants or advisers (Dumas, 1992).

However, in past decades, the professional and family roles of women have been changing. A large body of literature investigated the contribution of women in top management positions, stressing the importance of gender diversity in management (Joy, Carter, Wagner, and Narayanan, 2007). On top of that, the number of female executives keeps increasing worldwide (Grant Thornton, 2014). As a result, there is urgent need for further research in the area of women and their role in family firms.

Although the family business literature offers several exhaustive overviews of succession from various perspectives and presents a great set of generalized empirical findings (Handler, 1994; Brockhaus, 2004; Ip and Jacobs, 2006, Nordqvist, Wennberg, and Hellerstedt, 2013; Daspit, Holt, Chrisman, and Long, 2016), gender issues in family firms have been generally limited to brief comments and research notes. One of the few exceptions is the review of more than 200 studies presented by Sharma (2004), who concluded that women and their role in family firms have remained mostly in the shadows. According to the author, "no systematic research has yet been directed towards understanding the contextual and individual factors that buoy these women into leadership positions, their performance goals in terms of family and business dimensions, or the leadership and managerial styles adopted by them" (Sharma, 2004: 14). In the traditional family business succession literature, gender is merely one of countless variables rather than a significant factor that shapes conditions, process and context of the succession.

To date, only a few authors decided to review the fragmented findings on the marginalized roles of women in family firms. In a review of 48 articles published since 1985, Jimenez (2009) examined the obstacles and positive aspects of women's involvement in family firms. The author also focused on the issue of daughters and the obstacles they must overcome to achieve leadership positions in family firms. The review concludes that the question of how women enter and run family firms still remains unclear. Another review presented by Wang (2010) focused exclusively on daughters in family firms and their chances as candidates for succession. Wang is noticeably more pessimistic as he argues that there is evidence of traditional exclusion of daughters in the succession process, which results from both macro and micro factors.

Although there is an academic consensus on the fact that women in family firms, including daughters, play important, yet underestimated roles, the research on father-daughter succession as such is still very fragmented. The existing reviews have been based especially on pioneering articles, which emerged in the eighties and nineties. Our contribution aims to make a new step towards mapping the field by reviewing more recent studies and conceptualizing the basic prerequisites of a successful father-daughter succession.

The chapter develops as follows. First, we present a framework for classifying the factors that affect the success of father-daughter succession. Subsequently, we present a review of literature along these factors. Then, directions for future research are suggested. Finally, concluding remarks are presented.

2. Factors affecting the father-daughter succession process

As we already mentioned, the mainstream family business literature regularly omits the aspect of gender in empirical and conceptual models of the succession process. While performing the review of existing literature on intergenerational succession, and father-daughter succession in particular, we had to account for specifics that are commonly not addressed in the general succession-related

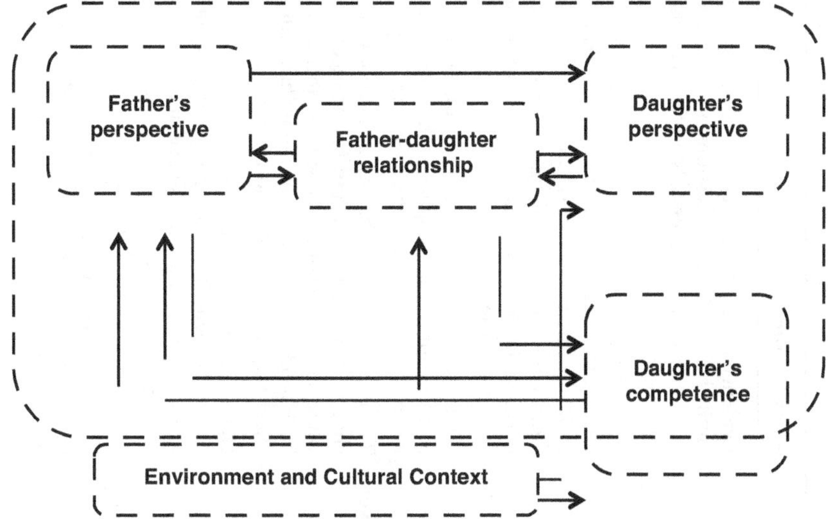

Figure 12.1 Framework for classifying factors affecting father-daughter succession

literature. These specifics were categorized into five broad areas representing the main factors of a successful father-daughter succession.

We suggest that the success of father-daughter succession depends on five partly overlapping and mutually interrelated issues: father's perspective, daughter's perspective, father-daughter relationship and daughter's competence, and environment and cultural context. Figure 12.1 illustrates a framework for classifying factors that affect the father-daughter succession process.

In order to answer the question of what we know about the determinants of the father-daughter succession process, the next sections review the existing literature along the five above-mentioned factors. Table 12.1 summarizes the studies that represented the basis for our work, including their main findings.

2.1 Environment and cultural context

The social and cultural environment indisputably shapes the general opinions and attitudes. In particular, gender stereotypes may play an important role in family firms, where the oldest son is historically predestined to take the reins of a business. Females, on the other hand, have played roles of "family members" and their involvement in management of family firms has been rather rare (Frishkoff and Brown, 1996). Incumbents typically determined their successors based on gender and age (Keating and Little, 1997).

To date, birthright (primogeniture) is still a tradition in various cultures. According to Stavrou (1999), first-born daughters were rarely considered for succession, even if it meant that the owners had to sell their firm. Daughters

Table 12.1 Overview of studies dealing with father-daughter succession

Author(s)	*Journal*	*Focus*	*Study type*	*Main findings/conclusions*
Ahrens, Landmann, and Woywode (2015)	Journal of Family Business Strategy	Labour market constraints in CEO succession contest	Quantitative	Evidence for gender preferences that favor male family heirs in CEO successions; in unplanned successions the predecessor's preferences play a reduced role.
Barnes (1988)	Family Business Review	How the daughters and younger sons deal with self-identity and family role expectations	Qualitative	Daughters and younger sons who become CEOs cannot ignore their family ties within the family hierarchy. As CEOs, they become key figures in incongruent hierarchies and so their positions in the two hierarchies are out of line with each other.
Barrett and Moores (2009)	Journal of Management & Organization	How women move onto the leadership stage	Qualitative	While women may be more likely than in the past to assume leadership roles, they are less often being systematically groomed for leadership.
Cao, Cumming, and Wang (2015)	Journal of Corporate Finance	How one-child policy influences succession in China	Quantitative	The results show that having a first-born male child is important for within-family succession while having a second son will also increase his likelihood of working in the family firm but not affect the first son's likelihood.
Constantinidis and Nelson (2009)	Management international	Role, condition and aspirations of daughters	Qualitative	Daughters who were positioned early as successors benefited from good long-lasting relations. When daughters have one or more brothers, the son is preferred as a potential successor from the beginning.
Curimbaba (2002)	Family Business Review	How the family and business structures affect the daughters' visibility	Qualitative	The professional experiences of female heirs categorized into three groups: invisible, professional and anchor.

Deng (2015)	Journal of Family Business Management	Factors of succession from father to daughter in China	Qualitative	Contrary to previous studies on female succession, daughters in this study were groomed to run the family business and encouraged to become involved in it at an early stage.
Dumas (1989)	Family Business Review	Father-daughter dyad in family-owned businesses	Qualitative	It is risky to give managerial advice to daughters based on studies conducted on fathers and sons.
Dumas (1992)	Entrepreneurship: Theory and Practice	Experience of daughters working as managers with their fathers	Qualitative	Daughters represent an untapped resource within the family firm.
García-Álvarez, López-Sintas, and Gonzalvo (2002)	Family Business Review	Socialisation of potential successors in family	Qualitative	Female successors typically have higher levels of education.
Haberman and Danes (2007)	Family Business Review	Power structures and interactions among father-daughter and father-son family business teams	Qualitative	Family farms never considered transferring the business to daughters until they made the request. As a result, family did much less transfer planning and business training of successor.
Henry, Erwee, and Kong (2013)	Conference paper	Gender differences in tacit knowledge transfer and the role of trust in the succession process	Qualitative	The evidence of a difference in the experiences of daughters and sons in the succession process.
Humphreys (2013)	Journal of Family Business Management	Issues that characterize the succession process for daughters	Qualitative	The findings indicate the women's journey to leadership was not dependent on gender but relied on having the right skills and the education to manage and lead their family firms.
Jimenez (2009)	Family Business Review	A review of obstacles and positive aspects of women's involvement in family firms	Qualitative	Little has been said about how women run their firms, what their leadership style is, or how they behave with other members of the firm.

(*Continued*)

Table 12.1 (Continued)

Author(s)	*Journal*	*Focus*	*Study type*	*Main findings/conclusions*
Remery, Matser, and Hans Flören (2014)	Journal of Family Business Management	Education, perceived capabilities and ambitions between men and women	Quantitative	Evidence of the gender difference regarding ownership. Male successors strive more often for full ownership, whereas female successors opt for shared ownership.
Schröder, Schmitt-Rodermund, and Arnaud (2011)	Family Business Review	Determinants of career choice, intentions of adolescents with family business background	Quantitative	Girls displayed a higher likelihood to opt for employment or to start a new company than to succeed into the family business.
Smythe and Sardeshmukh (2013)	Small Enterprise Research	Relationship in father – daughter successions	Qualitative	Findings indicated that daughters and fathers had an excellent relationship quality. Daughters were socialised in the family business early on.
Sonfield and Lussier (2012)	Journal of Family Business Management	Issues of gender stereotype between male and female owner-managers	Quantitative	The results indicate few differences between male and female owner-managers with the exception of individual vs. group decision-making.
Sonfield and Lussier (2009)	International Journal of Gender and Entrepreneurship	Comparison of men and women as owner-managers	Quantitative	Findings indicate no significant relationships between the percentage of family business owner-managers and the management characteristics.
Stavrou (1999)	Journal of small business management	Intentions of university students to join and take over	Quantitative	Birth order and gender did not have any statistically significant impact on offspring intentions, but first-born daughters were rarely considered for succession.
Otten-Pappas (2013)	Journal of Family Business Management	Successor commitment	Qualitative	The importance of a crisis or emergency for the development of normative commitment in female successors.

Author(s)	*Journal*	*Focus*	*Study type*	*Main findings/conclusions*
Overbeke, Bilimoria, and Perelli (2013)	Journal of Family Business Strategy	Factors contributing to daughters' self-assessments of succession	Qualitative	Daughters engaged in rational decisions about becoming successors only once a critical event occurred.
Overbeke, Bilimoria, and Somers (2015)	Frontiers in psychology	Drivers and barriers to daughter succession	Quantitative	Fathers who perceived that daughters were expressive or cooperative ruled out daughters' possibilities for succession, unless daughters developed a vision for the future of the company.
Vera and Dean (2005)	Family Business Review	Challenges daughters face during succession	Qualitative	All daughters reported feeling less visible than their brothers, forcing them to work harder to prove themselves as competent managers.
Wang (2010)	Journal of family and economic issues	A review of the literature on daughter succession	Qualitative	The topic lacks an overall direction or approach, and the aim of the present review is to stimulate greater research interest in daughter succession
Zellweger, Sieger, and Halter (2011)	Journal of Business Venturing	Locus of control and entrepreneurial self-efficacy, independence and innovation motives	Quantitative	Students with family business backgrounds who intend succession differ in terms of perceived behavioural control and motives from intentional founders and employees.

played the roles of assistants, advisers, or mediators between managing family members (Dumas, 1992). According to Barnes (1988), this fact can possibly be attributed to existing family hierarchy. Younger sons and daughters are often positioned at a lower rank than the eldest son, and when they want to participate in the family business they face greater difficulties and must make greater efforts than the eldest son. Even if an incumbent decided to choose his oldest daughter to become successor in order to ensure the survival of the firm, he was reluctant to provide his daughter with appropriate coaching and training, which undermined the daughter's success in the leading position (Lansberg, 1988).

However, past evidence suggests that daughters are receiving more support if they are the only child in a family. In a study focusing on 11 Belgian family enterprises, Constantinidis and Nelson (2009) found that daughters without brothers have experienced proper succession planning, entering the family business as regular employees and collecting professional experience in order to be prepared to take the reins. On the other hand, in families with one or more siblings, the son is usually the preferred successor from the beginning.

Gender preferences in succession also seem to be country-dependent. For instance, under the Chinese one-child policy, daughters were typically not considered for future appointment even if they were the only child. Therefore, it appears that the national context has a certain impact on daughters' positions in families without sons.

Sometimes, the occurrence of critical events in families may result in the need for unplanned succession; in such cases the incumbents' gender-biased preferences are reduced (Ahrens, Landmann and Woywode, 2015).

It seems that the preference for male successors over female successors is still a common practice nowadays, and the environment and cultural context shapes the expectations and preferences of family members, as well as the succession planning process. Therefore, we present the following proposition:

> *Proposition 1: In family firms, the environment and cultural context affects the father's perspective, the daughter's perspective, the father-daughter relationship and the daughter's competence.*

2.2 Father's perspective

Even the best-planned succession process may fail unless the family takes into account the emotional side of the business. A number of incumbents are not ready and willing to give up control even after the formal handover of leadership and tend to hold the reins of the family and the business past their tenure (Handler, 1994; Sharma, 2004). This phenomenon, also known as "founder's shadow", is discussed in the literature in great detail. Incumbents, often unwilling to accept their own mortality (Davis and Harveston, 1998), may be reluctant to leave the firm because it has become a part of their identity (Vera and Dean, 2005) and reputation. Since successors must cope with the omnipresence of the incumbent and dilution of decision-making, the "founder's shadow" is a source of pressures and tensions in the firm, as well as within the family. Over time, children can lose the interest in taking over the firm, or they may even refuse to work in the family firm (Stavrou, 1999).

To cope with the founder's reluctance to retire, researchers and practitioners proposed various formal measures, such as setting up retirement plans. From the emotional point of view, a father must have trust in the offspring's competence. Although successors have to deal with this issue regardless of their gender, it is clear that gender bias may play a role in assessing a daughter's competence.

Besides primogeniture mentioned in the previous section, the reasons why fathers prefer sons in succession seem to be psychologically determined. According to Hollander and Bukowitz (1990), fathers tend to be overprotective of their daughters, hence trying to shelter them from failure (Henry, Erwee and Kong, 2013). Parents who protect their daughters do not want to put them into the stressful position of managing a business (Vera and Dean, 2005). On the other hand, this reluctance may also indicate that in the eyes of fathers, daughters have limited managerial skills, and thus they are hesitant to transfer leadership.

A father may see his daughter as a business partner but at the same time as a child that needs protection (Vera and Dean, 2005). This ambivalent perception may generate tensions between both parties, making it difficult for the daughter to establish authority in the eyes of family members, but also in the eyes of other stakeholders in the company (Hollander and Bukowitz, 1990). A sound father-daughter relationship is thus an important prerequisite of a smooth succession, as the daughter has to be persuasive about her seriousness and demonstrate her value first as a business partner and, finally, as a leader (Stavrou, 1999).

Based on the above arguments, we formulate the following proposition:

> *Proposition 2: In family firms, the father's perspective is influenced both by the competences of the daughter and by the father-daughter relationship.*

2.3 Daughter's perspective

As we already mentioned, daughters are often "invisible" when it comes to a family business (Curimbaba, 2002) and their capabilities to become leaders are often underestimated in the shadow of their brothers. Prior findings about daughters' perception of being overlooked in terms of professional capabilities are overall consistent. They have to exert extra effort to prove to their families that they are capable to lead a business, often choosing to work outside the family business first (Vera and Dean, 2005). Even when female successors get proper business education and possess external professional experience, they perceive they are not equally treated (Dumas, 1992).

As compared to sons, daughters feel a greater emotional attachment to their family firms. Providing support to parents and keeping the business in the family is one of their motivations to join the family firm (Deng, 2015). However,

Humphreys (2013) reports that the initial motivation of daughters to help their families changes once they enter the family firm, as they start to be more interested in the leading position.

During adolescence, children perceive the jobs of their parents being important for their own career choice intentions (Matthews, Moore, and Fialko, 1999; Schröder, Schmitt-Rodermund, and Arnaud, 2011). Stavrou (1999) studied the intentions of university students to join and take over their parents' firms. While these intentions have been found to be generally low, he noted that the decision to enter the business is related to family rather than business issues. Therefore, it is not surprising that the thought processes that determine the intent to take over a family firm depend on the successor's gender. Daughters' mindsets, as compared to sons, are diametrically different.

Sons consider working in the family business from an early age and are fully aware of the fact that they can become leaders in the future (Overbeke, Bilimoria, and Perelli, 2013). This aspect shapes their attitudes and beliefs during adolescence. On the other hand, daughters are generally less committed to taking over the business, especially when the scope of the business does not fit to their personal wishes (Otten-Pappas, 2013). During their teenage years, they are not indoctrinated with the expectation that they will become future leaders. Therefore, daughters often choose to work outside the family business.

However, critical events in the family (such as illness or death of the founder, a brother's decision to leave the family firm or job loss of the daughter or her partner) may result in daughters' groundbreaking decisions. Should such events occur, daughters often change their attitude to the involvement in family business. The occurrence of critical events leading to succession of daughters is reported across all qualitative studies in our review. Overbeke et al. (2013) found that the vast majority of daughters who had taken over family firms by no means considered becoming successors before the crisis event occurred.

It turns out that it is often the potential successor who engages in the initiation of the succession planning process (Sharma, Chrisman, and Chua, 2003; Constantinidis and Nelson, 2009; Haberman and Danes, 2007). Haberman and Danes (2007) interviewed family farms in the US, finding that they never considered transferring the business to their daughters until the daughters themselves made the request. Obviously, these conditions resulted in less planning and a shorter knowledge transfer. The occurrence of crisis and the sudden necessity to involve a daughter into the company's management has a negative impact on their readiness to stand at the head of the company.

Contrasting evidence has been presented by Deng (2015), who examined four female successors in China. The interviewed daughters were groomed to run the family business from an early age. Although using only a small research sample, Deng provides partial evidence that when daughters are selected as successors at an early age, they greatly benefit from sound relationships and support from the family and employees (Constantinidis and Nelson, 2009), even in a country with a strong male primogeniture tradition, such as China.

Based on the above-mentioned findings, we propose that:

> *Proposition 3: A daughter's perspective is influenced by the fathers' perspective and by the father-daughter relationship.*

2.4 Father-daughter relationship

It is a generally accepted idea that besides traditional economic goals, family firms adopt family-centered goals. Good interpersonal relations often take priority over value maximization in family firms (Davis and Tagiuri, 1989; Stafford, Duncan, Dane, and Winter, 1999). Establishing family harmony and reaching consensus on the selection of a successor are vital conditions affecting the succession process as well as family cohesion. While potential successors need to look trustworthy in the eyes of all involved parties, the incumbent-successor relationship is definitely a crucial one.

A sound incumbent-successor relationship helps founders convey their values to the next generation. García-Álvarez, López-Sintas, and Gonzalvo (2002) argues that founders' values shape the socialization process of potential successors. Through this socialization process, founders can ensure that the culture of the firm will survive into the next generation.

As we already mentioned, the "founder's shadow", i.e. founder's reluctance to retire, may be a source of tension and conflict. As the female leadership is characterized by preference of cooperation and communication (Schmitt, Realo, Voracek, and Allik, 2008), the stalemate can be more challenging for sons than for daughters. What is more, open communication is a major factor that makes fathers acknowledge the commitment of their daughters to the business (Otten-Pappas, 2013).

Because of a better ability to cope with the father's continuing influence, daughters seem to benefit from a better tacit knowledge transfer (Smythe and Sardeshmukh, 2013). According to Humphreys (2013), one of the distinctive characteristics of the father-daughter relationship is shared values both in business and family. This suggests that when planning the transfer of the power to a daughter, the incumbent is better able to convey the culture of the firm and the family to the next generation.

Lansberg and Astrachan (1994) noted that the quality of the incumbent-successor relationship affects succession planning and successor training and, consequently, the likelihood of a smooth transfer of leadership. Hence, the success of succession depends on the cooperation of the incumbent and the successor (Brockhaus, 2004). This cooperation often takes the form of mentoring, which can become a powerful method of learning.

Since family firms are typical of long-term orientation (Lumpkin and Brigham, 2011), current owners, who possess a wide spectrum of knowledge and experience related to their firms (Lee, Lim, and Lim, 2003), may be unwilling to share them with their successors if their mutual relationships are poor. Past research provides empirical support for the necessity of an effective knowledge transfer between generations in order to prepare the successor and eventually enhance performance (Morris, Williams, Allen, and Avila, 1997). Successors even believe that mentoring experience was a vital tool for their success (Boyd, Upton, and Wircenski, 1999).

This proposition stemming from the mainstream literature is supported by studies that interviewed successful daughters (e.g. Vera and Dean, 2005; Smythe and Sardeshmukh, 2013). The interviewees described the relationship with their fathers as open, close and professional. Fathers were open to discussing business issues and daughters described their fathers as devoted mentors providing support over the succession process (e.g. Overbeke, Bilimoria, and Perelli, 2013; Humphreys, 2013). Mentoring proved to be invaluable for daughters in order to learn technical skills. Conversely, daughters who were not initially offered this form of learning had difficulties to gather relevant information for decision-making (Overbeke, Bilimoria, and Perelli, 2013).

Based on the above arguments, we present the following propositions:

Proposition 4: In family firms, the father-daughter relationship is influenced both by the father's and daughter's perspective.

Proposition 5: In family firms, the father-daughter relationship affects the daughter's competence.

2. Daughter's competence

As we already mentioned, daughters often do not receive appropriate succession planning and suffer from a lack professional training and experience (Barrett and Moores, 2009). As a result, a possibly worse post-succession may contribute to the "popular", yet most probably false, opinion that women are worse managers than men (Constantinidis and Nelson, 2009).

While there is still evidence of primogeniture stereotypes in the world, some studies report that the preference for male successors gradually started to play a minor role in successor assessment, and incumbents start to prefer skills and experience over gender predetermination. It is therefore appropriate to identify the successor's competence as one of the major factors affecting the father-daughter succession process. Three commonly mentioned sources of competence in the family business literature are education, professional experience in the family business and external work experience (Dyck, Mauws, Starke, and Mischke, 2002).

Generally, female successors seem to be more likely to become university graduates than men (García-Álvarez, López-Sintas, and Gonzalvo, 2002; Remery, Matser, and Flören, 2014). On the other hand, due to a perceived lower chance of becoming future successors, they often choose to study fields unrelated to the scope of the family business, which, in turn, negatively affects their potential for succession. It is not surprising that after graduation, daughters often choose to work outside the family business and do not consider taking over (e.g. Deng, 2015; Overbeke, Bilimoria, and Perelli, 2013).

On the other hand, external professional experience is frequently mentioned as a "must", since the successor can broaden his/her perspective and become better prepared for a wider range of potential problems (Brockhaus, 2004). The fact that daughters are more inclined to work outside the family firm was also supported empirically. For instance, Schröder, Schmitt-Rodermund, and Arnaud (2011) reported that girls displayed a higher likelihood to choose employment, or even preferred establishing a new company, than to remain in the family firm. Similarly, Zellweger, Sieger, and Halter (2011) found that gender has a significant effect on the preference for employment outside the family firm.

Several researchers tried to explore how a father's perspective affects the daughter's chances for succession. For instance, Overbeke, Bilimoria, and Somers (2015) found that fathers who perceived that their daughters were expressive or nurturing, caring, and cooperative, ruled out daughters' possibilities for succession. However, when daughters developed a vision for the future of the company and fathers recognized and shared their vision, daughters were more likely to become successors. What is more, the selection of family business successors depends on fathers' cognitions about women's roles in society (Overbeke, Bilimoria, and Somers, 2015). Hence, it seems that the father's perspective at least partly determines the daughter's succession plan (including training and education), and, finally, her competence.

Because the daughter's competence affects the father's perspective and is shaped by the environment and cultural context, which influences the father-daughter relationship, the arguments presented in this section are consistent with propositions 1, 2 and 5. Moreover, we also suppose that:

> *Proposition 6: In family firms, the father's perspective affects the daughter's competence.*

3. Directions for further research

The ultimate aim of family business research is to improve the functioning of family firms (Sharma, 2004). The little academic attention devoted to father-daughter succession issues is also faithfully reflected in practice. As the existing empirical findings suggest, incumbents may make a severe mistake in choosing the next generation's leader if their decision is built on inadequate criteria and overshadowed by gender stereotypes. On top of that, a number of important questions remain unresolved. Hence, we present possible directions for future research.

3.1 Need for comparative studies

In fact, everything we know about the intergenerational succession between father and daughter derives from a very limited number of studies. What is more, the findings are mostly based on qualitative studies that, by their very nature, do not provide an adequate basis for generalization. Hence, quantitative research is needed to test hypotheses about father-daughter succession.

To advance the topic forward, future research should take advantage of the existing knowledge on father-son succession that has long been the center of attention. The body of knowledge that has been developing and evolving over the past decades may help create a basis for comparison of similarities and differences in family firms where leadership is transferred from fathers to daughters. Comparative analyses (such as Haberman and Danes, 2007; Sonfield and Lussier, 2009; Henry, Erwee, and Kong 2013; Remery, Matser, and Flören, 2014) can provide a valuable insight into a number of dimensions that may help expand the existing knowledge. Taking into account the missing evidence on mother-owned firms, succession constitutes a complex issue from the gender perspective as the same-gender and cross-gender successions both require further academic attention.

3.2 Need for evaluation of the cultural context

Besides primogeniture, many other cultural factors come into play. The cultural context affects not only the behavior of families, but also family firms' operations (Chrisman, Chua, and Steier, 2002).

In some countries, the evidence suggests that an incumbent's dominance in the succession process may be culturally-determined (Tatoglu, Kula, and Glaister, 2008). We may also refer to studies examining succession in Chinese family firms (Cao, Cumming, and Wang, 2015; Deng, 2015) to provide a distinctive example that the cultural context unquestionably matters in the father-daughter succession process.

While there are several studies with multinational samples in our review, the authors do not elaborate on the possibilities of cultural influences on reported findings and, with the exception of Zellweger, Sieger, and Halter (2011) who controls for cultural influence, they combine international data to obtain large samples (Sonfield and Lussier, 2012).

This issue presents a valuable area for exploratory studies that may help explain the mixed findings presented by past studies. In this matter, we can refer to the book edited by Nason, Halkias, Thurman, and Smith (2012) that explores the cultural influences in father-daughter succession in 14 countries using the case study approach. These cases provide interesting insights into national contexts. However, comparative analyses of differences due to national specifics in father-daughter succession, or succession in general, have yet to come.

Cultural context thus opens an interesting area of research not only for succession in general, but also for father-daughter succession. Calls for a greater attention to this issue have already appeared in previous reviews (Brockhaus, 2004; Vera and Dean, 2005). However, we have not observed any theoretical or empirical progress since then.

3.3 Need for exploring the role of incumbent as a mentor

One of the distinctive features of a successful father-daughter succession is the father's role as a mentor. Successful daughters frequently commented that their fathers were open to discuss business decisions and willing to assist. Taking into account that daughters are not commonly considered for appointment as future successors in their youth, fathers represent one of the key pillars of their business education

(Humphreys, 2013, Overbeke, Bilimoria, and Perelli, 2013, Henry, Erwee, and Kong, 2013). A functioning relationship between both parties is an obvious prerequisite of an effective knowledge transfer. The future research should also be concerned with the incumbent and his role of mentor in successor development.

However, the mere presence of a mentor does not guarantee that intergenerational transfer ends successfully, and a daughter who inherited the family firm will effectively manage the family firm. Because of the well-known differences between male and female leadership (Schmitt, Realo, Voracek, and Allik, 2008), the daughter's ability to process the gained knowledge and adopt a preferable managerial style in the long term is a research area worthy of further investigation.

3.4 Need for focus on privately-held firms

So far, quantitative studies in family business research, including succession issues, focused predominantly on public listed companies. However, in most countries of the world, the main contributors to the national economy are privately-held companies. Therefore, it becomes essential to explore privately-held firms in order to understand their specifics. As an epiphenomenon, family business journals currently call for research focused on privately-held family firms (Carney, Van Essen, Gedajlovic, and Heugens, 2015).

While these firms receive growing academic attention (e.g. Uhlaner, Wright, and Huse, 2007; Sciascia and Mazzola, 2008; Arosa, Iturralde, and Maseda, 2010; Carney, Van Essen, Gedajlovic, and Heugens, 2015), quantitative studies focusing on intergenerational succession are still missing. Apart from case studies and small-sample surveys, quantitative empirical studies have been rather rare (Westhead, 2003; Scholes, Wright, Westhead, Burrows, and Bruining, 2007). To date, father-daughter succession in privately-held firms is an almost completely ignored, yet potentially fruitful, area of research.

3.5 Beyond father-daughter succession

Besides fathers and daughters, there are other family members whose relationship deserves attention. In particular, the relationships among the whole nuclear family members (father, mother, son and daughter) potentially influence the entire succession process. Besides the relationship between mother and daughter when a mother is not directly involved in the family business (Dumas, 1992; Vera and Dean, 2005), we have not addressed the very specific case of mother-owned family firms as in most studies focused on daughter succession; all incumbents were men. The existing literature on these family firms is limited and the findings are fragmented (Kaslow, 1998; Cadieux, Lorrain, and Hugron, 2002; Bjursell and Bäckvall, 2011).

Mothers, in the role of owners, are deeply connected to their family firms and apparently tend to hold the floor even after a successfully completed succession (Cadieux, Lorrain, and Hugron, 2002). Although some studies report that a father's influence lingers over the family business after his retirement (Barrett and Moores,

2009; Smythe and Sardeshmukh, 2013), daughters are able to cope with their interference, since women prefer a participative leadership style and care about interpersonal relationships (Eagly and Johnson, 1990). However, Vera and Dean (2005) report that in some cases, daughters found the mothers' influence to be stressful, as they demanded perfection and the last word in decision-making. That may result in poor trust and communication between the mother and her daughter/son, as reported by Cadieux, Lorrain, and Hugron (2002). Therefore, the limited findings suggest that in mother-owned family firms, the relationships between incumbents and successors may be different from father-owned firms. This provides a new, unexplored area of research, whose importance is highlighted as gender equality in economic, social and political aspects has gained dramatic momentum in recent years.

The proposed areas of future research are not exhaustive, and we could find a number of other implications based on existing research of succession in general. Another interesting area of research arises from the findings of Davis and Tagiuri (1989), who found that lifecycles of fathers and sons have an impact on the success of succession because their values, behavior and attitudes alter over time, and hence the quality of their relationship depends on their age. Smythe and Sardeshmukh (2013) propose to examine the influence of a daughter's lifecycle (marriage, child and upbringing) on the relationship with her father and the likelihood of her selection as a new leader of the family business. Since the sound relationship between the father and the daughter has been frequently reported as the pillar of a smooth succession, the lifecycles of both parties may have yet unknown influence on the process.

4. Concluding remarks

While succession belongs to the most studied topics of family business research, the existing literature frequently omits the aspect of gender. The goal of this chapter was to present the current state-of-the-art research about father-daughter relationships and identify the factors of father-daughter succession. Based on an extensive literature review, we classified these factors into five broad areas: father's perspective, daughter's perspective, father-daughter relationship and daughter's competence, and environment and cultural context. The literature provides evidence that these areas are mutually interrelated. Subsequently, we suggested directions for further research.

Although the research on father-daughter succession has progressed over the past three decades, it is still very fragmented and requires a broader empirical investigation. The cultural context, the daughter's ability to transfer the knowledge obtained in the course of successor preparation, as well as investigation of privately held-firms, will certainly deserve serious academic attention.

Nevertheless, we would like to conclude in a positive tone, and since more than half of the papers we reviewed were published in the last five years, it can be assumed that the topic of father-daughter succession will be addressed in the near future.

Acknowledgements

We appreciate the funding support received from the Czech Science Foundation for this project entitled, "Privately-held Firms with Multiple Owners: The Role of Family and Responsible Ownership" (registration no.: GA17–10948S).

References

Ahrens, J. P., Landmann, A., and Woywode, M. (2015). Gender preferences in the CEO successions of family firms: Family characteristics and human capital of the successor. *Journal of Family Business Strategy*, 6(2), 86–103.

Arosa, B., Iturralde, T., and Maseda, A. (2010). Ownership structure and firm performance in non-listed firms: Evidence from Spain. *Journal of Family Business Strategy*, 1(2), 88–96.

Barnes, L. B. (1988). Incongruent hierarchies: Daughters and younger sons as company CEOs. *Family Business Review*, 1(1), 9–21.

Barrett, M., and Moores, K. (2009). Spotlights and shadows: Preliminary findings about the experiences of women in family business leadership roles. *Journal of Management and Organization*, 15(3), 363–377.

Beckhard, R., and Dyer, W. G. (1983). Managing continuity in the family-owned business. *Organizational Dynamics*, 12(1), 5–12.

Bjursell, C., and Bäckvall, L. (2011). Family business women in media discourse: The business role and the mother role. *Journal of Family Business Management*, 1(2), 154–173.

Boyd, J., Upton, N., and Wircenski, M. (1999). Mentoring in family firms: A reflective analysis of senior executives' perceptions. *Family Business Review*, 12(4), 299–309.

Brockhaus, R. H. (2004). Family business succession: Suggestions for future research. *Family Business Review*, 17(2), 165–177.

Cadieux, L., Lorrain, J., and Hugron, P. (2002). Succession in women-owned family businesses: A case study. *Family Business Review*, 15(1), 17–30.

Cao, J., Cumming, D., and Wang, X. (2015). One-child policy and family firms in China. *Journal of Corporate Finance*, 33, 317–329.

Carney, M., Van Essen, M., Gedajlovic, E. R., and Heugens, P. P. (2015). What do we know about private family firms? A meta-analytical review. *Entrepreneurship Theory and Practice*, 39(3), 513–544.

Chrisman, J. J., Chua, J. H., and Steier, L. P. (2002). The influence of national culture and family involvement on entrepreneurial perceptions and performance at the state level. *Entrepreneurship: Theory and Practice*, 26(4), 113–131.

Constantinidis, C., and Nelson, T. (2009). Integrating succession and gender issues from the perspective of the daughter of family enterprise: A cross-national investigation. *International Management*, 14(1), 43–54.

Curimbaba, F. (2002). The dynamics of women's roles as family business managers. *Family Business Review*, 15(3), 239–252.

Daspit, J. J., Holt, D. T., Chrisman, J. J., and Long, R. G. (2016). Examining family firm succession from a social exchange perspective a multiphase, multistakeholder review. *Family Business Review*, 29(1), 44–64.

Davis, J. A., and Tagiuri, R. (1989). The influence of life stage on father-son work relationships in family companies. *Family Business Review*, 2(1), 47–74.

Davis, P. S., and Harveston, P. D. (1998). The influence of family on business succession process: A multi-generationalperspective. *Entrepreneurship Theory and Practice*, 22(3), 31–53.

Deng, X. (2015). Father-daughter succession in China: Facilitators and challenges. *Journal of Family Business Management*, 5(1), 38–54.

Dumas, C. (1989). Understanding of father-daughter and father-son dyads in family-owned businesses. *Family Business Review*, 2(1), 31–46.

Dumas, C. (1992). Integrating the daughter into family business management. *Entrepreneurship: Theory and Practice*, 16(4), 41–56.

Dyck, B., Mauws, M., Starke, F. A., and Mischke, G. A. (2002). Passing the baton: The importance of sequence, timing, technique and communication in executive succession. *Journal of Business Venturing*, 17(2), 143–162.

Eagly, A. H., and Johnson, B. T. (1990). Gender and leadership style: A meta-analysis. *Psychological Bulletin*, 108(2), 233.

Frishkoff, P.A., and Brown, B.M. (1996). Women on the move in family business. In C. E. Aronoff, J. H. Astrachan and J. L. Ward (Eds.), *Family and Business Sourcebook II* (pp. 446–450). Marietta, GA: Business Resources.

García-Álvarez, E., López-Sintas, J., and Gonzalvo, P. S. (2002). Socialization patterns of successors in first- to second-generation family businesses. *Family Business Review*, 15(3), 189–203.

Gillis-Donovan, J., and Moynihan-Bradt, C. (1990). The power of invisible women in the family business. *Family Business Review*, 3(2), 153–167.

Grant Thornton. (2014). *Annual Women in Business Tracker Finds Little Change at the Top of the Corporate Ladder.* Retrieved August 15, 2015 from: www.grantthornton.global/en/insights/articles/Women-in-business-classroom-to-boardroom/.

Haberman, H., and Danes, S. M. (2007). Father-daughter and father-son family business management transfer comparison: Family FIRO model application. *Family Business Review*, 20(2), 163–184.

Handler, W. C. (1994). Succession in family business: A review of the research. *Family Business Review*, 7(2), 133–157.

Henry, M., Erwee, R., and Kong, E. (2013). *Family Business Succession-Trust and Gender Issues in Family and Non-Family Succcession.* Proceedings of the 13th Annual Conference of the European Academy of Management (EURAM 2013) (pp. 1–27). European Academy of Management.

Hollander, B. S., and Bukowitz, W. R. (1990). Women, family culture, and family business. *Family Business Review*, 3(2), 139–151.

Humphreys, M. M. (2013). Daughter succession: A predominance of human issues. *Journal of Family Business Management*, 3(1), 24–44.

Ip, B., and Jacobs, G. (2006). Business succession planning: A review of the evidence. *Journal of Small Business and Enterprise Development*, 13(3), 326–350.

Jimenez, R. M. (2009). Research on women in family firms current status and future directions. *Family Business Review*, 22(1), 53–64.

Joy, L., Carter, N. M., Wagner, H. M., and Narayanan, S. (2007). The bottom line: Corporate performance and women's representation on boards. *Catalyst*, 3, 619–625.

Kaslow, F. W. (1998). Handling transitions from mother to son in the family business: The knotty issues. *Family Business Review*, 11(3), 229–238.

Keating, N. C., and Little, H. M. (1997). Choosing the successor in New Zealand family farms. *Family Business Review*, 10(2), 157–171.

Lansberg, I. (1988). The succession conspiracy. *Family Business Review*, 1(2), 119–143.
Lansberg, I., and Astrachan, J. H. (1994). Influence of family relationships on succession planning and training: The importance of mediating factors. *Family Business Review*, 7(1), 39–59.
Lee, K. S., Lim, G. H., and Lim, W. S. (2003). Family business succession: Appropriation risk and choice of successor. *Academy of Management Review*, 28(4), 657–666.
Lumpkin, G. T., and Brigham, K. H. (2011). Long-term orientation and intertemporal choice in family firms. *Entrepreneurship Theory and Practice*, 35(6), 1149–1169.
Matthews, C. H., Moore, T. W., and Fialko, A. S. (1999). Succession in the family firm: A cognitive categorization perspective. *Family Business Review*, 12(2), 159–170.
Morris, M. H., Williams, R. O., Allen, J. A., and Avila, R. A. (1997). Correlates of success in family business transitions. *Journal of Business Venturing*, 12(5), 385–401.
Nason, R. S., Halkias, D., Thurman, M.P.W., and Smith, C. (2012). *Father-Daughter Succession in Family Business: A Cross-Cultural Perspective*. London: Gower Publishing.
Nordqvist, M., Wennberg, K., and Hellerstedt, K. (2013). An entrepreneurial process perspective on succession in family firms. *Small Business Economics*, 40(4), 1087–1122.
Otten-Pappas, D. (2013). The female perspective on family business successor commitment. *Journal of Family Business Management*, 3(1), 8–23.
Overbeke, K. K., Bilimoria, D., and Perelli, S. (2013). The dearth of daughter successors in family businesses: Gendered norms, blindness to possibility, and invisibility. *Journal of Family Business Strategy*, 4(3), 201–212.
Overbeke, K. K., Bilimoria, D., and Somers, T. (2015). Shared vision between fathers and daughters in family businesses: The determining factor that transforms daughters into successors. *Frontiers in Psychology*, 6, 33–47.
Remery, C., Matser, I., and Hans Flören, R. (2014). Successors in Dutch family businesses: Gender differences. *Journal of Family Business Management*, 4(1), 79–91.
Schmitt, D.P., Realo, A., Voracek, M., and Allik, J. (2008). Why can't a man be more like a woman? Sex differences in Big Five personality traits across 55 cultures. *Journal of Personality and Social Psychology*, 94(1), 168–182.
Scholes, M. L., Wright, M., Westhead, P., Burrows, A., and Bruining, H. (2007). Information sharing, price negotiation and management buy-outs of private family-owned firms. *Small Business Economics*, 29(3), 329–349.
Schröder, E., Schmitt-Rodermund, E., and Arnaud, N. (2011). Career choice intentions of adolescents with a family business background. *Family Business Review*, 24(4), 305–321.
Sciascia, S., and Mazzola, P. (2008). Family involvement in ownership and management: Exploring nonlinear effects on performance. *Family Business Review*, 21(4), 331–345.
Sharma, P. (2004). An overview of the field of family business studies: Current status and directions for the future. *Family Business Review*, 17(1), 1–36.
Sharma, P., Chrisman, J. J., and Chua, J. H. (2003). Succession planning as planned behavior: Some empirical results. *Family Business Review*, 16(1), 1–15.
Smythe, J., and Sardeshmukh, S. R. (2013). Fathers and daughters in family business. *Small Enterprise Research*, 20(2), 98–109.

Sonfield, M. C., and Lussier, R. N. (2009). Gender in family business ownership and management: A six-country analysis. *International Journal of Gender and Entrepreneurship*, 1(2), 96–117.

Sonfield, M. C., and Lussier, R. N. (2012). Gender in family business management: A multinational analysis. *Journal of Family Business Management*, 2(2), 110–129.

Stafford, K., Duncan, K. A., Dane, S., and Winter, M. (1999). A research model of sustainable family businesses. *Family Business Review*, 12(3), 197–208.

Stavrou, E. T. (1999). Succession in family businesses: Exploring the effects of demographic factors on offspring intentions to join and take over the business. *Journal of Small Business Management*, 37(3), 43–62.

Tatoglu, E., Kula, V., and Glaister, K. W. (2008). Succession planning in family-owned businesses evidence from Turkey. *International Small Business Journal*, 26(2), 155–180.

Uhlaner, L., Wright, M., and Huse, M. (2007). Private firms and corporate governance: An integrated economic and management perspective. *Small Business Economics*, 29(3), 225–241.

Vera, C. F., and Dean, M. A. (2005). An examination of the challenges daughters face in family business succession. *Family Business Review*, 18(4), 321–345.

Wang, C. (2010). Daughter exclusion in family business succession: A review of the literature. *Journal of Family and Economic Issues*, 31(4), 475–484.

Westhead, P. (2003). Succession decision-making outcomes reported by private family companies. *International Small Business Journal*, 21(4), 369–401.

Zellweger, T. M., and Astrachan, J. H. (2008). On the emotional value of owning a firm. *Family Business Review*, 21(4), 347–363.

Zellweger, T., Sieger, P., and Halter, F. (2011). Should I stay or should I go? Career choice intentions of students with family business background. *Journal of Business Venturing*, 26(5), 521–536.

13 The 'Dowager' and her role in the governance and leadership of the entrepreneurial family business

Robert Smith

Introduction

This chapter spans both 'gender' and 'family entrepreneurship'. Its focus is on the role of gender in an unusual, 'business-context', and in common with other chapters, issues of family dynamics, personality, and behavioural traits feature. In business settings, the male as head of both the family and the business has traditionally adopted the heroic role of the entrepreneur, particularly in aristocratic business families (Anderson and Smith, 2007). This often leaves the wife, and mother, of the entrepreneur with role confusion, and in some cases an identity crisis (see Hytti, Alsos, Heinonen, and Ljunggren, 2016). Daughters in family business often face difficulties in entering family business management. They must carefully navigate family businesses and custom and construct their own identities as family business leaders. Daughters construct and negotiate their gender and leadership identities in their interactions with others by opposing, expanding and making use of the gendered scripts available to them (Hytti et al., 2016). Yet, women traditionally play a leadership and governance role (for example, consider the role of the governess) in both the family and in business. Whilst the role of the 'Matriarch' (Smith, 2014) is becoming increasingly accepted as a relevant entrepreneurial and leadership role model, little attention is given to the governance and mentoring roles of the 'Dowager' within the everyday politics of family business settings. The purpose of this descriptive study/chapter and embedded discussion is to begin to remedy this deficit and gap in the literature to pave the way for future studies into the phenomenon.

The genesis of this research began when the author was researching other gender role models and stereotypes in family business for other writing projects. During research, particularly into the business stereotype of the 'Matriarch', stories and anecdotes relating to strong women who had once been the entrepreneur in a family business, or had been the wife of an entrepreneur who had exerted considerable influence within the businesses, came to the foreground. These women had lived a full life and were now at the stage in their lives where they were ostensibly retired. In farming, for example, it is common for a retiring farmer and his wife to give up the reigns of the farm business and for them to move into a house on the farm or in a nearby village from where they can act as advisors, if required. This pragmatic business practice is very much overlooked in the literature, albeit there is a small literature on family boards. This phenomenon also impinges upon the succession literature.

A secondary influence on the development of this study relates to the British cultural stereotype of the 'Dowager', which is inextricably linked to class-based notions of aristocracy, to aristocratic families (see Thompson, 2001a) and, particularly, to the role played by Dame Maggie Smith as the fictional Dowager, Countess of Grantham in the iconic television period drama series *Downton Abbey.* In this respect, Dame Maggie plays the role of the Dowager brilliantly (see Fellowes, 2008,2011; Fellowes and Sturgis, 2012 for background information on the role). A third strand to the development occurred by chance when I happened to view a television book report in the book by Jung Chang on The Dowager Queen of China (Chang, 2013). On listening to the ensuing discussion, which centred on the book, I was intrigued to hear a story of governance that provided a potential theoretical framework around which he could base a justification of the observations and musings narrated herein. The 'Dowager' stereotype can be applied to family business settings and scenarios in their widest sense (as in the business of families and how it is conducted) and family businesses as a distinct category of entrepreneurial activity.

The above observations caused me to engage in a period of intense reflection in relation to methodology and questions of how exactly would one begin to research a governance phenomenon such as this. In the first instance, it was obviously necessary to locate examples in real life where the Dowager engaged in a business setting. The essence of this study and its purpose relates to interrogating Dowager narratives within contemporary family businesses. This chapter makes a dual contribution to the literature on gendered entrepreneurial identity and family entrepreneurship, thereby offering new and insightful additions to the entrepreneurship field.

Methodology

The primary methodologies used in developing this discussion are multi-disciplinary literature review and documentary research to develop a framework. This is, in turn, used to construct case studies of the late socialite and entrepreneur Deborah Vivien Cavendish, Duchess of Devonshire through which we can begin to explain the role of the Dowager (Devonshire and Upton, 2002). The case is supported by another example, the late Ena Baxter of the family business 'Baxters of Speyside'. These cases reinforce the importance of the dowager stereotype as an explanatory variable and develops the portfolio of leadership and governance roles associated with gendered entrepreneurial identity.

The Dowager stereotype revealed from the literature, media and custom

The Dowager stereotype is not normally associated with the literatures of business, entrepreneurship, nor family business. One is more likely to locate the genre in the literatures of history and politics (see Lewis, 2003;Thompson, 2001a). First, we must deal with issues of definition and etymology before examining the family business literature and before considering media representations of the dowager to assemble the stereotypical dowager.

Issues of definition and etymology

The dictionary definition of 'Dowager' when used as a noun is given as "*a woman who holds some title or property from her deceased husband, especially the widow of a king, duke, etc.* (often used as an additional title to differentiate her from the wife of the present king, duke, etc.[1] Alternatively, it is used to refer to "*an elderly woman of stately dignity, especially one of elevated social position* (e.g. a wealthy dowager). When used in everyday usage as an adjective it refers to "*pertaining to, or characteristic of a dowager*". It can also refer to a style of dressing. It is commonly found in colocation to the terms 'grande dame' and 'matron'. As such, it is a highly stylised title when used in British Society and the etiquette of its usage is explained in Deberetts.[2] Custom, titles and form are important. For example, the widow of an Earl is officially known as The Dowager Countess of [location] unless there is already a dowager countess in that family still living, in which case the widow of the junior countess is known by her forename e.g. Elizabeth, Countess of . . .". Not all those entitled to the term use it, and if the present holder of the title is unmarried, then the widow of the previous Earl does not use the term of either. Thus, being widowed (or without a life partner) seems to be a necessary prerequisite for triggering the title.

In studying the phenomenon, it is difficult to separate the concept from historical examples, which involve Royalty and aristocratic families. History is replete with examples of Dowager Empresses, Queens, Duchesses and Countesses who ruled after the death of their husbands or who acted as caretakers/ Regent until the King/Queen in waiting came of age. Likewise, it is difficult to divorce the concept from aristocratic notions and values to uncover the generic contemporary behaviours and values associated with the role per se. One is more likely to encounter the stereotype in examples of aristocratic entrepreneurship (Thompson, 2001b). Nevertheless, readings from history and the literature of class were helpful in enabling me to assemble a pen portrait of the characteristics we have come to associate with being a Dowager. In this discussion, we are primarily interested in the role and its capacity for adaptability into family business settings.

Interrogating the family business literature

Moult and Anderson (2005) have documented the role of strong women in entrepreneurial family businesses. Flexibility to accommodate familial and domestic roles and windows of entrepreneurial opportunity is important in women's' lives. Moult and Anderson suggest that such a window of opportunity could be expected to open when the demands of childrearing reduce as children become older. In the literature of family business, there is evidence of considering the roles of the matriarch and the widow, but the term 'dowager' is silent and unused. The dowager stereotype is a continuation of, and perhaps a subtypology of, the Matriarch stereotype (Martin, 2001). It is also an extension of the notion of matriarchal leadership. Indeed, it is also a potential, evolutionary stage in the ontological and epistemological development of a 'genre' of women in business. The natural habitat of the matriarch, and particularly the dowager, is the familial home and the boardroom. Indeed, Martin (2001) appreciated the role of the matriarch who dedicated her life to the family and their autocratic and didactic leadership styles in the directing of the business. See also the works of Cates and Sussman (1992), Dunn and Hughes (1995), Roessl (2005), and Colli (2012) in this respect. For Cates and Sussman (1992), the role of widower, or governess, in family business is important in terms of inheritance because there is an ever present fear that the widow or widower would remarry and divert the wealth to another family. Thus, widows are frequently named as executors of wills or power of attorney to ensure that the family system is perpetuated. The dowager was expected to perpetuate the patrician aristocratic values of the family and to expend her time and efforts to maintaining and protecting the family empire (Dunn and Hughes, 1995). Roessl (2005) documents the emotional turmoil of succession scenarios where the widow has an emotional attachment to the firm and its founder and flatly refuses to cooperate with takeover plans. See also Colli (2012) for an example of the widow of a family business dynasty where she stepped into the breach to manage the business until the 14-year-old entrepreneur in waiting came of age to take hold of the business. She held the reins until he had finished his period of training and of apprenticeship. The 'passing-away' of a family business matriarch or their medical incapacitation can also pose succession issues (see Galiano and Vinturella, 1995).

Prince (1990) highlighted the role of the matriarch in family business and the role of the wife of the founder (or entrepreneur) in family business mediation and conflict resolution. Prince acknowledged that although the matriarch does not always have a formal role in the business, she does in the family. The roles and responsibilities of the matriarch include resolving disputes between family members and between the family member and the business structures and employees. It is wise to involve the matriarch. Hutcheson, Jaffe, and Gilliland (2013) also acknowledge that the matriarch has a particular role to play in supporting members of a family business who have addiction issues and are abusing alcohol or drugs. They acknowledge that this can be particularly difficult if the founder has addiction issues. Jaffe and Lane (2004) appreciate the role played by matriarchs (and sibling spouses) in the governance of family businesses and the family council. Jimenez (2009) researched what happened to the 'invisible women' of a family business after their husbands die. She examined the role of the widow in taking over the business. It can be seen that the dowager plays a significant role in the domestication of Capital and the Capitalization of Family (Marcus, 1991) in aristocratic family enterprises.

Assembling the stereotypical dowager

From our readings above, we can state with certainty that the typical Dowager is a lady of mature years. She will possess matriarchal qualities of leadership and stewardship. She will most likely be a grandmother or perhaps even great grandmother. She will hold sway over a large extended family and be held in high esteem within the family and extended peer group. The Dowager will be in a position where she can still mentor, guide and influence the family by 'virtue' of her persona. Her power will stem from the fact that she has been the power behind the throne in all stages of the family's current history. In a business setting, she will have helped her husband run the business or estate and may even have acted in a managerial capacity whilst running the household. This dual seat of power provides her with two distinctive power bases. She will also have the roles of mother, grandmother and wife to draw upon. Normally, she will command respect, radiate dignity and exude power. However, with the mantel of leadership comes responsibility. The Dowager will have had to make difficult decisions and because of this will have a capacity for ruthlessness. The Dowager will have experience of governance and stewardship in family and in business settings where there is often a clash of interests. In rare cases there may be a malevolent and spiteful side to the advice or edicts dispensed. The Dowager is often seen as the guardian of family values and history, and it is often her role to act as the family conscience or the settler of scores. The Dowager also acts as an ambassador for the family and the business and will be prized for her wit and wisdom.

An important aspect of this scenario is that being a dowager is a position foisted on a woman of mature years. Yet it is a culmination of other roles, such as wife, mother, grandmother, matriarch and so on, and it is the life experience of the dowager that imbues her with the power and influence. The Dowager is also important in relation to the issues of fecundity and to the renewal and regeneration of the family bloodline. In aristocratic circles, the Dowager will most likely bring with her the shared wealth and social capital of her aristocratic family. The Dowager is also important in this respect because she is the familial Queen in waiting. She is expected to develop into the role over time and is groomed for this purpose. This can be difficult as there is often an existing matriarch in the role and perhaps even a resident Dowager. Coping with this situation can be stressful but is excellent training for future family diplomacy skills.

We now turn to consider the following two contemporary case studies of dowager stereotypes: Deborah, Dowager Duchess of Devonshire and Ena Baxter of the family business Baxters of Speyside.

The late Deborah, Dowager Duchess of Devonshire

Deborah Vivien Cavendish, Duchess of Devonshire DVCO was born Deborah Freeman-Mitford on 31 March 1920. She died 24 September 2014, aged 94. She was an acclaimed entrepreneur, businesswoman, writer, memoirist and socialite.

Deborah came from an aristocratic family. Her parents were David Bertram Ogilvy Freeman-Mitford, 2nd Baron Redesdale (1878–1958), son of Algernon Freeman-Mitford, 1st Baron Redesdale, and his wife, Sydney (1880–1963), daughter of Thomas Gibson Bowles, MP. She was the youngest and last surviving of the six Mitford sisters. She became a successful chatelaine of Chatsworth House, the great stately home and estate in Derbyshire.

Her childhood was spent pursuing her equine interests. She met her future husband, Lord Andrew Cavendish, at the races when both were 18. Andrew was the younger son of the Duke of Devonshire. He joined the Coldstream Guards. Andrew and Debo – as she was known to her peers – married in St Bartholomew's the Great in London. Andrew became heir to the Dukedom when his brother died in 1944. Andrew became the Duke of Devonshire in 1950 on the death of his father. Andrew's stewardship faced financial problems from the outset because his father died 14 weeks before he would have escaped the 80 percent death duties charge then in play. Andrew and Deborah inherited a portfolio of property including Chatsworth House, a stately home with 175 rooms. They also inherited a £5 million inheritance bill, which incurred £1000 interest per day. The couple worked hard and had to sell a large number of paintings, including Rembrandts and a Poussin. They also sold off superfluous ancestral homes, such as Hardwick Hall in Derbyshire. In 1959 the Duke and Duchess turned Chatsworth over to a trust. They kept an Irish holiday castle in Lismore but made a decision to run Chatsworth as an enterprise.

Over the years they worked hard together and helped restore it for opening to the public. Ever pragmatic, Deborah preferred to gold leaf the exterior window frames but only because it lasted longer than paint. At the same time, Deborah invited writers and artists to stay at Chatsworth. This fuelled her creative streak. Deborah also began a career as a writer and wrote biographies and a history of Chatsworth, which later became a steady seller in the Chatsworth Estate shop. She once jokingly referred to herself as a shopkeeper, but over the years she demonstrated an entrepreneurial acumen in directing the commercial activities of the Estate, including the Estate farm shop. Deborah evolved into a very competent businesswoman and prided herself in making money, not spending it. She pioneered the farm shop movement and made a profit on her aristocratic heritage. For example, she hit on the idea of having her signature printed on the labels of Chatsworth Food Limited chutney and sauce. Chatsworth farm shop is on a different footing than most farm shops as it employs 100 people. The Duchess was the main public face of Chatsworth for many decades. Deborah also initiated other retail and catering operations and assorted offshoots, such as Chatsworth Food and Chatsworth Design. She appreciated the commercial benefits of running a stately home. She was a hands-on leader and even manned the ticket desk herself, if required. She supervised the development of the Cavendish Hotel in a nearby village and the Devonshire Arms Hotel. Her fame was secured when she participated in a television documentary series on Chatsworth House and her life. She regularly served, personally, in the shop and reorganised the finances of Chatsworth Enterprises. She was also a shrewd farmer and could name every field in the Estate's 6,000 acres. Indeed, she became president of the Royal Agriculture Society and the Royal Smithfield Club. She retained her love of horses and animals. This interest manifested itself in a series of books on animals and on Chatsworth. The Devonshire marriage weathered many storms and the Duke's largess with commissioning paintings and jewellery. In 1999 she was made a DCVO, or dame, in the Royal Victorian Order. The couple celebrated their 50th anniversary and her accession to the ducal title. She became the Dowager Duchess in 2004 on Andrew's death. She wrote a memoire entitled *Wait For Me* in 2010 as a eulogy to their marriage. Deborah suffered many setbacks, and 3 of her children died at birth. She is survived by her daughters, Emma and Sophie, and her son, Perigrine, succeeded to the Dukedom. The family has a long tradition of producing notable Dowagers. Deborah collected various titles during her lifetime:

- *The Honourable* Deborah Vivien Freeman-Mitford (1920–1941)
- Lady Andrew Cavendish (1941–1944)
- Marchioness of Hartington (1944–1950)
- *Her Grace* The Duchess of Devonshire (1950–1999)
- *Her Grace* The Duchess of Devonshire, DCVO (1999–2004)
- *Her Grace* The Dowager Duchess of Devonshire, DCVO (2004–2014).

The late Ena Baxter, entrepreneur, artist, author and family matriarch

A contemporary example of a dowager in a family business setting is the late Ena Baxter of Baxters of Speyside. Ena Baxter is a classic example of the genre (See Smith, 2017 for a more detailed history of the Baxter family). She died January 15 2015, aged 90. She is credited with being the driving force behind the success of the family business. For many years she was the face behind their phenomenal success. Her story is a business romance story (Smith, 2017). Ena was a farmer's daughter raised in rural Aberdeenshire. She was born on 12 August 1924 at Drumblair House, near Forgue, and brought up at Huntly, Aberdeenshire. She went to Gray's School of Art in Aberdeen. She married into the business. Ena met her husband, Gordon, in 1952 when she was an Art teacher at the local school in Fochabers. After a whirlwind romance, she married Gordon in 1952. They moved into a small cottage beside the factory. Family legend has it that she adapted a recipe for Louisiana chicken gumbo soup that she had found in a magazine. She substituted ingredients. Gordon was so impressed that he coaxed her to swap her paintbrushes for a wooden spoon and a Bunsen burner. She was soon formulating new soup recipes, which led to the introduction of a new range of the firm's tinned soups. One of her new soups was Gumbo soup. Initially she suffered frustration and setback, but Gumbo soup went on to sell one million cans in the first year. Another success was Royal Game soup and Cock-a-Leekie. She also developed new jams, chutneys and marmalades and their award-winning Tomato soup.

Ena soon proved herself to be a shrewd businesswoman. She is described frequently in the press and in interviews as being tough. Under joint stewardship with her husband, the company grew quickly and together they travelled the globe exporting soup to Japan, Minestrone to the Italians and Haggis to Korea. Together they built the business into the corporate giant it is today. Their range of foods won 3 Royal warrants. Ena proved to be a natural marketer and soon the firm won the Queen's Award for Export. Ena is credited with much of the success of the business. It appears that she ran the business with the same ethos of running a household. She avoided the gimmicks and one-upmanship of 1980s corporate strategy. She avoided borrowing money from banks and instead financed reinvestment in the factory through their own cash flow. Gordon and Ena successfully held off over 170 takeover bids and continued to grow the family business. They avoided the corporate trend for buying up other companies and chose to grow Baxters with family values. They also chose to concentrate on their core business and did not diversify into farming or haulage, as did other food businesses. One of my favourite quotes from her obituary was the quote attributed to Gordon Baxter – "Where's Mrs Heinz? Collecting French Impressionists. Where's Mrs Baxter? In the kitchen making soup!" Ena became the star of her own television cookery programme before celebrity chefs and foodies became all the rage. This turned her into a local celebrity and she soon became a regular fixture on the annual list of Britain's wealthiest women. By the mid-1990s the company was employing 800 staff with an annual turnover of £45 million and exporting to more than 30 countries.

Ena and Gordon Baxter had three adopted children, a daughter and two sons, all of whom were groomed to run the family business. Ena continued to play a pivotal role in the business but kept a low profile in the press. Her husband, Gordon, was the visible head of the business and their sons took up management positions. Their daughter, Audrey, went to university and other relatives joined the family business. Ena became a published author of Ena Baxter's Scottish Cook Book. She personified Baxters as a symbol of Scottish family wholesomeness. Ena was adroit at playing roles and in television commercials played the role of a sweet old dear in the kitchen. This belied her genius in creating new products in the kitchen. Her life was stressful as she coped with family, business and the pressures of work. Ena regularly rowed with Gordon but in a playful way and on many occasions was close to exhaustion, collapsing at the kitchen table to weep from sheer frustration.

After their daughter, Audrey, became managing director in 1992, Ena and Gordon had more time to devote to outside interests. Gordon enjoyed fishing on the Spey whilst Ena rediscovered her love of painting. Together they set up a charitable foundation raising many thousands of pounds for charity. Her life at the helm of Baxters was eventful, and her final years were overshadowed by the deaths of her husband and her son, Michael, who had left Baxters to set up his own food consultancy. Ena personified the family business matriarch and although Audrey remained in control, anecdotally there is evidence that Ena continued to support her as an advisor and mother carrying out many of the roles and responsibilities attributed to the Dowager. After Gordon passed away, Ena continued to play an active advisory role at Baxters.

Discussion and implications for future research

There are no findings/results as such – simply fascinating stories with potential theoretical insights. The two narratives discussed above are useful because they can be used as narrative templates by other researchers or consultants to restore selected aspects of the 'Dowager' or 'Widow' stereotypes and use these to investigate and interrogate their research knowledge base to populate a spreadsheet with examples that can be tested using the framework.

The obvious limitations is that this is a single case study, but there are obvious implications for future research in that expanding the case study to include other examples would help develop the typology. The stereotype has real practical implications in that the lady who fits this typology need not usurp her partners or children's entrepreneurial identities. There are also implications in relation to class-based explanations and theories of entrepreneurship. This is obviously a novel explanatory framework of value to family business and entrepreneurship scholars. This study in presenting and analysing two case stories and scenarios begins to address this neglected issue and open up new vistas in gendered explanations of enterprise and leadership.

This discussion has raised some important issues in relation to methodology and developing methods capable of unearthing data and capturing it in a robust framework. This is because very little has been written about the role of the Dowager or other gendered stereotypes (such as mistresses or consorts). One possibility is to engage in a prolonged study using documentary research methodologies or histiography. However, this methodology, although it would uncover a vast array of supporting historical data, would do little to build up a robust picture of the utility of the role in contemporary family business. Documentary research may also produce a dry monographic article, which may only be of use to business historians. Another important factor is that, in researching existing examples of Dowagers, as a researcher the author was frustrated by having to resort to accessing journalistic and internet sources that only contained skeletal biographic details. It was obvious that the data he sought was not available in the current format. It is also of note that the two case studies used in this discussion paper are of ladies who are now deceased. Ironically, extensive use was made of their obituaries to piece together a coherent and cohesive story of their individual enterprise. It is obvious that this study will require locating temporary examples of mature women in business that are in a Dowager role or are matriarchs with a similar level of experience. From personal experience, the type of data the author was trying to uncover will require skills of diplomacy and a high level of interview skills to document because much of the proof will be anecdotal. It will be required to build trust to access such data because what happens in the family often stays in the family.

The stories of ruthless leadership and tough management may only be told by familial black sheep or by outsider employees. To uncover the Dowager stereotype will require further patient scholarship.[3]

Notes

1 From Dictionary.com. It is also used as a label, thus we hear of a queen dowager or an empress dowager. It is derived from Old French *douagiere*, from *douage or dower.*
2 www.debretts.com/forms-address/titles/earl-and-countess/widow-earl
3 This will be a similar research experience to what I experienced during the writing of the matriarch paper (Smith, 2014). This study began in 2004 during a family business research seminar at Lancaster University when I presented a PowerPoint presentation and handout suggesting the relevance of the matriarch stereotype to contemporary family business. The presentation was well received by the audience, many of whom were mature family businesswomen. However, the resultant study took several years and several iterations and numerous rejections before finally be published in 2014, 10 years after its inception.

References

Cates, J.N., and Sussman, M. B. (1992). Family systems and inheritance. *Family Business Review*, 5(2), 205–226.

Chang, J. (2013). *Empress Dowager Cixi: The Concubine Who Launched Modern China*. London: Jonathan Cape.

Colli, A. (2012). Contextualizing performances of family firms: The perspective of business history. *Family Business Review*, 25(3), 243–257.

Devonshire, D., and Upton, S. (2002). *Chatsworth: The House*. Frances Lincoln.

Dunn, B., and Hughes, M. (1995). Themes and issues in the recognition of family businesses in the United Kingdom. *Family Business Review*, 8(4), 267–291.

Fellowes, J. (2008). *Mud and the City: Dos and Don'ts for Townies in the Country*. London: The Book List.

Fellowes, J. (2011). *The World of Downton Abbey*. London: Collins Publishing.

Fellowes, J., and Sturgis, M. (2012). *Mrs Isadore Levinson and the Dowager Countess of Grantham*. London: Harper-Collins.

Galiano, A.M., and Vinturella, J.B. (1995). Implications of gender bias in the family business. *Family Business Review*, 8(3), 177–188.

Hutcheson, J.O., Jaffe, D., and Gilliland, K. (2013). Addiction in the family enterprise. *Family Business Review*, 26(1), 104–107.

Hytti, U., Alsos, G.A., Heinonen, J., and Ljunggren, E. (2016: Online First). Navigating the family business: A gendered analysis of identity construction of daughters. *International Small Business Journal*, Online first, https://doi.org/10.1177/0266242616675924

Jaffe, D. J., and Lane, S. H. (2004). Sustaining a family dynasty: Key issues facing complex multigenerational business- and investment-owning families. *Family Business Review*, 17(1), 81–98.

Jimenez, R. M. (2009). Research on women in family firms: Current status and future directions. *Family Business Review*, 22(1), 53–64.

Lewis, J. L. (2003). *Sacred to Female Patriotism: Gender, Class, and Politics in Late Georgian Britain*. London: Routledge.

Marcus, G. E. (1991). Elites: The domestication of capital and the capitalization of family. *Family Business Review*, 4(1), 75–111.

Martin, H. F. (2001). Is family governance an oxymoron? *Family Business Review*, 14(2), 91–96.

Moult, S., and Anderson, A. R. (2005). Enterprising women: Gender and maturity in new venture creation and development. *Journal of Enterprising Culture*, 13(3), 255.

Prince, R. A. (1990). Family business mediation: A conflict resolution model. *Family Business Review*, 3(3), 209–223.

Roessl, D. (2005). Family businesses and interfirm cooperation. *Family Business Review*, 18(3), 203–214.

Smith, R. (2014). Assessing the contribution of the theory of matriarchy to the entrepreneurship and family business literatures. *International Journal of Entrepreneurship and Gender*, 6(3), 255–275.

Smith, R. (2017). Reading liminal and temporal dimensionality in the Baxter family 'public-narrative'. *International Small Business Journal.*, Online first, https?doi.org/10.1177/0266242617698033

Thompson, F.M.L. (2001a). *Gentrification and the Enterprise Culture: Britain 1780–1980.* Oxford: Oxford University Press.

Thompson, F.M.L. (2001b). Aristocrats as entrepreneurs. In F.M.L.Thompson (Ed.), *Gentrification and the Enterprise Culture: Britain 1780–1980.* Oxford: Oxford University Press.

Index